W9-AZS-334

JAMES T. CAREY, Assistant Professor of Criminology at the University of California, Berkeley, presents the case of the hip youth. Carey has recently been carrying out research on drug users through the Haight-Ashbury Free Clinic in San Francisco.

The College
Drug Scene

The College Drug Scene

James T. Carey

A SPECTRUM BOOK

PRENTICE-HALL, Inc.
Englewood Cliffs, N. J.

Copyright © 1968 by PRENTICE-HALL, Inc.
Englewood Cliffs, N. J.

All rights reserved. No part of this
book may be reproduced in any form or
by any means without permission in
writing from the publisher.

Library of Congress Catalog Card Number: 68–27489

PRINTED IN THE UNITED STATES OF AMERICA

Current printing (last digit):
10 9 8 7 6 5 4 3

Preface

My initial interest in exploring drug use by college age youth in and around Berkeley emerged out of discussions with several faculty members and graduate students in the University of California School of Criminology who were working closely with a self-help group of older ex-narcotic users. It became clear very early that the group we were working with was considerably different from the college students becoming a part of the wave of illegal drug use in the early 1960's. The most obvious differences between the young people who took mind-altering drugs and their older counterparts were in terms of age and social class. The college group came from respectable middle-class and upper middle-class homes and associated almost exclusively with people of similar background. They appeared on the surface to be clinically no "sicker," "needier," or more inadequate than others of their age and social status.

A proposal was made to explore the meaning and significance drug use had for these young people as part of a larger study under the sponsorship of Professor Herbert Blumer. The college age inquiry under my direction was one of three sub-studies that were initiated. The standard tools of the ethnographer were used to gain access to drug-related scenes, gather brief life histories, and observe the social situations of use. The end product is this book. The case study materials were developed within the context of the sociologist's theoretical concern with deviance. A description of the economic character of the drug world in and around the Colony is also included to escape some of the limitations of the case method. There are certain tasks which must be performed if the drug marketplace is to maintain itself. Understanding them is critical if one wishes to focus on the kind of criminal or deviant career which is becoming increasingly available to middle-class youths.

My thanks go first to Herbert Blumer for his sage and helpful observations at each stage of the project and for his critical and detailed reading of the manuscript. This is over and above his contribution as a continuing source of inspiration and intellectual stimulation during my graduate years at Chicago and my teaching career at Berkeley. The insights of Jerry

Mandel were also invaluable. He collaborated with me on a description of the drug traffic which is summarized in Chapters 2, 4, and 5. I am indebted also to Norm Linton who assisted in the development of the chapters on the recreational user and the head, as well as exchanging many ideas with me on the meaning of college age drug use. Thanks, too, are due to other graduate students who worked with me on various facets of the research: Alice Huberman, Roxanne Sweet, David Bentel, Martin Thimel, Paula Shelton, and Daniel Haytin. An expression of gratitude goes to my colleagues who read the manuscript and suggested revisions: Joel Fort, Israel Gerver, and his colleagues at the Office of Juvenile Delinquency, Arline Daniels and Gil Geis. Whatever defects there are in the book are my responsibility, not theirs. To James Clark of Prentice-Hall a note of thanks is also extended. He encouraged me to think in terms of publication originally and was a constant friend and constructive critic throughout.

My wife and children were also very supportive during the long months of writing and revising. I am especially indebted to them for allowing me one summer of freedom from family obligations to complete the final draft.

A final note of thanks is offered to anyone else who assisted me on various phases of the research and writing whom I have inadvertently omitted from this list and to the Office of Juvenile Delinquency in the Department of Health, Education, and Welfare whose research grants (nos. 65029 and 66022) made the book possible.

Contents

The College
Drug Scene

Introduction:
Deviance Theory and
Deviant Worlds

An explanation of deviant behavior is in large part the product of the theoretical approach and concern of the investigator. Generally, there have been four such methods of approach to deviant behavior, one of which was employed in this study.

The least commonly employed approach is the use of autobiographical materials to conceptualize deviant motivations. The concern here is to illuminate the motives, goals, values, and experience of individual deviants. The tool employed is the descriptive material provided by the deviant himself. Clifford Shaw's description of the development of criminal and delinquent behavior, as well as other studies of the early Chicago school, are examples of this approach.[1]

A much more popular approach to the study of deviant behavior is the application of psychoanalytic categories and assumptions to the personality of the individual deviant in order to develop a motivational theory of deviant behavior. The goal here is a motivational model for a particular form of deviant behavior. The tools, however, are not naturalistic or descriptive materials, but clinical data and test scores on selected persons who have come to the investigator's attention. This material is interpreted in terms of psychoanalytic assumptions and theoretical constructs. This kind of approach has developed, for example, the theory that heroin addicts are passive-submissive personality types, latently homosexual, emotionally unstable, who use and seek drugs for sexual gratification, to escape feelings of low esteem and insecurity, and to ward off psychotic states. Cohen has given a similar description of individuals who use psychedelics illegally.[2] This approach has been used to explain the motivations to participate in a wide range of deviant behavior.

[1] Clifford R. Shaw, *The Natural History of a Delinquent Career* (Chicago: University of Chicago Press, 1931); C. R. Shaw and H. D. McKay, *Brothers in Crime* (Chicago: University of Chicago Press, 1938); C. R. Shaw, *The Jack Roller* (Chicago: University of Chicago Press, 1930).
[2] S. Cohen and K. Ditman, "Prolonged Adverse Reactions to Lysergic Acid Diethylamide," *Archives of General Psychiatry*, VIII (1963), 475–80.

THE STRUCTURAL APPROACH
TO DEVIANCE

A third approach involves the application of analytic, sociological concepts in an attempt to explain deviant behavior. Implicit in this approach is the assumption that, regardless of the personality characteristics of deviants, certain social conditions tend to produce deviant behavior. Proponents of this view therefore attempt to outline the structural aspects of deviant behavior and examine the relationship between certain social features and deviance. Usually dealing with deviant behavior in gross terms, i.e., not distinguishing between particular forms of deviant behavior, they argue that such variables as class, social disorganization, social milieu, anomie, cultural discontinuity, or role conflict lead to deviant behavior. The perspective is from the standpoint of the system of rules, or role expectations. The implication is that deviance is independent of the perspectives of either the enforcer or the deviant actor. This is the position of Parsons[3] and Merton.[4] They begin with a static model of social order and pose the question why there is a violation of norms. Merton, for example, maintains that deviant behavior is the result of the particular condition of the social structure in which there is a dissociation between culturally defined aspirations and socially structured means to achieve these aspirations. The dysfunctional social structure exerts pressure on the individual to behave in a deviant manner.

The analysis usually begins with official rates of deviant or criminal behavior. The official fact of higher incidence of heroin use in low-income areas has led to an exploration of the conditions of life in those areas which make narcotic use so prevalent. Finestone has provided us with an intriguing picture of a social type that emerges in the lower-class Negro slum.[5] The lower-class resident lives in an environment which places limits and restrictions upon his advancement and self-fulfillment. He reacts to this by setting up his own standards of esteem and success which invert those prized in the larger community. The goal of life becomes the achievement of a pattern of living which disavows work through some form of "hustle" which may involve begging, borrowing or stealing, but not through violent means. The role model is the "cat," whose pattern of living is a consciously cultivated and gracious work of art. The "cat" not only has his distinctive "hustle," but also his distinctive "kick" which disavows the regulation of conduct in terms of future consequences. The "kick" is likely to be some form of drug use with its own lore of appreciation and connoisseurship. Finestone interprets this life style as an adapta-

---

[3] T. Parsons, *The Social System* (New York: The Free Press, 1951), Chap. 7.

[4] R. K. Merton, *Social Theory and Social Structure* (New York: The Free Press, 1957), Chap. 4.

[5] H. Finestone, "Cats, Kicks and Color," *Social Problems*, V (1957), 3–13.

tion because of the inaccessibility of legitimate avenues for attainment. The result of this blockage is that a segment of the population turns in on itself and constructs new criteria for achievement.

Cloward and Ohlin[6] develop an explanatory scheme taking into account the higher number of addicts who come from lower socioeconomic groups as analyzed by Finestone. Their general aim is to make sense out of or normalize the circumstances of use. The penalties associated with drug use are so harsh that one is led to ask why anyone should take such risks. One possible response is that the user is mentally disturbed. Another is that he is in a situation where drugs are available and the norms against their use neutralized. This is the situation of the low-income Negro or white in the urban slum. The lower-class person is faced with an environment that sets limits on opportunities to achieve goals highly valued by our society. If he cannot attain these goals legitimately, he is moved to achieve them illegitimately. But not only are legal opportunities limited; illegal ones are also. The individual so circumstanced—unable to make it legitimately or illegitimately—retreats from the situation into drug use. He is characterized as a "double failure" and his response as a "retreatist" one.

THE LABELING PERSPECTIVE

The fourth approach to deviant behavior also attempts to ascertain the structural or situational features of deviant behavior, rather than the motivational features; but instead of analytic concepts and variables derived from or imposed upon statistical data, its tools are naturalistic, descriptive data and observation. This perspective views deviance from the standpoint of the enforcer. For example, Goffman[7] considers that "mental illness" is, in part, a function of administrative decisions by persons in positions of power: lawyers, judges, and psychiatrists—those who have the power to define some behavior as deviant and to apply sanctions. The structural or situational features which are described are not gross societal conditions of deviance, but situational contingencies which the deviant himself perceives or the sociologist observes. The focus is on the process of deviant behavior, i.e., the interaction between situational demands which are the products of the larger social structure and the individual who must confront these demands. Alfred Lindesmith's work on opiate addiction is the first and most obvious example of this approach.[8] Through informal interviews with persons who defined themselves as

---

[6] R. Cloward and L. Ohlin, *Delinquency and Opportunity* (New York The Free Press, 1961).

[7] E. Goffman, *Asylums* (Chicago: Aldine, 1961).

[8] A. R. Lindesmith, *Opiate Addiction* (Evanston, Ill.: The Principia Press of Illinois, 1947).

addicted to heroin he was able to isolate the sequence of events which constituted the causal process in which addiction was generated. Each stage of the process was accompanied by variable rationalizations or motivations which went along with them. These rationales or motives do not precede addiction but are generated in the process of becoming addicted.

Becker's later work on the sequence of events leading to marihuana use is also an example of this approach.[9] The emphasis is on being in a situation where drugs are available and norms against their use are neutralized. The focus is on the development of a commitment to use. This longitudinal view which isolates the stages leading to systematic use enables us to perceive the system and the possible places within it progressively. Becker traces the individual's willingness to use marihuana through several stages. The person is in a congenial setting where marihuana is available. He learns to smoke and produce real effects. He learns to link the effects with marihuana and enjoy the sensation. He is now a beginning user. He moves further into the user scene if he neutralizes the community's moral judgment against it, if he gets closer to the supply, and if he can keep his information control tight. The user moves from occasional use to regular use and he moves closer to the source of supply. Becker delineates the "social control" problems—the problems of supply, secrecy, and morality —which the user must confront by virtue of the illegality of his acts. The way in which the deviant meets these situational contingencies and the skill he develops, through interaction, in confronting them determines in large part the development and maintenance of deviant motivation. Others have shown in differing connections that the successful labeling of an act as deviant or illegal almost invariably constrains the deviant to structure much of his identity and activity in terms of this.

The theory underlying this approach has been derived from George Herbert Mead.[10]

> In [Mead's] theory objects, (including the self), have meaning for the person only as he imputes that meaning to them in the course of his interaction with them. The meaning is not given in the object, but is lodged there as the person acquires a conception of the kind of action that can be taken with, toward, by and for it. Meanings arise in the course of social interaction, deriving their character from the consensus participants develop about the object in question. The findings of research on the character of drug induced experience are therefore predictable from Mead's theory.[11]

Some studies also have been conducted on the social life, personal

[9] H. S. Becker, "Becoming a Marihuana User," *American Journal of Sociology*, LIX (1953), 235–42. H. S. Becker, "Marihuana Use and Social Control," *Social Problems*, III (1955), 35–44.

[10] G. H. Mead, *Mind, Self and Society* (Chicago: University of Chicago Press, 1934). See also H. Blumer, "Sociological Implications of the Thought of George Herbert Mead," *American Journal of Sociology*, LXXI (March, 1966), 535–44.

[11] H. Becker, "An Exploration of the Social Bases of Drug Induced Experiences," *Journal of Health and Social Behavior*, VIII (3) (September, 1967), 166–77.

relationships, and problems of adjustment of the addict that highlight the gradual process of immersion into a special world. This special world is, in a sense, connected with the general process by which addicts have been cast out of respectable society. Fiddle[12] states explicitly that the narcotics laws and their enforcement have given special form and meaning to addiction and created an addict subculture. He describes the circulatory system —or the system of roles and interrelationships by which the addict secures illegal drugs—and a survival system which includes: (1) an ideology of justification; (2) the requirement of new members to maintain the system; (3) defensive communication; (4) a neighborhood warning system; and (5) ritualistic and magical cyclical patterns and intense personal relationships with other addicts.

Lindesmith[13] first explored the criminogenic character of the law and enforcement policies related to drug use. He saw society's response as a partial determinant of the very behavior it was designed to discourage. He compared the law enforcement-dominated system of control in the United States with the medical control system used in Britain. His early articles suggested the harmful effects of American policy when contrasted with the more benign British model. The laws governing drug use in the two countries are similar, but their implementation differs. Subsequent interpretations of the two drug control acts—England's Dangerous Drug Act of 1920 and America's Harrison Act of 1914—and differential implementation of the laws have led in different directions in the two countries.

Schur[14] emphasizes not only the modification of self-image by being defined as criminal, but the formation of deviant subcultures as a direct result of repressive drug control policies. Secondary deviation, including secondary crime, he points out, may be crucially related to the criminalization of this and other kinds of deviance. The criminalization process establishes the economic basis for black market operations or helps produce situations in which police efficiency is impaired and police corruption encouraged.

THEORETICAL ORIENTATION
OF THIS STUDY

It is the fourth approach that has been used in this case study of a group of persons who use drugs in a college community. Descriptive and naturalistic material taken from lengthy interviews with drug users is the

---

[12] S. Fiddle, "The Addict Culture and Movement Into and Out of Hospitals," as reprinted in U.S. Senate, Committee on the Judiciary, Subcommittee to Investigate Juvenile Delinquency, Hearings, Part 13, New York City, September 20–21, 1962 (Washington, D.C.: Government Printing Office, 963), pp. 3–156.

[13] A. R. Lindesmith, "The British System of Narcotics Control," *Law and Contemporary Problems*, XXIII (Winter, 1957), 138–54.

[14] E. M. Schur, *Narcotic Addiction in Britain and America: The Impact of Public Policy* (Bloomington; Indiana University Press, 1962).

means attempted to discover the structural and situational components of deviant behavior. Inherent in choosing this approach are certain assumptions about the nature of deviant behavior itself. It is assumed, first, that an individualistic, motivational model cannot give a comprehensive picture of deviant behavior. The psychoanalytic approach assumes that if an individual is deviant, there is something *in him* that causes his behavior. However, this assumption presents two problems: there is the problem of generalizing from studies of some deviants to all who carry on particular categories of deviant acts. This characteristically leads the investigators to state that for a phenomenon like drug addiction, there are several "personality types" involved. More seriously, this approach cannot show that deviant behavior is the product of the peculiarities of personality. All behavior is the product of individual actors with particular personality structures and processes. To say, for example, that drug addiction is the result of passive dependency tells us nothing about why a passive dependent becomes a drug addict, for surely there are many passive dependents who are not drug addicts. Why, then, do some individuals with certain personality types become deviants, while others with similar personality characteristics do not?

It is assumed further that the social structural approach does not offer an adequate explanation of deviance. The trouble with this approach lies in its concern with describing the social system rather than with describing the process of deviant behavior from the standpoint of the deviant himself. The proponents of this view tend to make very general statements about the dysfunctional conditions for deviant behavior, without focusing on the process of deviant behavior which emerges from a confrontation by the deviant with the situational demands created by the social system. Like the psychological approach, the social structural model is unable to explain the selectivity involved in deviant behavior. For example, Merton is able to state that deviant behavior is a product of the dissociation between ends and means within the social system, but he is not able to state how individuals, confronting the same conditions, behave in different ways. In the end, then, the social structural approach is only able to give us certain broad systemic conditions of deviant behavior.

It is assumed, finally, that the situational approach to deviance offers certain advantages that the other approaches do not provide. Rather than making general statements about the conditions which may result in deviant behavior, it can, by evaluating naturalistic data, determine the particular situational conditions which, if confronted by the individual, will lead to a deviant career. In this way, it becomes possible to make statements about the situational contingencies of deviant behavior and the relationship between those contingencies and deviant motivation. This approach is obviously closer to the social structural approach than to the individualistic approach, because it assumes that deviance cannot be explained by reductionist psychoanalytic principles. On the other hand, since its primary concern is not with the social system and its relationship to deviant behavior, but with the process of deviant behavior which emerges from the confrontation with situational contingencies created by the social system, it is able, unlike the social systemic approach, to make statements about the particular concerns and problems of particular individuals. In other words, it looks at the social system from the perspective of the individual. But it does not attempt to develop a motivational theory; instead of concerning itself with the impossible task of elucidating "dispositional types" for particular deviant acts, it attempts to examine how motivations toward deviant acts are maintained, enlarged, and refined in the process of deviant behavior. In sum, by focusing on the situational demands, it can relate the social structure to the individual actor.

The individual is seen, in this perspective, as an active agent in giving meaning to his symbolic and physical environment. That which mediates between social structure and individual behavior is the self. Individuals have selves and act by making indications to themselves.[15] Every item of behavior is sifted through the meaning system or self-indicating system of the actor. This view tends to reject that social system approach which emphasizes the binding character of norms. It is more accurate to see individuals who bring their own meaning system to norms and make of them what they will. This is not, however, to deny the importance of more general dimensions, but only to say that values and consciousness intervene between them and behavior. The economic character of the drug market (discussed in Chapter 2), the more general problem of the American response to drugs, and the structural changes in American life which affect young people (discussed in Chapter 8) are instances of objective circumstances which set the stage for the evolution of the Colony herein described.

[15] See H. Blumer, "Society as Symbolic Interaction," in A. Rose, ed., *Human Behavior and Social Processes* (Boston: Houghton Mifflin Company, 1962), pp. 179–92.

1

The Colony

I don't like a lot of things about America. I mean I don't like a lot of American people and I don't really feel comfortable among poor uneducated . . . you know, opinion polls and TV ratings just seem, you know, almost every time anything is approved by a majority of the people it seems to me I can almost immediately say that it's the wrong thing . . . minorities might not always be right but I think the majority is always wrong. And yet there's this thing of having some sort of feeling for the people, having some kind of feeling of obligation to the society. And so, real hang-ups, like wanting to work in slums yet not liking slum people . . . and I don't feel at home with any party or candidate . . . or a group of people to be with except in very out-of-the-way places with very out-of-the-way kinds of people . . .

The strategy for coping with the larger society, the "square world"—the response to the dilemma poignantly expressed above by a young collegian —is the subject of this book on drug use among the college-age segment of contemporary society.

The phenomenon of questioning, disenchanted youth seems to be universal. However, it is particularly manifest in communities which have attracted a disproportionate number of rebels and nonconformists. Localities exhibiting such a population composition can be considered to harbor colonies of a new bohemian subculture. These colonies are especially suited for research on the adaptations of youth to the challenges posed by the adult world, and therefore our investigation focuses on Berkeley, California, as a major example of a colony.

One of the distinctive features of a colony is drug use among its members. Although drugs do not necessarily occupy a central position in their life, use is sufficiently widespread to influence the social relationships between colony members and the rest of the community, an effect which in turn acts to bind members to one another regardless of whether they take drugs or not. For these reasons the sentiments, opinions, and values revealed

8

by those most committed to drug use reflect fairly closely the attitudes of general colony membership.

This study is based on direct field observations, conversations, and interviews with admitted drug users who acted as key informants over a period of one year. Approximately eighty subject-informants participated in the study. Three-fourths of them took drugs regularly, one-fourth occasionally.

Information on drug trafficking was obtained from interviews held with five persons who periodically dealt in amounts over $500, five middle-level dealers, reports from lesser traffickers of twenty dealers on this high level, dozens of formal and informal interviews with pushers periodically buying anywhere from $50–$500 of non-opiate drugs and selling from one-half ounce to several kilos of marihuana or 3–50 capsules of LSD, and scores of discussions about drug trafficking with various Colony members who use drugs.

One of the difficulties involved in doing research of the type reported here is the fact that systematic users are poor sources of demographic information about their peers. Habitual users are often able to state whether or not another person is a user and might often be in a position to give a fairly reliable account of the extent of his drug-related activities. But they do not know and, furthermore, are not interested in somebody else's educational attainments or his occupational status. These normally important determinants of status do not play a strategic role in the social stratification system of this drug scene. Participants in this study represent a completely accidental sample of drug users. Their number, however, is compensated for by their broad range of experience.

A DIGRESSION ON METHODOLOGY

A major source of distortion in the depiction of life styles of persons defined as deviant has been the condition under which the information was gathered. As Lindesmith[1] pointed out many years ago in speaking about heroin users, the manner in which they are characterized is strongly influenced by the nature of the observer's relationship to them. More recently Polsky[2] made the same point about the study of career criminals, i.e., that they are studied in captivity. Apart from the sampling bias involved, the relationship of researcher to respondent is suspect. In the language of intergroup relations it is not one of "equal status" in which the respondent is free to disagree or has developed the kind of trust in the investigator that will enable him to disclose himself.

One possible way to get information on drug usage among college students is to draw a random sample in a particular community and ask

[1] A. R. Lindesmith, *Opiate Addiction.*
[2] N. Polsky, *Hustlers, Beats and Others* (Chicago: Aldine, 1967), pp. 122 ff.

them what drugs they have used and how often. The validity of the outcome very much depends on what the respondent thinks will be done with the information since he is disclosing something which could hurt him. The problem of validity is greater if one is querying persons whose major identity component is linked with the area under investigation. If the subject is very important to him, he may be unwilling to translate his experience into someone else's categories.

Unfortunately, if good descriptions are to be made of deviant behavior and illegal business there are few ways to get "hard data." The problem is underlined in attempting a picture of drug trafficking in the Colony. Who should be surveyed? Would a random sample of Berkeleyites yield a picture of what is a reasonable price? If only a fraction of the population uses drugs, would it be worthwhile to get three or four interviews that would tell us nothing for every "useful" questionnaire?

But even before raising these questions, there is a problem of what to ask. Contemplating a survey seemed like putting the cart before the horse. A survey might be relevant after a good deal of preliminary investigation, but even then a new problem is posed. There were numerous persons interviewed and instances observed or heard about where small amounts of drugs were passed around. Hence confidence about understanding the lower levels of trafficking is high. This declines the higher up we go. The number of cases of 10 or 250 pound marihuana deliveries is simply too small to permit a survey, apart from the problem of getting access to the transactions.

The social scientist interested in styles of drug using and dealing must use field observation if his account is to reflect reality. Animal ecologists have noted that when studying an animal in his natural habitat you discover important things about him, things not discoverable when he is behind bars. What is true of animals is more so of humans. The picture of what this world is like can only be discovered by becoming a part of the world of users and dealers. The information has been drawn primarily from what they say and what they do in their daily round of life. This has been supplemented by official statistics and mass media reports when these illuminated some aspect of this world. An observational or knowledgeable informant approach can be justified on its own merits as proper for this subject, but a simpler justification is one of expediency. It is difficult to figure what or who else to consult.

A more detailed methodological appendix is included after the last chapter to allay the skeptical.

The group we are concerned with has many internal differences and distinctions. Of particular importance is the intimate life style of the individual drug user as affected by his drug use. This involves differentiation along a spectrum that ranges from the well-ordered and occasional habit of the "recreational user" to the casual, daily use of the "head."

The principal focus of our investigation will rest on the heavy user inasmuch as this approach provides several advantages. For the "heads" drugs constitute a more important aspect of one's life experience than for the "weekender." Consequently, the former are more articulate about the process which led to their present situation and the extent to which their values differ from those of the larger community. A study of systematic use goes beyond earlier descriptions of initiation and concentrates on adaptations developed in the face of society's moral disapproval. However, it is our intention to describe in this chapter the overall characteristics of the Colony and indicate its shared views, norms, and rationales; the distinctions and differences between users will be treated later.

For a group of people who value the beauty of their environment highly the city of Berkeley and its University of California campus have marked appeal. The city is located on San Francisco Bay with spectacular views of the ocean and the surrounding hills and mountains. The vegetation is lush, variegated, and everblooming. Fertile soil, mild climate, and abundant moisture make gardening a year-round activity and can provide the most ramshackle dwelling with a complement of color. Even a modest garden will reward its tender with an array of hues and aromas. The trees which dot the town and the adjoining hills and valleys display a multitude of textures and shapes. The city's architecture is a combination of styles ranging from midwestern clapboard and pastel stucco to tileroofed Mediterranean and western redwood shingle with a sprinkle of Victorian. Where rezoning has permitted conversions or multiple-dwelling units, these too, if not always the best, are for the most part interesting.

There is a lack of front lawns and the social system built around them. The presence of large cheap homes and many back houses with innumerable trees has implications for the life styles of Colony members. Such a physical setting then, both affected by and acting upon a relatively liberal city population, has made Berkeley an attractive place to pursue an existence that is colorful, unusual, varied—and in some aspects illegal!

The subculture (hereafter referred to as the Colony) which has grown up in Berkeley is primarily composed of young people in the 18–25 age bracket. These members of the Colony are likely to be regular students at the University, part-time students, or drop-outs somewhere along the line; and a few have never attended college at all. They are usually the products of the arrived middle class, who, confident of their position in society, are able to criticize and react to its shortcomings from this perspective. They are urbanites or, more precisely, metropolitan dwellers who have been raised in middle- to large-sized cities or their suburban rings. A disproportionately high percentage of this group is Jewish. At the ends of the age range, however, there are some older and younger persons who relate themselves to the scene either as professional "beats" or aspiring experimenters.

There are also numerous related offshoots of this scene which will not be described here. Persons drift into and out of the Colony and into and out of various levels in it. People service the Colony and differentially feel themselves to be part of it. Some are total strangers to it who contribute an anoymous, non-plasticized presence because they are older, and do not sympathize or do not understand. Others are highly sympathetic elders or dabblers in drugs, and almost all are long-term bohemians. There are the professional people, university professors, architects, artists, and businessmen whose professions provide them with a major identity component but who feel themselves to be a part of the Colony.

The center of the Colony is a two-block area one-half mile south of the University. Residents call it "The Avenue." It serves as the main street for the Colony and is located several blocks from the main downtown shopping area which is rarely visited by Avenue habitués. The area's special character depends on certain architectural and zoning features. The lots are small, the buildings old, and the rents cheap. Traffic is congested and moves slowly. This gives an opportunity for those on foot to stroll leisurely, look around, and stop to listen or chat.

On the Avenue are a number of places to eat or buy food: several restaurants, a coffee shop, two pizza places, a number of hamburger stands, a donut shop, a bakery, and a small grocery store. There is also a hardware store, several laundromats, a poolroom, a pharmacy, four record stores, a gallery and the ubiquitous used and new bookshops. Absent are large stores, auto lots, bars, supermarkets or nightclubs. From the point of view of the outsider nothing seems to be happening there. A conventional middle-class observer would immediately take note of the crowds, the color, the cosmopolitan air, the casual—sometimes unusual—dress, and the range of social types. Closer inspection reveals the Avenue to be a place for gathering, sipping coffee with friends, playing pool, browsing around the bookstores, looking at prints, and performing minor chores such as buying small amounts of food or doing laundry. And it is a place to be *seen*.

Most important, the Avenue functions to keep the Colony together. Information is passed along about absent friends or partners, new people in town, events in San Francisco, and on other college campuses, and especially the activities of the police.

For a small number of Colony members, the Avenue constitutes their "living room" or, more precisely, a "playroom." For these people, such living arrangements as do exist are quite irregular. They may be sleeping in cars, in laundromats, or in the apartment of someone who has been kind enough to put them up for a while. They view the Avenue, or certain parts of it, much as delinquent youth view their street corners.

The Avenue is also a place where many roles can be tried out, and possible new ones developed. One 22-year-old Colony member and hard-core drug user characterized the role he developed as a "watcher."

I always sit over there, smile knowingly. What you're doing is watching; you're being a watcher, the guy who knows better, the guy who's been there and knows what it's all about, who doesn't have to do it anymore. I was just going to sit out and watch . . . make a snide comment every so often. (I make) more and more snide comments as time goes on. That gets to be a thing too. They expect sarcasm and I still have that. Even in just a tone of voice.

The "watching" or observing is acceptable if it is done within the framework supporting the Colony. This means that the observer must be familiar. "Watching" on the part of persons who are not known or only slightly known evokes almost immediate suspicion. The new face can easily hide an undercover policeman, an informer, or, as one person characterized several people he knew, "student bounty hunters." A 24-year-old woman, married and a systematic user, described a variation on this role of the watcher:

I used to go to Robbies and stay in there all day and draw and talk and watch people. Don't know how we didn't get busted or picked up or something. It was absurd. We'd go up to get something to eat and we'd come back laughing hysterically because we just couldn't, you know, we laughed. We'd stand in front of the food for a half hour, you know. I don't know how they didn't arrest us.

Another Colony member described the Avenue as a place where he liked to work occasionally when he got "high," much as a middle-class father might putter around in his workshop (though presumably not high—at least on drugs). A 21-year-old part-time carpenter, deeply involved in the drug scene, reported one experience:

You'll be doing something and then all of a sudden realize you're really loaded and you're doing this absurd thing. You know, taking a clock apart in the Forum or something and you stop and look around and say, "Oh no, I blew it!" kind of thing . . . but if you just keep taking the clock apart, put all the parts in a bag and walk out, there's no change of pace, you know and because you haven't thought about it, that's what you did. You just took a clock apart in the Forum.

The Avenue also acculturates the newcomer to Berkeley. Some Colony members felt that they no longer needed to frequent the Avenue once they had made a handful of friends and started moving in a specific social network. Free time for them was mainly spent socializing in people's homes. But the Avenue is a place to return to at slack times, when looking for a party or a connection, or when out of girls. It is also a place to be avoided if you are holding or pushing drugs and have a stable distribution system.

GENERAL ATTITUDES

The Colony is not an isolated community with its own norms, values, and social arrangements. It exists within a larger order and, to a considerable extent, arrives at its own identity in response to this larger order. The Colony characterizes the Great Society as straight (as in "straight and narrow") "rigid," "up-tight," "inflexible," and accuses it of imposing its outlooks and its institutions on persons who want and need something else or something more. Television is rejected as laughing gas for the masses. Values related to single-mindedness, the double standard, violence, and cleanliness are all called into question. The Colony is most critical of the larger community's hypocrisy: on the one hand an unrealizable standard of behavior is idealized while on the other hand all sorts of unethical behavior are condoned. The fact that Colony members come generally from families with liberal orientation gives a peculiar bite and sharpness to their view of American society. As one 21-year-old ex-college student and systematic drug user described it:

> We're so aware of the realities . . . we realize the things our parents have been telling us over and over and over again are lies. We feel that because we've been lied to . . . well, it's not a case of not being able to fit into the society, we just don't want this society anymore. We're going to form our own society. Most of the kids I know are tremendously intelligent. The average IQ I'd say of people involved in the movement is . . . is 120 plus . . . in five years the majority of the population will be in an age group of 19-25, maybe 50-60 per cent. The thing is, it's a very mild revolution that's going on ah . . . five years ago when I was in high school, I felt that I was alone in respect to what I was doing, alone. The more and more I delved into the situation, the more I realized that I wasn't alone. There was a mass of people moving in the same direction—people who were tired of the old system, people who are fed up with the old attitude and people who feel that what these people have contributed to the other generation is ridiculous. We're tired of wars. We're tired of social striving. We're tired of the class system . . .

The values most highly treasured by American society, as seen by the respondents, are those which emphasize earned pleasure and leisure, as well as social independence. In the Colony all such convictions are subject to re-examination if not actual challenge through a number of activities, the most widely known of which is drug use. This is not to suggest that the initial motives for drug experimentation are mainly rebellious. Attraction to use is experienced as a pull rather than a push. Defiance is, at least in the beginning, an important motivation for a small group. In response to a question as to what led to his use of drugs, a 19-year-old student and occasional user said:

It was an outlet for anti-social feelings—a lot of anger towards my parents for making me stay in the dorm; toward the dormitory for making me try and conform—wearing a beanie in the dorm. I just didn't feel like the kind of sociability at the time. At the time it was a way of rejecting them (parents). And so I find that they (drugs) are an outlet for me.

Others explained the widespread use of marihuana on college campuses in terms of the larger numbers and proportion of youth going to college. The fact that these students enjoy the benefit of a temporary status with relatively few commitments and have the time to read, think, and discuss leads inevitably to some fundamental questioning. A 19-year-old heavy drug user and part-time dealer stated:

I think more people are going to school and learning, and that the process of life in this country is such . . . is that it's inevitable that at one point or another you are disillusioned. And you learn that what you have been told is wrong, and that justice doesn't prevail, and that the cake wasn't cut evenly when you were kiddies and stuff. And I think it's on such a widespread scale in this country, and that a man questioning, you know, . . . real ignorance becomes more apparent. This leads to questioning taboos . . . regarding drugs. And also, the whole society has become (an) inverted mind type of thing. Everybody is talking about their heads, and drugs are, of course, associated with this.

ATTITUDES TOWARD EDUCATION

The Colony reserves perhaps its most salient criticism for education. Because our respondents are of college age, they have had firsthand experiences with educational establishments. A 21-year-old ex-college student and heavy user characterized university education as a waste of time:

University is great, man, sure is nice all the things you can learn there. But it's too bad that you're supposed to go there and learn these things so that you'll forget them the next day. And that's generally what it's for. You know the University is a test. You make it through the University and you get your grade, and then you go with your grade and somebody pays you to do something.

Criticism seemed to center on the bureaucratization of education, which encouraged anonymity, mechanical presentation of factual material, the lack of logic in requirements for a B.A. degree, and their profound irrelevance to what is happening in America today.

Other criticisms of college concerned the social activities that were a part of college life. They were perceived as meaningless or designed to prolong some kind of second-class status for the student. A 24-year-old married woman and hard-core user described her own reaction:

At every school you went to, at every school you heard something
about Yale, Dartmouth, Harvard, all those places, the same guys
putting on the same drunk, you know, and that was the whole scene.
That's all they wanted, that's all they were, that's all they were doing,
you know. And so, in my sophomore year, you know, I just stopped
making that scene. . . . I just couldn't stand it . . . you know, like
I saw everything at . . . [college] like a hypocritical evil thing. All
these girls, all these gold bracelets, all they wanted was, you know, a
certain kind of house, and a certain kind of snobbish tennis court
existence, you know. . . .

Not all the attitudes described were negative. Members of the Colony
spoke of their admiration or respect for outstanding teachers and expressed
appreciation of the atmosphere a large university provided. Several mentioned the university library and the kind of people that seem to be drawn
into a university community. One 20-year-old occasional user, a student of
drama, focused on individual faculty members:

The University . . . was a small geographic location, where somebody had taken, had the courtesy to bring together a large body of
knowledge and a few people who it was worth listening to, and they
talked. And so, you know, I was going because I wanted to hear what
this cat had to say. I went down to a college south of here because
there were three or four people on the faculty that really knew where
they were at. And I got into symbolic logic and semantics [with] a
cat who had studied with Korzyoski and electronics from a dude who
had an Associate of Arts degree in anthropology from 1941. That was
the only degree he held then. He's probably one of the few people who
understands the mechanics of physics, mathematics and electronics
well enough to take absolute dunderhead freshmen kids and make
them see, you know, like the relationship of the sine to the radius to
the voltage to mathematical symbolism. You know, a beautiful cat,
just incredible.

No one mentioned any university-sponsored "activity" or "happening"
growing out of class work as central to their lives. Colony members were
likely to use university facilities, e.g., the library, pick the brains of university scholars occasionally by attending classes, go to events by student
organizations such as Cinema Psychedelica, Vietnam Day, a SNCC benefit, rock dance, or an Alpert lecture. Football, student government, faculty-
student retreats, departmental picnics, and the like are rejected by the
Colony. These aspects of university life are too closely tied to university
administration and are judged as having no relevance or impact on any
living society including the one the university is presumably preparing students to enter.

POLITICAL ATTITUDES

The political orientation of the Colony ranges from slightly left of center to active involvement in New Left politics to political rejection. Frequently members of the Colony described their progression through various left-wing organizations to a pronounced state of political alienation. Many of the most committed Colony members were former student activists. They described the exhilarating surge of student activity that burst upon the academic scene in the early 1960's. The activists evinced a burning concern for the injustices associated with student powerlessness, the black man's place in American life, and the war. At first there was a strong conviction that the educational and social order could be rearranged so that some of its more obvious inequalities would be remedied. This view, unfortunately, was dashed by the reaction of university and college officials in the face of pressures for academic reform. No real concessions, from the Colony's point of view, seem to have come from politically sophisticated administrators. The inability to effect university reform led to a profound disaffection on the part of those most deeply involved in student protest groups, and to the development of a distinctive life style which celebrates political disengagement. The feeling is that the situation within the university cannot be changed, that the educational structure is beyond correction.

Concomitant with this diagnosis is the sense that larger political and social structures in America are also unresponsive to change. They are rigid and inflexible—like our Vietnam policy. The components of this attitude will be discussed in a later chapter, but an overall understanding might be achieved through the following statement of a 20-year-old male who had dropped out of the university and characterized himself as a hard-core user:

> The group I use to be with was politically active . . . I don't know, maybe not really active . . . but we were always talking about political stuff and what are we going to do about it. We gotta get down to the train station, you know . . . this whole bit. The group I'm with now—I like it much better—it's more down to earth. I mean, we say the war in Viet Nam, there's nothing we can do about it . . . tear up your draft card and forget it, you know. We're not that active. We say yay! the pickets, and we stand and watch them and agree with 'em but we're not gonna be the ones right in there because, you know, nothing much is gonna get done, and it's just being ridiculous.

The conclusion reached by many young Colony members in the face of this situation is to eschew attempts to rearrange the social order. The belief has emerged that the only change for which one can work is change within oneself, and that massive change can come only from individual transformations. This is the fundamental precondition for improving the world.

WHY DO THEY COME

Their pungent observations of University life, the American system, and the like give rise to the general question of why young people migrate here and become members of the Colony. Perhaps many come initially to go to school. Nevertheless, the simplest reason stated by a number of respondents is that, with all of its faults, Berkeley is one of the few spots they can tolerate in this country. A 20-year-old occasional user explained what persuaded him to enroll at the University:

> I don't know. I feel comfortable here. Finally, you know, after travelling all the way across the country with my sleeping bag and the whole bit, I find myself comfortable. And like I looked around here were all these theatres, and all these book stores, and this great school, and a lot of people who maybe sort of looked like me, and maybe this is it—nobody looked at me (as being odd) . . . It's a very free community. I think maybe I sensed it right in the beginning. And I sort of said, you know, things, you know, you've heard about Berkeley from before and I was sort of excited—that thing with the HUAC in 1960. And things like that. You know, looked like this was the place where things were happening.

A 24-year-old married woman and systematic user told what she found Berkeley to be:

> What's life in Berkeley like? All right, three days ago we went to Ukiah and went camping out. Sang under the trees, ran into the water, floated downstream in the currents, you know, had hot dogs, you know, outside, going back and forth to Sausalito, all these things that are outdoors. Canyon, you know, that's what life is in Berkeley . . . just very open and very free and very uncomplicated.

The migration to Berkeley which was experienced by most of the respondents reflects in its own way the tremendous and continuing migration of newcomers to the state of California. The "Go West" theme is an active one for adventuresome Americans who believe the cross-country trek will reward them with beautiful weather, bountiful land, and fruitful experience. The goal of the migration, however, has been narrowed considerably for Colony members. Going West means specifically the Bay Area, not Laramie, Wyoming, and rarely Denver or Boulder, Colorado. For some of our respondents their move represented not a westward one but a northward one since they had migrated from San Diego and Los Angeles.

For young Americans, particularly those of college age who are themselves products of a mobile society and who are tuned into the student grapevine—"you haven't seen it if you haven't spent some time in Berkeley." The risk and reputation of the University are the challenges by which they define themselves and implicitly make decisions about tomorrow. The student who seeks the University in this spirit, and with the scholarship to be admitted, is also the student most likely to encounter the Colony and to associate with it to some degree. For others the existence of the Colony itself, not the University, is what draws them here.

Some of those who come take up residence and actually settle in Berkeley or the Bay Area. Many of them complete what they came to do and go on or return to a life still to be made. Some remain as Colony members; a few remain marginal to the Avenue; but all have been touched by the "Berkeley Scene."

MAKING A LIVING

Employment patterns in the Colony seem to fall into four main categories. First, there are the professional people: graduate students, architects, doctors, dentists, and people whose profession provides them with a major identity component. Usually the professionals are at the beginning stage of their career. Second, there are the artists: painters, rock musicians, sculptors, writers, film makers, and actors, who are primarily involved in creative activities which provide them with a livelihood. Third, there are the financial dependents: they are mostly students receiving family support although part-time or occasional work may supplement their budget. Fourth, there are a large number of marginally employed. The relationship of this last group to the world of work is an unstable one. Few respondents had conventional jobs appropriate to their educational background, and those who did were less involved in the drug-using subculture.

Many respondents worked episodically. Their motivation was survival, and employment was therefore considered to be only a temporary necessity. Jobs performed generally entailed menial tasks at the bottom of the economic ladder. But this dead-end aspect was part of what made work tolerable and justifiable. A 24-year-old former user described his employment:

> . . . in the last year, I've worked as a mail clerk in a bank, and presently I'm working in a laboratory. Neither of them are especially skilled, just something to get money from.

One 24-year-old man, a systematic user, described some of the impressions he gathered as a low-level laboratory technician:

> You don't even have to be alert when you get up there. You just have to stumble down to work somehow and spend about six hours there, rather than eight, you know, get the work done in less time than they think it takes.

Later, the same person described his experience of going to work under the influence of LSD.

> The only time I had some kind of problem was [when] I took LSD once, on a Sunday, and had to go to work on Monday . . . it's not a matter of hung-over, but it was a matter of still having things that [I] want[ed] to set straight in [my] mind, figure out what happened, and what it meant to you and sort of put things in their place. So you have a lot of unsettled thoughts and at my job it's not really such a problem because my work gets very automatic and I can pretty much think about whatever I want to, you know, as I'm working.

Another pattern of work activity is based upon an occupational choice that enables the Colony member to earn money whenever needed without committing himself to the economic value systems of society. The skilled trades, for instance, provide such opportunities. A 21-year-old hard-core user described the freedom his work provided him:

> I never worked a lot—and I'm a carpenter when I do work because I dig working with wood and building things, . . . The only reason I don't work now is because I refuse to work on tracthouses and all those atrocities they're building—I mean, there's no handicraft in it—there's no beauty in it man. I built three houses by myself, completely, back East. I started working for my father when I was 13 or 14. . . .

An alternative survival strategy is to live off someone else. Generally this means parental support, but it may also involve attaching oneself to a person who has a regular income and can supply room and board. One 22-year-old art student and hard-core user described the support she obtains from her family:

> I haven't been working for a year and a half . . . it's beautiful. My father's putting me entirely through school. As soon as I filed for divorce I was let back in the fold, . . . (laughter) and he decided that the only way for his daughter to have a happy, useful life was for her to get a degree. So as long as he wants to continue thinking this, I'm all the happier—because after a bachelor's, I'm sure I'll want a master's . . .

In general the informants' attitude toward work appeared to be quite negative. They seemed to feel that unless you were doing something creative or something you enjoyed then it was only to be endured. A 21-year-old ex-student deeply involved in the drug scene characterized his attitude toward work:

> Work is a hangup because if you've gotta work eight hours a day on somebody else's gig man, that doesn't leave you too much time or energy for your own. Prospect of working, you know, on something that I didn't particularly care about for the next twenty years is a drag. I mean it's no fun.

Notion of a Gig

Whatever reservations about conventional work prevail in the Colony, the fact is that the major demands made by the larger society on Colony members are in terms of employment. For some individuals this is not a problem because they are students and can easily find low-level university-related jobs which pose no serious ethical conflicts. Assisting the library staff or hashing in a dormitory are examples of such noncontroversial tasks.

Those individuals, however, who have never been students or have ceased to identify themselves with this status have a more complicated problem. Similar to what Goodman[3] observed about the pacifists, not any job will do. A person's work participation might make him a direct party to an abhorred activity and thus compromise his integrity. Therefore Colony members are, because of their convictions, confined in their job selections to occupations which they do not consider to be exploitative of others, i.e., mainly unskilled labor. An acceptable choice is to be a hospital attendant, a messenger, or a farmhand. To work as an artist, writer, or musician is another alternative. It simply means that one occasionally sells a painting or some poetry or gets paid for a one-night performance in a small folk rock band. Jobs of this nature are preferred because they allow their holders the maximum amount of freedom to do as they wish.

The low-level bureaucratic job, if possible in some large public organization, is valued to some extent for the same reasons that make other occupations acceptable. For instance, one can work in the post office because it is an essential service, it will be around after the revolution, and besides, people communicate with one another by mail. In a society where real communication is a problem, post office employment is prized. One of our respondents a 22-year-old hard-core user, described a job with the post office as ideal.

> The post office is anonymous to be a little gig of my own, or really main gig, thinking the way I do, in a sense.

The massiveness of the organization provides some freedom to those individuals who are at its lower levels. There are no demands made to move up. Persons holding such jobs rarely feel any pressure for advancement and are subject only to general supervision. As a consequence, the person can be pretty much left on his own. The work is not taxing and allows for a certain contribution of one's own. Taken together, all these features make up a gig: a job which provides one with a modest salary, where one's integrity is not compromised and where there is room for a sprinkle of initiative. An advantage added to this way of earning a livelihood is that you are likely to find others who also consider your job to be a gig. A 21-year-old systematic user who had a variety of work experiences described the kind of jobs those involved in the drug scene gravitate to:

[3] P. Goodman, *Growing Up Absurd* (New York: Vintage Books), pp. 63–68.

You know it's funny . . . no matter what area you go into, whether it's sheet metal work or if you go to work for the bridge painting crew. . . . A year ago I worked at the post office; it's not very long before you find somebody else that works there too who is sitting at his machine punching away, just digging it and you say 'yeah man, hi.' You just find them everywhere. I don't know what's happening in this world. . . . I don't understand it.

THE HUSTLE

The need for an appropriate survival strategy has encouraged some Colony members to develop other than conventional means to obtain money, notably various forms of hustle. A hustle is a nonviolent, illegal means of making money. The most frequently used hustle involves dealing in drugs.

An ex-student, 21-years-old and a systematic user, reported on his own "employment":

(How have you been managing to live?) Through various hustles. Selling LSD for one. There are a variety of nice things, I mean you can sell . . . machinery, like motorcycles, out there I usually get pretty good deals on them and I'll fix 'em up and sell 'em and get parts and sell them. A guitar that I sold—I bought it for $80 in Denver, and a girl who sings in the group called the "Woman Folk" was over at the Hungry i . . . was staying here for a while and I sold it to her for $100 plus her old guitar so . . . things like this.

Supplying drugs is considered legitimate by Colony members. Hence many of them sell some drugs at one time or another. In the face of the huge and many-faceted use of non-opiate drugs in the Colony it is natural that entrepreneurs have stepped in to provide the drugs. An elaborate system of production, transportation, and distribution has developed. The network provides numerous job roles that need to be filled and that place certain "demands" on the "employee." Somewhere in the system users "require" suppliers who can obtain marihuana or LSD, and these suppliers must have reliable sources who supply them in a few days. At the bottom there is a vast need for persons who can deliver small amounts of marihuana or a capsule or two of LSD at a moment's notice. Dealing at the lower levels requires that the dealer be outgoing, gregarious, and friendly to make the numerous contacts necessary for success. The many drug-dealing careers seem lucrative and attractive, especially with a market of respectable size. There are niches for almost anyone in the Colony who wants to enter the illegal trade. The jobs are tax free and exotic, require no elaborate past job histories, can be part-time or nighttime, and offer plenty of room for rapid advancement.

Other minor hustles can also be found in the Colony. One respondent told of stealing auto and motorcycle parts and selling them. Another described how he set up a package entertainment night club, gourmet restaurant, and Wild West saloon. He worked out a plan of operation and then looked for someone with capital to invest. His way of making a living required deception, a good deal of information on the night club business, and the ability to win the trust of gullible investors. The qualities necessary for this kind of work are precisely those which are characteristic of the professional thief described by Sutherland.[4]

A more pedestrian survival strategy is begging, or as one disapproving respondent put it, "leaching." Some respondents panhandled meals and a place to sleep daily. Essentially, they lived by their wits, inviting the same kind of response from strangers, friends, or acquaintances.

In sum: all Colony members come to terms with the fact that they must survive economically. The major problem as viewed from the Colony is how one can keep his own integrity and work. Some try conventional jobs and report the dilemmas they face. A more characteristic response is to work episodically or in those kind of jobs where autonomy is a built-in feature. For others an acceptable alternative to a conventional job is to become part of the illegal drug distribution network in and around the Colony.

IN-WORLD RELATIONSHIPS

There is some question as to whether or not the Colony can be considered a community in an anthropological sense. It may be more precise to say that in general there are highly differentiated combinations of drug preference which are accompanied by a pattern of social relationships. The respondents themselves spoke of their involvement in "scenes" rather than in a community. They represented social groups in which marihuana and LSD were used. Persons who participate in such a scene, whether tangentially or systematically, constitute a market for particular drugs. But simply being a consumer of marihuana and LSD does not in and of itself necessitate that the consumers know one another or view themselves as part of the same world, nor does it mean that users socialize exclusively with other users. Since these drugs are illegal, the process of making them, or growing the ingredients, is underground.

A good deal of secrecy also surrounds the distribution system. Groups spring up around the supply, distribution, and use of these illegal drugs. To work effectively, the information and supply system must bind the members of particular drug scenes more closely together than would be the case if the drugs were not illegal. However, since the drugs under consideration are illegal their production and distribution tends to be secret and underground. In addition, any individual who takes drugs will be

[4] E. Sutherland, *The Professional Thief* (Chicago: University of Chicago Press, 1937), Chap. 1.

forced to reexamine his position with respect to the larger society. In response to the question "In what ways have drugs altered your views?" one 23-year-old woman who used drugs occasionally said:

> Yes, a great deal. Mostly I became aware of the law givers, or the law makers, 'cause I had to think of the fact that I was doing something illegal, endangering myself and other people, and I became interested in trying to find out why such a thing was considered illegal. And also to be put in a certain category, a certain group of people, [I] had to become aware that I was being labeled, and why. And trying to find my own position in that group, and what I really stood for.

Thus legal and social pressures force the users to organize in groups which, in order to be effective, must have much closer relationships between their members than would be necessary if no unlawful activities were involved. Clearly, associations including hundreds of people do not satisfy this condition, and therefore we find the social structure of the Colony to be a collection of the aforementioned scenes which are bound together only by a very loose alliance, the term alliance to be understood in the following sense: a person who is a member of any particular scene is much more likely to meet people connected with different scenes than is one not linked to any scene whatsoever. A scene then is composed of a small number of individuals who are close friends. A 20-year-old student who used drugs on weekends characterized his group:

> (Is your group close knit?) . . . yeah, as a matter of fact it is. But the way—generally the way, it seems to me is that there are close knit groups, you know, and within that group everyone will use drugs. I don't see it as any different from, let's say, a close knit bowling group.

Another 24-year-old animal caretaker deeply involved in the drug scene put it this way:

> At first I thought there was only one scene, and I was in a little corner of it. But I'm convinced that there are a lot of scenes, people who came from some sort of high school scene, people who came across it at other colleges, people who came across it hanging around some of these cats from Oakland and so on.

The essential quality of these friendship groups is that they share certain values. These values will be described more fully in later chapters. However, the various scenes are not "total" groups in the sense that they are mainly organized around use or that members have no other friends. If this were so, any user could become a member of one of these loosely organized friendship groups, and this is decidedly not the case. People may be excluded for a variety of reasons: because they are escapist, because they're defined as sick, or untrustworthy, or "uncool." Also, if an individual is a recreational user, he will only find access to scenes whose participants share his own commitment to drug use and similarly a "head" will be restricted to scenes composed of persons like himself. The reasons for the relative exclusiveness of the two scenes can be found in the opinions the two different groups have of each other. Recreational users view heads as "outrageous" in dress and manner. Heads view recreational users as dishonest and hooked on conventional values. The relationship between a recreational user and a head is likely to be something like the relationship of a buyer to a seller. They may be found in the same public places, but generally not at the same parties, and never living together.

The Colony is narrowly defined to include recreational users, heads, and those persons who service their demand for marihuana and LSD. There are a wide assortment of scenes in Berkeley, however, in which drugs are not characteristically used yet values are shared in common with Colony members. If one visualized the Colony and its context there would be a small core of systematic users surrounded by a larger group of occasional users. Another and larger ring would consist of those who had experimented with marihuana and/or LSD at one time or another. Beyond that ring would be a larger circle of "sympathetic outsiders." All of the persons in these various scenes would share a vague sense of community. The sympathetic outsiders are mainly white and middle class. They share the Colony's anti-authoritarian and anti-bureaucratic stance but do not use drugs and feel that politics still provide a viable alternative to individual transformation.

LIVING ARRANGEMENTS

The differences between the scenes of the recreational users and the heads do not appear to be confined merely to disagreements on the philosophy of drug use but extend to other aspects of social life as well. According to the information supplied by our informants this trend is particularly pronounced in the area of living arrangements.

Colony members who were less involved in the drug scene tended to live by themselves with roommates, or occasionally with a partner. Attitudes toward premarital relationships seemed to be more liberal than those of the general student population and some respondents (usually males) spoke approvingly of the trend toward sexual freedom which would permit affectional-sexual liaisons between persons, without love being involved.

Colony members viewed boy-girl relationships in a different perspective than did their parents. One of the most conspicuous changes was in the conception of love. It was not viewed as a deep, romantic involvement. To love someone means simply that they "turn you on," that you respond to them at a physical level and are attuned to them. The former requirement of romantic love as a prerequisite to sexual intercourse is no longer necessary. It was viewed as acceptable to sleep with a girl whether you had affection for her or not. Physical relationships were considered legitimate in their own right. There was no expectation among Colony members that an affair would be a permanent one. Affairs which were unhealthy, i.e., where a partner demands something you can't or won't deliver, were expected to be terminated. Relationships which began as temporary, however, could become long range. Colony members saw a number of levels of involvement between two people which might give it a permanent character. The de-emphasis on romantic love seemed to allow for the maximization of personal freedom in a relationship. There was a dilemma inherent in this approach. You were free not to get involved, but others have the same freedom also. The relationship where each partner tries to maximize the other's freedom is a very fragile thing.

Heads, on the other hand, were more likely to be involved with one partner, and sanctions were strong against promiscuity. A kind of serial monogamy seemed to prevail. In this sense, the relationships between men and women were quite traditional. Heads spoke of their female partners as "my chick," or "my old lady."

A number of systematic users were involved in what resembled experiments in communal living: A group of people would cooperatively occupy a large apartment or house, pool its resources and possessions and run its affairs with a strong sense of mutual responsibility. One respondent, a 28-year-old graduate student, told about the residence at which she first turned on to LSD:

> Like everybody was sleeping on one house, in [one] of their houses, you know, there'd be ten or twelve, or God knows how many people would just zonk out, taking stimulants, and staying up, kind of a weird running party.

A 23-year-old housewife and heavy user described a place she moved into after joining an LSD scene:

> It was a completely open pad. The first time I went there there were like a dozen or more people out on the floor, and they probably had been turning on the night before and were just sleeping on the floor, and there was this one guy sitting up on a card table, reading. He was the only one that was still on his feet. And he turned out— he was one of the most beautiful people. But there were people in and out all the time, and people who would shoplift, like and buy food to feed the whole place. And they would come, you know, like turn on and bring food, and stay there and talk. And this one guy . . . was making his living stealing books and selling them back. And in the meantime he was doing paintings. It was just, you know, all kinds of people.

RELATIONS WITH A LARGER
BOHEMIAN WORLD

Within the overall marihuana–LSD scene a distinction was made between the person who was a non-using nonconformist and the one who was a user. Generally writers or artists who for one reason or another do not use drugs though they may have experimented with them were considered to be "bohemians." One 24-year-old animal caretaker and hard-core user described this group as follows:

> Then there's the rest of them. Most of them are people who are sort of not in it, but around—a sort of Bohemian community. And they are very tolerant of it, and they've smoked it, and choose not to do it. I think actually they didn't give it a fair trial. Like one guy said: "oh yeah, I've tried it, and didn't particularly like it."

Another informant, an unemployed 21-year-old hard-core user, identified people living in his apartment house as straight, yet described them later as bohemians. In response to the questions: "But didn't you say these people were straight?," he replied:

> Yeah, but that don't—they're not like you're straight. They're all artists. They're good artists . . . and there are some artists that aren't [users]—not very many.

One difference between the bohemians of another era and the group described by our respondents as bohemian is that the latter constitute only a fraction of all the people that are at present associated with unorthodox life styles. In short, the proportion of non-using bohemian to users is very small.

However, whether or not certain writers, painters, musicians, folk singers, salesmen, or scholars used drugs or not did not seem to be the critical factor for Colony members. The kind of personality an individual displays was seen as a much more important criterion. As a consequence the Colony maintains contact with a larger group of people defined as "straight but understanding." A person can be hip or cool and not be using drugs. If queried on the subject, an acceptable response might be something like: "that's just not his bag man." An interesting side note on the relationship between the drug scene and the world of the artist is the conviction voiced by most of our informants that the innovators of popular culture are very much influenced by the psychedelic revolution whether they take drugs or not. One 24-year-old animal caretaker put it this way:

> The straight world generally doesn't recognize the head world when it sees it. It doesn't know that the head world is very involved in all the rock and roll songs, disc jockeys, modern artistic movements and

so on. Ah . . . they are a little terrified of those people sometimes, but they point them up as the scroungy beatnik types. And, so, they get a little panicked once in a while which comes out in stereotypes like that. Usually they don't know what's going on.

A 28-year-old librarian and hard-core user described what she thought was the connection between popular literature and popular art:

I see a connection, yes. It's related to disrespect, you know. It's like disobeying the laws of art, of making fun of traditional thought of art. It's a new dada, and from this will come a whole new reaffirmation of art, I'm sure. And, I can see that this type of person perhaps that . . . type of person who would, or has tried drugs—those who separate themselves from the straight people, the square people, the hangers on.

RELATIONSHIP WITH "STRAIGHT" PEOPLE

As has been mentioned before, anyone who takes drugs will seek the company of others sharing this experience. However, it appears that drug use will not only encourage a person to participate in some new scene but it will simultaneously effect changes in his standing relationships with non-users. In particular, it seems that the more deeply a Colony member is involved with drugs the less likely it is for him to associate with straight people. This lack of contact with the "outside" world was discussed by a number of our informants who gave varying accounts of the causes and consequences of their isolation from the straight society. One 21-year-old head said:

I really started getting upset about that when I realized that I—I spoke of the restrictions of this dope and that was one of the things that I began realizing how few straight friends I had anymore and how little I saw of those too.

Often a distinction is made between straight people who are "with" it and straight people who are "uptight." A 23-year-old recreational user made this distinction:

(Have drugs caused you to move away from straight friends?)
Yeah, but I don't think that the drug bond is what brought me closer to my friends who do happen to use drugs. I think it was another characteristic which has perhaps made them this type that does use drugs—being unafraid of society's rules. If you believe in something, you know, you do it.

Later on she described a straight friend with whom she continued contact after turning on:

I found [her] to be quite liberal-minded in every aspect. I'm not surprised that she easily accepts the fact that I use drugs. She's one of those who early came up with the idea "if other people do it, I'm not going to like them any the less for it, that doesn't mean I have to do it." And it goes with politics, sex, and drugs—She's, I've found, very tolerant.

A 22-year-old unemployed head explained his difficulty in communicating with straight people, but recognized that with some people it was possible:

> I don't know a hell of a lot to say to them (laughter). I can say hello and, you know, go through a pretty basic riff with them . . . just maybe asking directions or something like that. . . . I had a conversation about music with a cat from Northern California who was (a) very college type, you know, and I got through to him, but I think it was probably mainly because he dug the same kind of music I did, and having listened to that kind of music, turned on. I really— I just raved all over the place. And he started digging it and he got in there and he started goofing out in his own way, but he talked about it differently. He talked about different aspects of the thing, all these planes of conversation that come together . . . between each other . . . I dug what he was saying. He dug what I was saying. . . . And it was interesting to me and I mean, it was kind of like in a buzz state after . . . when my chick and I decided to leave. I was thinking, wow, that was a great conversation with a straight person so I haven't—I don't talk to that many straight people. They don't even have, you know, much reason, or I'm not involved so much with straight people these days.

In the Colony contact with disapproving straight people is minimal. When asked about this type of relationship, members were likely to mention their parents, previous friends, employers, or occasionally a professor. Yet even these relations were limited because Colony members function in a milieu where they are not likely to encounter many strongly disapproving conventional persons. The conventional people who service the colony are often so sympathetic they are not perceived as straight. They are not the stereotype of the American legionnaire who runs the snack stand in small towns across America. If there are disapproving straight people who service the Colony, they are likely to be quiet since they are not in their home territory. Sorties to San Francisco or home for vacation are parallel worlds to the Colony they leave. As one of our respondents put it: "I don't want to visit the suburbs or try to find out what the 'real America' is like. I already know."

This overview of the Colony outlines briefly the main themes which will be discussed in the following chapters. A clearer picture of what the Colony represents in terms of new life styles possible for college-age persons today requires a more detailed analysis of how a newcomer gets initiated into the Colony.

2

Patterns of Drug Organization
in the Colony*

Before a Colony member can experiment extensively with marihuana or LSD he must be in a setting where these drugs are available and must be willing to try them. A person may be highly motivated to try marihuana and LSD, yet be in a situation where they are unavailable to him. Or conversely, a person may have these drugs available and be unwilling to experiment with them because of beliefs about their effects or because of his perception of the character of those who use drugs. This chapter will deal with the pattern of drug organization in the Colony which has made marihuana and LSD available to anyone who wants to use them. The following chapter will explore the interpersonal relationships which predispose a young person to try these drugs.

The description of drug organization is based primarily on observations in the Colony and its peripheries and on numerous taped and off-the-cuff interviews with drug users on up to traffickers in thousand-dollar exchanges. To the extent possible, statistics or other quantifiable evidence are used. The question might be raised at this point as to why prior reports on drug organization are not used to build up our knowledge of trafficking. The answer is simple: the problem is so new that today's analyst has little to build on. The prime source of data remains the users and pushers themselves.

The standard version of drug organization was forcefully stated fifteen years ago in a book by a former narcotics agent in collaboration with the popular writer Will Oursler.[1] A narcotics underworld was reported spreading drug use among students and teen-agers. Marihuana was the bait. Marihuana trafficking was controlled by a single criminal apparatus. Bulk marihuana was broken down and sold as individual cigarettes.

The view of marihuana pushers being strange-looking outsiders, employed by mobsters, who seduce innocent youngsters by giving away

* With the assistance of Jerry Mandel.
[1] H. V. Anslinger and W. Oursler, *The Murderers: The Story of the Narcotic Gangs* (New York: Farrar, Straus & Giroux, 1961).

marihuana under false pretenses first appears in 1937 testimony by expert government officials at the congressional hearings on marihuana legislation, and in several articles by the FBN Commissioner, H. S. Anslinger, from 1930 until his retirement in 1962. The standard version of a criminally controlled organization still has currency, even among some officials and other experts. An FBN pamphlet, *Living Death—The Truth About Drug Addiction*, reprinted as late as 1966, reported:

> Ordinarily, a person is tempted first with marijuana cigarettes. He may not even know they are dope. . . . When a person realizes that anyone is trying to snare him, he should realize he is having a terrifying look, face to face, at what probably is the foulest racket in existence.[2]

There is some reason to question this description of drug organization. There has never been evidence substantiating this version. Presumably, it was drawn from the secret files of the FBN, and any attempt to substantiate it would reveal too much of the agency's operation and the way it gathers its information about criminals involved in drug trafficking. A more serious question is raised, however, if we look at the profits to be made from selling marihuana in today's booming college and Colony markets. As we intend to demonstrate, the profits are very small. The social scientist can then reject this older version of drug organization, either because it is questionable or because it does not relate to the present middle-class college drug scene.

The professional literature in psychiatry, psychology, sociology or criminology provides hardly anything on non-opiate traffic and very little on trafficking. The problem is so new, non-ghetto popular usage so unexpected even five years ago, evidence so difficult to obtain precisely because of its illegality, that today's social scientist has nothing substantial in past literature to build upon. All relevant sources will be taken into consideration, but the primary data come from field observations and learned informants.

A THEORETICAL FRAMEWORK

Speaking to Colony members in order to "see things through their eyes" is an example of induction—of building description from small bits of data. Throughout the gathering of data and its analysis we also applied basic economic models to deduce certain aspects of the trade, to check on cost and profit statements by traffickers and users, and to organize the

---

[2] U.S. Bureau of Narcotics, Bureau of the Treasury (Washington, D.C.: Government Printing Office, 1966).

numerous pieces of information. An economic model as an analytic framework was suggested in trying to interpret mass media stories of dealers arrested who were dealing in hundreds of thousands of dollars worth of marihuana. Agents estimate the value of bulk marihuana in terms not of what they pay for it (which is always considerably lower than their estimates of worth), but of what they conclude will be the total profits after the bulk is broken down and sold as individual "joints." Official estimates fit in with the standard version of syndicated dealing, of top-to-bottom mob control, but are contrary to the occasional reports of what agents actually are paying for large purchases as well as numerous statements by dealers.

One could make several hundred thousand dollars only if he had: (1) a huge concentrated market; (2) purchasers of individual joints willing to pay $1 each; (3) no competition, which requires limited production or the possibility of limiting supplies; and (4) low distribution costs (though it would take 100 street pushers, averaging 40 joint sales per day, over three months, to sell 400 pounds of marihuana). Except for the huge demand, these conditions (as will soon be demonstrated) are not met with marihuana, and only partially met for LSD.

The type and extent of drug organization—the jobs, outside contacts, profits, social status of sellers, etc.—depends largely on economic factors such as the demand for the drug, production costs, ease of supplying, and the risks at every level. This is essentially an issue of supply (how cheaply can the drugs be placed on the market?) and demand (how many persons will be willing to pay that price, or more, and how much will they want?). However, supply and demand analysis only takes us part of the way, for two reasons. First, our concern is mainly with one facet of the picture—namely, the distribution apparatus and the demand in and peripheral to the Colony. Second, several aspects of supply and demand (particularly concerning low-level distribution and demand) are hard to determine quantitatively but instead require an understanding of the motives, and possibly the life style, of those involved in the buying and selling. Our concern, fundamentally, is with patterns of drug organization in the Colony, and an economic framework of analysis is only an aid in this pursuit.

The factors which influence the supply are: the cost of production, the pay scale for which distributors are willing to work—reflecting how well they like their jobs and what economic alternatives are open to them—and risk, which not only includes the law itself but the producer's and distributor's perception of how the law is enforced.

The factors which influence demand are: the perceived effect of the drug, the availability of the drug or the supply contacts, and the risks, which include both the law itself and the users' perceptions of how that law is enforced.

SUPPLY FACTORS

Several elements affecting the supply of marihuana and LSD can be easily noted. Neither is scarce, and the manufacturing or growing costs of both are inexpensive. Marihuana's source—Indian hemp—is a tenacious weed known to thrive in California, Kentucky, and Brooklyn as well as in Mexico, Panama, and Siberia. The toxic component in its flowering tops is reportedly much stronger when grown in hotter, more tropical climates. Most American users make do with a poor-quality Mexican grade, far below the fabled "Acapulco Gold," "Panamian Red," or "Moroccan Hashish." Possibly the Mexican harvesters save the very best top cuttings for themselves. In any event, monopolizing marihuana is very difficult. If prices were too high, customers would begin growing the weed in warm California, and southwestern or southern areas, as a relative handful are already doing. LSD is not scarce now or in the foreseeable future, although the future is problematic. If demand soars considerably, then the current supplies may dwindle. On the other hand, other drugs (like STP) may replace LSD partially. Also, a chemical breakthrough in its manufacture seems inevitable. Though it only costs pennies per dose to manufacture (even illegally), the price of equipping a laboratory to manufacture *good* LSD from a lysergic acid base currently runs into thousands of dollars. Reports that any advanced chemistry student can manufacture LSD in the lab are true only in the technical sense that he can manufacture very poor LSD—which the market will reject after once coming in contact with the fraudulent product: A 23-year-old marihuana and LSD dealer and regular buyer of grams of LSD stated:

> There is nowhere as much acid being made in school laboratories now as they would have you believe, mostly because a total synthesis of LSD, which is the only worthwhile one, is capable of being made only by people with real chemical experience and real chemical facilities. Otherwise, what you consider to be 500 micrograms will test out after impurities have been removed to be anywhere from 90 to 140 So it's trash . . . and there's enough of the other stuff available.

The manufacture of LSD, therefore, is not a bathtub operation, as is the case with methedrine crystal. Lysergic acid, the crucial ingredient in LSD, can be synthesized or derived from an ergot preparation. But that technology is not yet available to any graduate chemist. Working from ergot is a very technical, very expensive, and not totally satisfactory method. Some LSD dealers claimed that the low-grade LSD occasionally distributed in the Colony was due to the lack of expertise on the part of the chemist: A 22-year-old LSD dealer and regular buyer of grams reported:

. . . a lot of people are making acid who don't know what they're doing and the acid's not good acid. It doesn't work, you know, it's not strong enough.

It takes the investment of a lot of time and several thousand dollars to produce even poor-quality LSD. Obtaining the lysergic acid is also a problem. But though LSD is not scarce, it requires considerable skill to make it, considerable financing to set up the lab, and fairly good contacts to get the raw ingredients. Some examples of the "normal" costs of manufacture are indicated by "typical" prices. In the San Francisco–Bay Area a kilo-buyer pays 5 cents a joint for marihuana (about $100 for 2.2 pounds, 50–60 joints per ounce). The same $100 buys from 30–45 capsules of, supposedly, 500 micrograms of LSD. Before federal and state laws, in 1966, a gram of LSD, which made 2,000 such capsules, could be bought for $750–$1,500, and at that the chemist and his "front" or "backer" were taking profits from 80–90 per cent of that price.

The other elements of supply are much harder to describe. Obviously, most of the costs to the consumer result from distribution expenses. Some of these can be described without knowing the motives of the traffickers. The costs of making and consolidating contacts, smuggling and other shipping costs, storage, and numerous miscellaneous expenses (such as wining and dining contacts, phone bills, "waiting" costs, etc.) can be estimated without probing the minds of the dealers. However, the major aspect of distribution can be summed up as "how little money will persons work for at any given level of distribution, given what they perceive as the other rewards of their job?" The other side of the "perceived rewards" is the risk involved. These risks depend not only on the state of the drug laws and their enforcement, but also on the "visibility" of the drug, its bulk. Marihuana is a far bulkier drug than any other popular illegal drug, and is therefore, hard to conceal and risky to ship; it is unwise to risk exposure by growing it in the United States. On the other hand, in a standard capsule dose, there is less LSD than "filler." With risks also, it is not the reality which determines the cost of drugs but the perceptions of risk by dealers, and how great a value they place on keeping out of the hands of the law. In later chapters, we will be interested in precisely these intangibles of how the dealers perceive their jobs and risks, the profits and precautions they deem necessary to engage in selling drugs, and the actual work and expenses that go into maintaining their life styles as pushers and dealers.

In many ways, the supply factors of most concern to us are not easily separated from several components of demand. For example, how well the pusher likes his job depends largely on how his clientele views the services he renders. Colony members who do not "crave" their choice drugs feel positively toward those who supply them with pleasurable experiences.

Demand is also relevant to our analysis because only by estimating it do we have some gross notion of how many drug-dealing jobs are available at various levels. The situation would be vastly different if, in an area like Berkeley, the monthly consumption of marihuana was 2 kilos or 200 kilos. Likewise, if 2,000 Berkeleyites smoked it, the social context of using and dealing would be very different than if there were 20,000 consumers.

Supply Summary

The production costs of marihuana are negligible. Its cost is related solely to importation and distribution expenses. There are diverse sources of marihuana supply for the Colony, which will be described in more detail later, but the major source comes in bulk from Mexico and is distributed through a three-level distribution system. Contact is made from the American side with Mexican farmers who can supply marihuana. It is then smuggled across the border and delivered to persons at the top of the network, usually living in the Bay Area. If large amounts of bulk marihuana are imported, then costs tend to be lower though the attendant risk is higher. This lower cost is eventually reflected in street prices. If we speak of bulk purchases, i.e., over 100 pounds, it costs under $15 a pound to purchase marihuana in Mexico and have it delivered to the United States. It will be packed probably in a dried, pressed form, often in kilo (2.2 pound) bricks. Each brick will be about the size of a shoe box.

It is then sold to a small circle of persons known to the top distributor. It may be sold in bulk, i.e., about 10–50 kilos to each distributor for about $60–$80 a kilo, or a kilo at a time over a long period. Gross profit on 100 kilos would be about $5,000 for an effort involving several months' work. If expenses were deducted from this, the net profit would be about $3,500, or an average of approximately $1,200 a month. The common pattern is to move the merchandise as quickly as possible to the next level to avoid storage problems, although occasionally big dealers will store very large shipments of marihuana in order to appear "normal" before selling or in order to line up customers before exposing their big supply.

The marihuana at this stage is usually sold to street pusher a kilo or two at a time. The average cost at this level is $100 a kilo. If we assume that the big middleman has paid $75 a kilo to the big importer and sold it for $100, he could make $250 a month gross profit if he sold 10 kilos. If he sold 25 kilos, he would earn about $625 a month. The kilos of marihuana are broken down at the street-pushing stage into ounces called "lids" which are sold for $10–$15. "Nickel bags" or one-fifth–one-sixth of an ounce selling for $5 are seldom sold in and around the Colony because the work and risk is too great for all parties to the sale considering the small amount of marihuana and money involved. The pusher usually makes about 30 ounces from his kilo (a certain amount of leakage and personal use keeps this figure down), from which he makes a gross profit of $450. Net profit may range from $200–$350. If he sells only to friends or friends of friends, he is likely to dispose of the kilo in a month. There are numerous opportunities for part-time pushing jobs at the lower levels, and the amount of money is variable. These roles will be described in later chapters.

We can speak of two different distribution systems operating in the Colony—one for marihuana and one for LSD. Both consist of three strata: top, middle, and street level (not including the producer, i.e., the farmer or chemist). They are separate at the top, but linked at the second stage. The equivalent of the Mexican farmer in the LSD distribution system is the chemist, though he may take more initiative than his counterpart in setting up his own network. Like marihuana, the production costs are minimal if one has lysergic acid. If regularly manufactured, the chemist can make LSD for about 2 or 3 cents per 500 capsule. He usually sells grams of LSD for the equivalent of 10 cents a 500 microgram capsule to the top distributor, and sells enough for approximately 5,000–20,000 such capsules at a single sale. If he sold enough for 10,000 capsules, his profits would be about $750 a month, though he would work but a few days.

The top of the LSD distribution system looks somewhat like the one for marihuana though the social class of the personnel may differ, and the risks are considerably less and the profits higher with LSD. After purchasing enough LSD for 5,000 capsules from the chemist, the top distributor delivers a half-gram or more, i.e. enough for 1,000 or more capsules to a small group of middlemen at about $1.00 per capsule. If we assume that 75 cents per capsule is profit, then the gross profit per month for the top distributor is about $3,750. It is at this point in the two distribution systems that large profits are to be made.

The middleman usually sells in bulk, seldom under 100 capsules to a customer for $1.75–$2.00. The profits to be made at this level are about $900–$1,000 per month gross. Working expenses reduce this amount to about $600.

The street peddler usually buys 100–200 capsules for about $2.00 and sells them for twice that much. Gross profit from the sale of 200 capsules of LSD per month is about $400. Deducting expenses at this level, the net profit is about half that.

In short, the cost of production is low, there is enough money to be made at all levels, and there is a belief among those who are part of the system that the risks involved are slight and diminishing if one regularizes his purchase and sales.

DEMAND FACTORS

The drug most widely used in the Colony is marihuana. Next comes LSD. Far behind is the demand for amphetamines or pep pills, purchased as methedrine crystal in heavy drug-using circles, and usually injected rather than swallowed. However, comparing the demand for different drugs is difficult because the effects, significance, and costs of drugs vary so much. A pound of marihuana costs under $100 in the Bay Area and can be finished in a month by fifteen regular users. A pound of LSD would supply the Bay Area for years. A person who drops acid once a week is considered a head, but using marihuana twice a week is considered recreational. A dozen or so LSD trips are often considered major events in one's life, but marihuana sessions twice a week over several years are usually considered sensual fun and games of not nearly the same significance. The Director of Psychiatry at the University of California hospital in Berkeley put it this way:

> Although the takers of marijuana and LSD overlap . . . Pot smoking is likely to be a relaxing, convivial affair . . . few pot enthusiasts would claim that it initiated one into life's mysteries. Devotees of LSD, on the other hand, have surrounded the ingestion of this substance with a mystique. . . . Some students claim that LSD experiences provide deep insights.[3]

At "street" prices, $5 buys a single capsule of LSD, but enough marihuana for at least 10 joints, each capable of an evening's high.

Later in this chapter we will analyze the growth trends of various drug use to determine how new the phenomenon is and what direction it seems to be taking, and we will try to specify the actual extent of drug use within the Colony and its peripheries. But initially we will discuss the perceived effects of the various drugs used and the social attitudes toward drug use in and on the fringes of the Colony, in order to make more comprehensible the local demand and (in later chapters) the acceptability of drug selling.

Perceived Effects of Drugs

Colony members state that the main thing about marihuana is that it is pleasant. It is used more than any other current illegal drug because it is relatively mild. Most tasks can be easily performed under its influence, and a high lasts only a few hours, with no aftereffects like a hangover.

So long as the stories of marihuana's association with criminality, violence, rape, opiate addiction, and the like were believed, or considered distinct possibilities, the demand for marihuana remained relatively low in the Colony and its environs. These beliefs declined in importance as more and more people were exposed to the experience of users. In the early 1930's in the United States such exposure was limited to Mexican-American communities, a handful of Negro ghetto areas, and a few jazz bohemian circles. In the late 1940's and early 1950's experience with marihuana seemed to spread rapidly in Northern ghetto areas. Soldiers in Korea and Japan during the early 1950's were also exposed to heavy marihuana usage. However, neither the knowledge of the pleasant

---

[3] Mervin Freedman and Harvey Powelson, "Drugs on Campus: Turned On and Tuned Out," *The Nation*, January 31, 1966.

effects of marihuana nor rejection of previous beliefs about marihuana penetrated the white middle class, or lower middle class, until the 1960's.

Because marihuana is perceived as mild, it does not generate fears of bad trips, and regular users turn on their friends to it virtually indiscriminately. Many systematic users treat marihuana as the factory worker does beer. It is so abundant and inexpensive that it is often given as a gift or to friends upon request. Within the Colony, it is probably the equivalent of a martini as the offering to visitors.

In contrast to marihuana, there is general agreement on the effects of LSD. This seems to be due to what might be characterized as an "LSD Lobby" centered around Timothy Leary, the *Psychedelic Review*, several researchers who have published their results, and numerous middle-class "creative" people who write and paint about their LSD experiences. Unlike the early clusters of marihuana users, the LSD scenes contain very articulate, confident people. The research on LSD has been much greater than that on marihuana, and the researchers have been more impartial and scientific than the handful who studied the effects of marihuana. The Alpert-Leary experiments at Harvard, for example, used far more subjects than any marihuana research. They had their subjects take LSD under natural conditions of environment, conducive to maximizing certain major effects of LSD, something which has never been done in any experiment with marihuana.[4]

What, then, are the effects of the drug? Users agree on two basic types of effects. One is intellectual, and pertains to material or symbolic "structures." Man-made artifacts are seen as just that—unnatural and artificial. Institutions, roles, statuses, symbols, especially including "words," concrete-aluminum-glass-steel buildings, freeways, material possessions, etc., are seen as so much bric-a-brac standing between a human being and his environment. The second type of effect is sensate. Colors glisten and shimmer. Sounds explode and ripple. Textures come alive or split. These effects will vary from person to person, and from one LSD high to another, but users agree that something very powerful occurs in these areas of the senses. There is a third type of effect which though common is not universal and may only be the second type of effect extended and picked up by the mind in the form of hallucinations. Certain perspectives seem to follow the LSD experience. Users often hear "silence" and are at once aware of the enormity and continuity of the world and their own limited essences. Simultaneously, many feel an intimate part of the "overall design of the universe." An 8-to-5 job, 30-year home payments, an expensive car, one's socioeconomic status, all lose significance when stacked up against tens of thousands of years of past, present, and future human development.

These effects are not easily forgotten. Sometimes, the peak of these feelings will last from three to fifteen hours. Even on the second day of

---

[4] See Chapter 8 for a discussion of research conducted on marihuana and LSD.

an "acid trip," the user may feel very high. The user must, therefore, be prepared not only to experience vast new things but to be able to spend two days in a setting which would not be upset by the LSD experience.

The effects of LSD may even extend beyond the one- or two-day trip. Temporary psychoses have often been reported, and most Colony members accept such reports as having validity, even if vastly overemphasized. LSD "visions" have recurred in some users many weeks or months after a trip. Many regular users attribute bad trips, breakdowns in the ability to cope with the LSD-induced stimuli, and swift chaotic changes in a person's life to the interplay between the person and the drug, not to LSD itself. They feel that the user might have had "too much artificiality surrounding himself" or might have refused to accept the cacophony of stimuli about him—or might refuse to be a minute atom in the unfolding of an infinite universe. The regular user tends to consider such bad trips as revealing "inadequate people," and therefore many of the vast changes are improvements in life styles. Still, such strong effects of LSD are heavily and negatively weighted by nonusers and novice users, thus hindering the demand for LSD.

Regular users accept the possibility of bad trips, even for themselves, for everyone has severe hang-ups. Regular users often claim to benefit from bad trips, and they accept and indulge in the subtle uses to which LSD can be applied.

There are also limitations on the extent of demand. The effects are so strong that there is little desire to take it more than once a week, even among "acid heads." More than twice a month is considered very heavy usage. Furthermore, repeated usage breeds greater sensitivity to the drug and makes it easier to reach neo-drug states without the "acid." "Acid heads" often reduce their dosage after many months of usage.

LSD is not often given away as is marihuana. Its effects are so strong that only the most irresponsible indiscriminately offer it to virtual strangers or straight friends. Because of fears of bad trips, many Colony members will not take LSD except in very controlled settings. The perceived effects are that under "correct supervision," and often otherwise, LSD is consciousness-expanding and psychologically beneficial, possibly even spiritual.[5]

LSD's effects are unmistakable, but the marihuana high is often so mild that initiates miss it, especially if it is of poor quality, if the setting does not foster sensual awareness, or if the user has not learned to inhale properly, is concerned by the odd behavior of his fellow smokers, or is in constant fear of being arrested.

Generally heroin and the opiates are rejected by Colony members. Rec-

---

[5] LSD's spiritual aura is recognized by evangelist Billy Graham who, when speaking at Berkeley and other colleges during 1967, offered a "Christ trip" as "the real alternative."

reational users reject heroin because it is perceived as addictive and expensive, and one has to be in contact with "hard criminals" to purchase it. It also requires using the feared hypodermic needle. Heads reject heroin basically because its effects are desensitizing.

Methedrine or amphetamine crystals, though used occasionally by Colony members, are generally avoided because of the reputation for being physically debilitating. Many Colony members seemed familiar with what they characterized as "speed" scenes—involving young people whose drug of choice was methedrine. The disruption of social relations between regular methedrine users and their friends is a feature of this scene that is unappealing to Colony members. Methedrine users, or "meth heads," are viewed as quite inconsistent. Their ups and downs make them too unpredictable and upsetting for someone not knowledgeable about the drug or not willing to bear the burden of the relationship.

Those in the Colony who have tried methedrine and found it appealing have tended to move out of the Colony. Others admit to using it infrequently. A handful describe themselves as having "passed through" a methedrine crystal stage, sometime on their way to the Colony. Because methedrine is not chemically addictive, is much cheaper than heroin, and is said to be instantly euphoric, its use in and near the Colony is greater than that of opiates, but is still only a small fraction of that of marihuana or LSD.

Social Attitudes Toward Drug Use

The standard "pusher myth" assumes very few users and virtually no information about drugs among novices or potential users. Youth, according to this assumption, are lured and seduced into trying something unknown. Similarly, a major sociological perspective that marihuana users are socialized into a deviant group also assumes few users. The situation in the Colony, however, is nearly the opposite. The non-marihuana user is likely to be a rarity. Firsthand and secondhand information about drugs is so quickly and thoroughly disseminated that even the open-minded non-user can fairly easily determine the effects of various drugs. A Columbia University physician was recently quoted:

> The case could be made that if a male goes through four years of college on many campuses now, without the [marihuana] experience, this abstinence bespeaks a rigidity in his character structure and fear of his impulses that is hardly desirable.[6]

Regarding marihuana, the Colony reads official and medical statements to see how closely the authorities are approaching "reality," not for any enlightenment. A major adviser on drugs for the U.S. Crime Commission, psychologist Richard Blum, considers that the new wave of drug-users in many ways know more than the "experts."

[6] Quoted by David Sanford in "Pot Bust at Cornell," *New Republic*, April 15, 1967.

The exploratory uses of kids are way ahead of our classification. Pharmacologically, the kids have made some of the pioneering advances in drug effects, so if we are good researchers we will be watching them.[7]

The market is not growing because of subterfuge; more and better "drug education" by authorities will mean nothing to the Colony. To smoke marihuana—even daily—is not socially disapproved by most Colony members. Rather, to argue seriously for current laws against it, or to be opposed to its use because of its medical and psychiatric dangers, would make one a deviant in the Colony or almost all its peripheries. The social disapproval of "the outside world" is considered as an absurd tragedy by those most removed from the straight world, or reaffirmation of the reasons for rebellion by those engaged in making their separation from such authority.

The attitudes in the Colony toward LSD, on the other hand, are varied, and many individuals have mixed feelings. However, there seem to be some common views: LSD should not be given indiscriminately, for there are some people for whom it might not be beneficial; there is nothing wrong or immoral about the person who does take LSD; it should not be forbidden by law as it recently has been; and the official position on LSD is often silly.[8]

Social attitudes toward drugs have an impact on demand, just as heavy use influences the social attitudes. A contagion effect has developed: the more users, the less viable the official "lines" re marihuana and, to a lesser extent, LSD; the less respected the sanctions against drug use and the less respected the rationale for such sanctions, the greater the experimentation with drugs; the more widespread the use, the easier it is for novices, non-users, and relatively straight persons to obtain drugs; the more varied the user groups, the less any potential user has to change identities to begin using a drug; the more users and the more peripheral areas of use, the more jobs open for drug traffickers and the more pushers will operate among "their own kind"; the more pushers blend in with their clientele, the harder it becomes to catch them; the less the risk, the greater the desirability of drug dealing. To stem this contagion, official policy must be based on reason, but the Colony is convinced that this is virtually nonexistent regarding the drugs of their choice.

[7] Speech to Attorney General's Conference on Drug Abuse, San Francisco, July, 1966. Quoted in *San Francisco Examiner*, October 27, 1966.

[8] Recent statements such as the following by California Senator George Murphy are merely "proof" of the "consciousness-shrinking" required of Establishment leaders: "[LSD] seems to have the capability to destroy the minds, the morals, and the mentality of many of our young people and could possibly change them from potentially sound, constructive, productive members of our society into dangerous, mentally-depleted psychotics."

(Testimony before the Special Subcommittee on Narcotics, Senate Judiciary Committee, May 23, 1966.)

Over time, the contagion effect reaches a tip-over point where serious doubt about official positions is replaced by disregard. Social pressure influencing drug use then tends to come solely from within the Colony, and the less-convinced peripheral elements become inquisitive rather than inquisitional.

A Summary of Demand

If the effects of marihuana are perceived as pleasurable and easily manageable, if there is increasing social pressure to try it or at least not to "put it down," if it is available to everyone in and near the Colony, if the risks of taking it are diminishing as constitutional issues are raised concerning its illegality, the demand in the Colony should be soaring.

As for LSD, the users have increased geometrically over the past two years and will in all likelihood continue to expand—except, perhaps, if there is convincing evidence of LSD's damaging effects. Cost is a small barrier; $2.50 to $5.00 for an all-day trip once a month or so is hardly a burden to most of the Colony LSD market. As both the market expands and the technology improves, we can expect prices to continue to drop and production outlets to increase.

The punishment in California for using LSD is not as severe as for using marihuana or the opiates. From the Colony member's perspective there is no sign yet of any significant enforcement apparatus and no cases of severe punishment of possessors of LSD. Media reports of enforcement have emphasized cracking down on producers and distributors, which does not have the effect of deterring users. LSD is not associated with illegal behavior in the minds of the Colony members. The law is associated with repression rather than with society's protection. It will not reduce demand appreciably unless it has far stronger teeth and unless it is enforced far more stringently than the marihuana laws. There is no indication that this is likely to happen.

THE LINK BETWEEN VARIOUS ILLEGAL DRUGS. Marihuana seems to be attractive to a wide assortment of people. If we were to look at the social composition of marihuana users, we would find they come from various age and income levels. Marihuana is linked to LSD and amphetamines by virtue of the fact that people who use these drugs also use marihuana. Though marihuana may have a distinctive supply and production system, much like the other two there is some convergence at the middle levels. What this means is that the middle-level dealer in LSD and amphetamines is likely to stock marihuana as a service to his customers. The middle-level dealer in marihuana, however, may not stock other drugs. Because of the demand for it which far exceeds the demand for other drugs, there are many persons who sell only marihuana. The pattern of the marihuana dealer specializing only in that drug and no others may be changing. The risks are great, and there is more money to be made if he moves up to LSD. In view of the numerous sources of kilos, the low costs involved in the initial purchase of bulk marihuana to the initiate pusher, the presence of a ready market for marihuana which any regular user knows about, and the aura of free play which surrounds most marihuana-using circles, the pusher who begins to traffic usually begins with marihuana alone.

The social composition of those in the Colony who use marihuana and LSD seems to be substantially the same. This is not so when we compare them with heavy amphetamine users. The heavy amphetamine users seem to be younger, may come from a lower educational strata in the community, and seem to prefer the experience of "going outwards" rather than "inwards." The regular LSD users in the Colony seem to be somewhat older, which may account for their rejection of amphetamines. Heavy amphetamine users often remain on sprees which extend well beyond the weekend, while LSD users view their drug as inappropriate for sprees. In short, the social composition and the motivations of users in the marihuana-LSD scene and the amphetamine scene are different. The rationales for using hallucinogenic drugs preclude any interest in heroin. Its use is considered antithetical to the value of opening up one's perceptions. Hence dealers in marihuana or LSD do not usually stock heroin as a service to their customers, though presumably, if there was a demand for it, heroin would find its way into the Colony. By contrast, the heavy users of amphetamines, who are unattached, young, and gregarious, tend to be found at the fringes of many drug scenes. Since a premium seems to be placed by them on experimentation with all sorts of drugs, the amphetamine dealer is likely to stock a variety of drugs.

There are several ties between heavy amphetamine usage and heroin, however. The nalline test for narcotic addiction is a major threat to thousands of heroin users. Some have found that injecting methedrine crystal a day or two prior to taking the nalline test allows the traces of opiates to disappear.[9] At about the same time this was discovered, young heroin users who were experimenting with the drug reported that they liked the high and the scene but wanted to avoid getting addicted. They began at that point rotating methedrine crystal with heroin. In one midwestern city a dispute was reported between the younger and older heroin users, the former arguing that methedrine was far preferable to heroin and did not lead to addiction, the latter contending that heroin was more benign and did not destroy one's body.[10]

[9] J. T. Carey and A. Platt, "The Nalline Clinic: Game or Chemical Superego?" *Issues in Criminology*, II, No. 2 (Fall, 1966).

[10] J. W. Rawlin, " 'Street Level' Abuse of Amphetamines," A *Presentation to the Conferees Attending the First National Institute on Amphetamine Abuse*, Southern Illinois University, February 21–25, 1966.

Methedrine crystal has several characteristics which make it fit easily into a heroin scene. It is taken by needle, and requires all the preparation of heating with water or some other substance. There is an instant of feeling when methedrine "rushes" to the brain. There is also the ritual with paraphernalia and repeated injections.

All of these ties are ways in which the opiate world incorporates methedrine crystal, and the obvious link between the heroin users and "speed freaks" who come out of a non-ghetto world is through the dealers. At the upper levels heroin becomes available, and the person who regularly shoots methedrine may be able to acquire some heroin. Aside from the dealers, the methedrine scene is conducive to heroin experimentation because of the presence of needles. This apparatus seems to be a barrier for most young people in the Colony. The feeling is that once you possess a shooting kit you have entered a new dimension of risk and lawlessness.

There seems to be no clear-cut chemical link between methedrine crystal and opiates. Most heavy methedrine users have no desire to enter the world of the junkie. Clearly the main link with the heroin world, with methedrine as with any other non-opiate, is the social context within which drugs are taken. It is the meaning which drug users apply to drugs which leads them to or away from "graduating" or "flunking out" to heroin.

RECENT TRENDS IN DRUG USE

The disregard of official warnings and traditional sanctions against drug use has indeed reached a tip-over point in many areas besides the Colony, if one believes the official arrest and seizure figures. This is a nationwide phenomenon, although California seems "ahead" of the nation, and (among young middle-class users) the Colony and its neighboring community in the Haight-Ashbury seem to be forerunners in California. Before discussing the numerous consequences of this trend in drug arrests upon the style of drug use and the policies of law enforcement, some relevant statistics will be cited to demonstrate that a "tip-over" has in fact been reached.

In California, from 1962 to 1966 non-marihuana arrests for narcotics and other dangerous drugs remained about the same, but marihuana arrests for adults increased from 3,291 to 14,293 and for juveniles from 248 to 3,869. These enormous increases are not spread equally throughout the population but are concentrated among the young and among whites.[11]

---

[11] The average age, even of adult arrestees, is decreasing. The changes in the racial composition of arrestees is illustrated by statistics of juvenile marihuana arrests for 1964 and 1965. White arrestees increased 118 per cent from 342; Mexican-Americans increased 15 per cent from 335; and Negroes increased 41 per cent from 336.

CALIFORNIA STATE NARCOTICS ARRESTS, 1962–JUNE 30, 1967

	1962	1963	Percentage Increase Over 1962	1964	Percentage Increase Over 1963	1965	Percentage Increase Over 1964	1966	Percentage Increase Over 1965	First Half of 1967
Marihuana										
Adults	3,291	4,677	42	6,055	29	8,349	38	14,293	71	11,587
Juveniles	248	503	101	1,224	141	1,623	33	3,869	138	4,526
Other Narcotics or Dangerous Drugs										
Adults	12,959	12,051	—	13,189	9	13,095	—	14,026	8	8,547[a]
Juveniles	1,077	936	—	781	—	1,068	37	1,165	9	1,209[a]

[a] Much of the rise in Other Narcotics and Dangerous Drugs for the first half of 1967 was due to the implementation of anti-LSD laws for the first time.

—a trend reported in many other states.[12] The statistics illustrate a trend which, because of its size and because it is repeated throughout the area, state and country, cannot be attributed to the numerous quirks in law enforcement and crime statistics which often invalidate small, short-run statistical changes. The statistics do not specify the extent of drug use because there is no easy way of determining what percentage of users get caught.

As a result of the great increase in use of marihuana (and LSD), persons in the Colony and other heavy drug-using communities are getting much bolder in their public statements about drugs; this is reflected in buttons, magazines, song lyrics, and plain old-fashioned political statements. One 23-year-old middle-range dealer stated:

> It's not only happening at Berkeley but all over the place, because that's what's happening. People are getting to the point where they all say, "Screw you, I'm getting high; I think it's good for me."

Older drug users, brought up at a time when smoking pot was a deviant act requiring secrecy and concealment, are constantly taken aback by such public boldness. Recently, and increasingly, smoking joints of marihuana in certain public settings has become noticeable, especially when there is a large, apparently pro-drug crowd present (as at rock dances, be-ins, etc.) or in settings where law enforcers are not likely to be present and the mood of passers-by is likely to be peaceful. A 24-year-old female, a former pusher who had been involved in a heavy drug scene for several years, observed:

> I'd been living in Los Angeles a few years, and people there tend to be a bit cooler at their drug taking than here. Berkeley and maybe the Haight-Ashbury is the only city that I could walk down the street and pass people smoking a joint walking—the only place that I've gone to a dance or to an open-type of party—not private—and people sat around and smoked grass. Everytime I come up here I see it constantly.

If the users are feeling emboldened by the recent trends, the law enforcers seem to have lost control. Various strategies have apparently been tried, but none works. Close surveillance and arrests of all types of users, and obtaining evidence by any means, merely clog up the jails

---

[12] Boston in 1967 reported a record marihuana seizure of about 140 pounds, approximately double the previous record set less than a year previously. New York, in 1966, seized 1,690 pounds of marihuana compared to approximately 100 pounds in 1960. In New York City narcotic felony arrests during the first eight months of 1967 were running 44 per cent above the same period in 1966. In the two counties of Long Island, Nassau and Suffolk, the increase in drug arrests approximates that of California. Narcotics arrests in Nassau rose 117 per cent in 1966 and through May 1967 appeared to be moving toward another 50 per cent rise. Average age of arrestees decreased from 22.7 in 1966 to 20.6 during the early part of 1967. For Suffolk narcotics arrests appeared to be in for a 60 per cent increase in 1967, with half the arrestees aged 16–21.

and courts with young persons not very different from average. Overlooking small bits of evidence even when apparent merely sanctions drug use. This, however, seems to be the policy which has evolved in Berkeley and San Francisco, and probably many other cities of heavy non-opiate drug use where the general population is generally tolerant of nonviolent bohemians. A 25-year-old graduate student who occasionally delivers quantity marihuana to Berkeley commented on what would provoke a drug arrest in Berkeley:

> The only time there's going to be a big bust around a university area, even like Berkeley which is obviously a pretty freaky scene, where there are certainly freaks within a block of the University where there isn't anybody who isn't high, the only time is if you're sitting there with a sign that says, "We deal in drugs here, and we think it's good, and I'm high." That's probably what it is when there's a big Berkeley bust.

Rough limits seem to be drawn on the extent of drug use or sale, the flagrancy of drug selling, and the general outrageousness of the individual.

If the "tip-over" seems beyond containment, and sophisticated police strategy seems to be concerned merely with heavy selling and flagrant and outrageous use, the drug arrest statistics may well taper off. For now though, the statistics show a trend of vastly increasing drug use, although the extent of usage requires a more sophisticated analysis using official statistics and other information.

3

Involvement in the Drug Scene

This chapter will attempt to describe the routes into the drug scene in and around universities. It does not take account of the many other paths into this same scene. Some of the participants in our inquiry were inducted into drug use before they came to Berkeley. This may have been in some artistic or theatrical circle or as part of growing up in a disorganized section of a large city where, by all reports, drug use is widespread. Our concern here is to sketch one typical route into a college-related drug scene.

The typical cycle of involvement described here is an idealized one. There are probably several alternative cycles which could account for an individual's increasing involvement in a university-connected drug scene. As was implied earlier when describing the trafficking in drugs, there are somewhat different processes at work in introducing persons to scenes other than the marihuana-LSD one. Our investigation was formulated in terms of a sequential model, but the empirical reality did not fit that neatly. Some persons experiment with marihuana and it ends there. Others move into a marginal position in the drug scene and remain there. A smaller group move into the core of the marihuana-LSD world. Some of them go into drug dealing and embark on an illegal career. At each point in the process some are dropping out or remaining stationary so that at the end of our cycle we are only talking about a handful of people. The stages of involvement described in this chapter begin with the potential user's critical stance toward the larger society and ends with drug dealing. In between are reported the circumstances of first use, development of rationales for using marihuana, more systematic use, turning on to LSD, rationales for its use, and finally hard-core use.

SENSE OF DISILLUSIONMENT

The beginning for everyone seems to be some critical awareness of the way things are in society. A sense of disillusionment is strong. As a 24-year-old reformed head and laboratory technician put it:

I guess it takes a dissatisfaction with—first you have to be dissatisfied with what you see around you in society. Because if you're satisfied with other people and yourself, and just whatever you see when you walk down the street or look out the window, then you'll probably never take it, because, because, if you're satisfied with it, then you accept all the norms. One of the norms is that you don't smoke pot. And, eventually, somebody is going to come along and offer you some. And, eventually if enough people offer it to you, you are going to take some.

Our questions focused on our respondents' situation prior to initial use: the kind of scene in which they were moving, what their feelings were about it, and so on. There are some problems in retrospective reporting. Our respondents' replies may be inaccurate. They may not remember or, more likely, their present situation may distort their recollections. The critical stance of Colony members might be much more a function of later involvement in the drug scene than something which existed prior to their first using drugs. Suffice it to say that they perceived themselves as more disillusioned with society than their peers, prior to "turning on" for the first time. This usually went along with a sense that they were defined by others as different—too "restless," or "loners" or "too imaginative" by parents and school authorities. One 26-year-old systematic user and part-time artist put it this way:

I'd been drawing all my life, and scared my folks to death. They didn't like that at all. They didn't like the idea of me not adapting to the dog eat dog world, and being in what everyone calls a dream world.

A 27-year-old married woman who eventually became a hard-core user linked up her own personal dissatisfaction with the shape of the large society:

I've always been dissatisfied and I think this holds true for my husband, too. With ourselves, as well as with things around us, the way we see things as being and how wrong-headed people are. And what in the hell is wrong with the world, and why do people have wars and that sort of thing?

The fundamental disillusionment comes because of society's hypocrisy—proclaiming one set of standards and doing something else. They say we're interested in peace yet we are involved in a war against a weak nation; they say we are interested in equality yet we have segregation; they say we're interested in freedom yet we suppress divergent views. A 22-year-old user-dealer expressed this same view:

[Society's] morality has had hassles with every other type of morality, you dig? They have suppressed people. They suppress right here in this country . . . The Indian was smoking grass, and hunting buffalo, having his little fights amongst himself, and all that, you dig? But the cat wasn't that bad, man to get to be damn near wiped out, so that there is only a population of [of Indians] in the United States a population only big enough to fill Rhode Island. Man, that's terrible! And there were more than 900 different tribes of Indians on this continent, man.

Not only is society hypocritcial; it is rigid or "up tight." It is unable to be spontaneous, to let go. But more than that it doesn't want anyone else too, either. A 24-year-old hard-core user stated the case forcefully:

> (Speaking of reaction to beats) They're afraid of our place. They're afraid of our divergence from their solid norm, because they're so afraid to step out of theirs. You know they couldn't. They couldn't anymore go and turn around and grow a beard and wear dirty clothes and not wash for several days than . . . most of the hip people that I know are, have more, stand more on principle, than those people. It seems to me that those people aren't really taking their principles seriously, they're not taking too much at all seriously, . . . so that they really get an insane sick thing out of putting everything down, you know. Like an angry, drunk, clean slob, frat rat. He's angry at everything you know. He's angry at his next door neighbor. But it's a game there. . . . They call each other bad names all the time and they call some people on the street bad names all the time. Because that's their game—call everybody down you can.

The term "up tight" seems to point to a certain kind of wooden or martinet behavior exhibited by straight people. It refers to an inability to bend or to accept different ways of doing things or different notions of what constitutes right and wrong. The same young man continued:

> They feel that every action they do has to conform to a ritual, otherwise it's not right. You can't do anything that's spontaneous or from yourself. You make love like in the toothpaste ad, talk to your children like, like "Father Knows Best." . . . they've lost the natural ecstasy of living, man. Rigid is sort of a hollow block of wood so that you're kind of tight on the outside but if you konk it a couple of times,—sounds like a drum—like Is there anything going on inside of there?

Other themes are connected with the acute sense of the hypocrisy and rigidity of the straight world. One relates to the kind of status striving which does not permit any kind of enjoyment. An unemployed 21-year-old head voiced this criticism:

> Ah, knowing that "yes, you have to work, you know." But you don't have to work in order to buy a 1965 Buick for your wife. All you need is a 1953 Plymouth, man to get you from here to there. . . . See, all these people are working for status. To build a house and live in—to build an image and live in it.

The sense of disillusionment leads to questioning the legitimacy of society's norms. Initial use of illegal drugs such as marihuana commonly occurs when structural circumstances favor it and when the novice is aware that ideas which neutralize its stigmatized character are known.

The structural circumstances and the neutralizing ideas are so inter-related that little is gained by insisting on historical priority. A 24-year-old reformed head spoke about the gradual awareness of official deception about marihuana:

> I remember seeing movies when I was a kid, and they showed movies on drug addicts and everything, you know, little dramatizations of, of junkies and people that smoked marihuana and they painted a really bad picture like, look kids, don't ever get involved in this . . . this is what it's like, really bad people sitting around, shooting up dope, or smoking pot, really criminal type people. And they'd actually come out with lies, you know. They'd say "well marihuana was addicting and that if you take it twice, you automatically turn into a raving maniac, or something . . ." and then you find out, well these people lied to me, society in general has really lied to me, he said that, . . . They said a lot of things about drugs that weren't true.

A 19-year-old heavy user and part-time dealer further described the process:

> A person . . . can't have helped but hear that grass is, you know, when you're growing up that grass is, you know—marihuana and juvenile delinquency and all that. And . . . I think a person who tries it, having had all this knowledge about it before, suddenly he realizes something he has been told is wrong all his life is suddenly not wrong, that this can't help but lead him to think the same way about other things.

The claims society makes on its members to comply with norms relating to drug use cease to have meaning at this point: A 25-year-old graduate student much involved in the drug scene noted:

> . . . the thought of that when you take drugs you recognize that the frameworks don't have such absolute value as you had once seen . . . people who take marihuana are less concerned with the trivia of American values. In America as a country which spends more sometimes for the packaging of an article in the supermarket or an automobile than it does on the substance itself and it does the same with people and their characters and their attitudes and their jobs and their livelihood. . . . Often, much more attention is put to the packaging than to the content. People who smoke marihuana—this is usually one of their immediate reactions—they slow down a little. . . . They slow down and they say "hmm," they start noticing things in people's character that they have been moving too fast to see. . . .

CIRCUMSTANCES OF FIRST USE

While a profound state of dissatisfaction with the larger society and the values it proclaims usually precedes extensive experimentation with marihuana, the dissatisfaction by itself is not an explanation for use.

Many alienated young people do not resort to drug use. Two other things must be present: the person must be in a setting where drugs are available and he must be introduced to drugs by someone he holds in esteem. In a previous chapter we described the pattern of drug use as it has developed around large universities close to metropolitan areas. Drugs are now available to the student who is willing to experiment with them.

Commonly a person becomes aware of the possibility of using drugs when it comes to light that a friend is using them. If the novice is a girl, this person is likely to be a boyfriend; if a boy, a roommate or relatively long-time intimate. That a person standing in such a relationship to a novice takes drugs at all is a strong argument for the novice to take them as it dispels prior ideas that only "dope fiends" and "derelicts" of one kind or another would ever consider doing so. Perhaps other persons that he respects are considering the use of drugs, and this dispels some of the initial disfavor and apprehension.

A 23-year-old woman, an occasional user of marihuana, spoke of her boyfriend's reaction to his roommate's use:

> He was very willing to accept the fact that I didn't want to have anything to do with it so he just went along with his turning on (but not very much when you were around?) No, but doing it did effect me and, it made me—seeing him do it and suddenly realizing, you know, let's look at this again. You know, it's not hurting him and all this. Then my roommate, ah . . . who, she was much more interested in experimenting and "why not, let's try it." And she finally decided she was gonna try it and then, oh, another good friend was into the drug scene to a point that she rarely, but occasionally, had a joint and a lot of her friends were in it. And you know, I saw her and got into it thinking in terms of it being more widespread than I thought with her too. And I can't remember who influenced me to try it the first time. But it was a combination of either my roommate—she was gonna try it, you know "tonight," and that sort of thing. And my friend who I know as a perfectly sane person, you know, doing it and so, you know, then I tried it.

This is a situation of trust between a small group of friends which extends from introduction to drug use through the period of using occasionally as others make drugs available and therefore only periodic experimentation is possible.

RATIONALES FOR USING MARIHUANA

On occasion persuasion is involved in moving the novice to try drugs for the first time, but this persuasion takes the form of arguments which neutralize the effect of the customary restraints on using drugs instead of more straightforward directives to experiment. Such neutralization usually covers the following points. Marihuana is non-addicting and is, therefore, unjustly included under the narcotics laws. A 21-year-old part-time artist and systematic user observed:

> I think it should be legalized. I don't see any reasons why not. They have now a cruel and unusual punishment, and that's ridiculous, because it's not half as destructive as alcohol.

A 21-year-old heavy user-dealer and former student agreed:

> [this] is a misconception of the majority of the population . . . that it brings about a physical addiction. Ah . . . this is stupidity, it doesn't, because there is no addiction, no physical dependence on these particular drugs. I can stop, abruptly, not worry and whenever I feel like it.

Another statement that is rejected relates to drug dealing: drug dealers are wicked men who hang around playgrounds hoping to inject small children.

A 22-year-old woman, a casual user, agreed:

> I think a lot of fairly tales are passed down. I distinctly remember girl scout movies that I watched when I was a little girl. You know, along with ones, the one on the facts of life, they had one, about drugs and about alcoholism. There were 3 of them: sex, drugs, and alcohol. Quite a combination and, it started out with a scene—kind of a grubby city high school and a man in an overcoat with a package under his arm going through all sorts of little things and going down to the basements of their houses, or maybe in the stock of a grocery store they worked in, something like that.

A third statement concerns the ultimate consequences of using marihuana: that it will eventually lead to heroin. A 21-year-old heavy drug user thought the association between marihuana and heroin was misleading:

> . . . The best thing that could happen is that marihuana could be completely removed from its association with heroin. . . . No longer do they go hand in hand. Marihuana smokers won't become heroin addicted all the time, or in fact, as it goes on, most of the time. . . . You have all of these students becoming involved and in many cases the only things they are exposed to is the psychedelics—marihuana, LSD, occasionally peyote, because they've read about it so try to get it. Heroin in most cases isn't available to them and so there's nothing that will lead them on. You usually have to go looking and digging to find heroin up here in the Bay Area. It's just not that free.

A fourth point raises some questions about whose interests are involved when "non-addicting" drugs are included under the law. A 21-year-old hard-core user-dealer addressed himself to this point:

> Because of the nature of the drug the main groups that are against legalization you'll find are the tobacco and liquor interests. The

people who have tremendous amounts of money involved in one of the two industries. These two lobbies are the main reason why the Federal government has not legalized it because they have tremendous amounts of money that they can throw in to the Senate to force them not to legalize it.

A fifth point compares marihuana and alcohol. Marihuana is held to be physically safe and much less debilitating than liquor and does not impair functioning so severely. A 25-year-old housewife and systematic user distinguished the effects of marihuana and alcohol:

> Getting high [on marihuana] is much, much better than getting drunk. . . . You have more control, . . . you're much happier than getting drunk. . . . That you have much more control, that you're much happier, that you come down much more gently, that your feelings are not wild, in short, even if you are very high you are still responsible for what you say and do.

The justifications which emphasize the positive reasons for using marihuana consume a much larger proportion of the interviews and conversations than do those rationales which seek to neutralize society's objections.

Marihuana is described as increasing a person's awareness, making one more open to colors, sounds, and other people. It has a generally relaxing effect and makes people feel peaceful, not violent. The effects are sharply distinguished from alcohol. Marihuana sharpens your perceptions, alcohol dulls them. If the person is engaged in some kind of artistic or creative enterprise, it aids them. The freedom from anxiety which marihuana induces enables the person to focus much more clearly on the present. This makes immediate, natural responses possible. A 21-year-old systematic user and part-time artist described the increased awareness attributed to marihuana:

> . . . you notice many things, you become very interested in the little details. For instance, you may have noticed things like handles, or bottles, or pebbles, and children's attitudes, and you'd find that children aren't so young as you think and that you aren't as old as you think and that you don't become an adult if you don't understand that you aren't going to become any greater than a child.

In short, it enhances appreciation of sight, smell, taste, and sound and is beneficial in many otherwise less-rewarding circumstances, e.g., movies and concerts.

EARLY USE

Early use is defended on intellectual grounds. It also continues to offer the protective insulation of small friendship groups far from the sources of supply. The fears that exist in these circumstances are not those of the criminal more or less openly confronting hostile laws, as the chances of being apprehended by the police are actually quite remote. However, there are other sources of anxiety. As Becker notes, the novice user will be concerned with whether or not he is able to control disclosure of being high.[1] A 23-year-old woman who characterized her use as occasional reported her own anxieties:

> I was petting the dog until all of a sudden I thought "I think I'm squishing him," you know . . . Oh, I was so frightened and I was sure that I was going to squish this dog because my hands were so sensitive to it. But I thought I was doing very strange things and trying to get the composure to say something, just anything. I couldn't say hello because I was afraid it wouldn't come out right.

But, as Becker indicates, this passes and the marihuana user becomes more confident. He can be around straight people even while high and not suffer detection. A 21-year-old head described how he exhibits his own confidence:

> I've learned to control most of the drugs that I take, on practically every experience that I have I end up going out and so I never have any worries at all along those lines. I have been confronted and sometimes I bring it on myself by asking directions or something and . . . other times I've been so crass as to walk into the Hall of Justice and visit a friend who had been arrested and in jail. . . .

A 23-year-old laboratory technician who saw himself as a weekender reported his own lack of concern about disclosure:

> Oh, it's easy, people hardly ever know. I mean it's happened to me too. When I've been straight, people come in the house, or perhaps they come to a party, people, even on LSD, or something, they don't talk much. But they don't look glazed or don't do crazy things. And several times I've gone to straight parties and have turned on before I got there, or gone outside and turned on. And, I don't think anyone has any idea that was anything but booze. And sometimes I've even in places where there wasn't even any booze, even, was completely straight, and I guess just thought I was a very outgoing person or something, you know . . .

The beginning user is afraid that someone will inopportunely come into the surroundings of use unheralded, and will find some telltale sign of use like the butt of a marihuana cigarette. These feelings are largely directed toward other authorities than the police: parents, non-using friends who would become upset, school officials, and the like. These fears seldom act as a positive deterrent, but persons who are anxious about

---

[1] H. Becker, "Marihuana Use and Social Control," *Social Problems*, III (1955), 35–44.

them will confine their use to "safe" circumstances within the confines of the friendship group away from prying eyes. They will not be likely, for example, to take the drug home with them when they return to their parents for a school holiday.

At this stage use is loosely ritualized. Special preparations are made for the occurrence: doors are locked, shades are pulled, foods are prepared, perhaps room lighting is altered, the drug is passed in a routinized fashion from one to another of the participants, and feeling states are commonly remarked upon. The presence and expectation of use of the drug provide a rationale for such a structured occasion. A 20-year-old student recreational user described the ritual connected with marihuana usage at this stage:

> And the reason this all impressed me so much—I think this was the finest time I had on pot. He brought out a little box and he opened it up and he was extremely ritualistic about the whole thing only not in a phony way—just it was a medium of hospitality for him, it was like the same care with which one would pour a cordial for somebody or with which one would serve sandwiches or something—only better, you know . . . And it was great to watch this, this ah . . . very beautiful man ah . . . just in terms of his movements and his mannerisms, taking this pot, and, you know, just arranging it in the cigarette paper and very slowly and carefully . . . if it ever comes to a time when this is respectable, it is going to be an eminent mark on sophistication because so much is involved in preparing pot.

MORE REGULAR USE

If the novice passes more deeply into drug use, several important events occur. To regularize use (say, the use of marihuana several times a day), one must get closer to the source of illegal drugs, to information about the market and to the more public hazards associated with use. The user who wants to increase his use both in type of drug and in quantity must forsake the protection of the small group of friends. He must move into circles where users are *mutually known* as users but where not much else is known. This is nearer the relationship of acquaintanceship than friendship and may involve not even being acquainted but *known about*. The realization that this has happened, sometimes unwittingly, is a rude shock to persons who, for one reason or another, require secrecy.

The circumstances of introductory use are typically situations where someone was sometimes able to procure drugs from a third party that the others did not know personally and who did not know them. The situation from the point of view of the user is a relatively safe one. The circumstance of regularized use, however, puts the user into a broader arena of action. He tends to become a "known" figure, involving a reputation. Others may know about him but not know him intimately. This entails moving out of the small friendship group with all the protection that afforded. The discretion that holds between friends is not a feature of relationships between persons only known to one another. This observation is at odds with Becker's when he asserts that becoming a marihuana user necessitates tight information control. It involves just the opposite as the user tends to become known and dependent on the goodwill of persons he has no firm grounds for trusting. In short, the regular user loses control of the information that others have of him. A 30-year-old professional described the situation that caused him concern and limited his further involvement in the drug scene:

> I like to maintain a reasonable amount of discretion with people that I choose as friends, and I no longer had such a choice, 'cause I'd go over to somebody who was a friend and all kinds of outrageous types would show up. And, people I never knew, never saw before, would never see again but any one of them could have been a plant. So, I withdrew, it was time to move on.

Precautions are usually taken at this point to protect oneself from the police. The concern shifts from being found out by straight friends or school officials or parents to being found out by the police. The strategy for dealing with this threat of police exposure is to exercise discretion in buying or selling drugs, keeping drugs in one's possession, or "turning on" in public. One 21-year-old hard-core user-dealer in reply to the question, "Have you ever supplied anybody that you didn't know?," replied:

> No, first of all because ah . . . of the police aspect which is always prevalent and second because ah . . . I like to know a person pretty well before I let them know I use.

Another 21-year-old part-time artist and part-time dealer discussed his fears of the police:

> I'm always a little bit leary of it, and that's good, because it gives me caution. And, that's one of the penalties I pay. I've always had this little fear of having somebody knock on the door, just because it's illegal.

A 25-year-old housewife and systematic user spoke of her experiences with the police, which increased the precautions she took in using drugs:

> Well, one time the police came into the house and busted everybody but me and my husband. We had [lived in] one room that was clean. And he had never made sales. In fact he had warned all the other occupants of this very large Victorian house that there was a lot, you know, that there was danger, that there were agents coming into the house, and he was yelling about this all the time, so we were clean.

. . . And so they [the police] were constantly cruising by our house, and you know, several times our back door was broken down and nailed back up. In fact, it still happens to me every time I move, my back door is broken down, and what do you call the little frame that goes around the door is always nailed back up. Maybe 2 weeks after I move into a house, I look and I see that someone has broken in, the screen door latch has been rebored. But I never have anything in my house, never!

To progress into regular drug use it seems to be necessary to overcome the fear of giving oneself away while "high." The main fear now is being caught in possession of the drugs by the law, either on the streets or through undercover informants. Being caught in this position is prima facie grounds for conviction or the opening wedge for being compromised into the position of informer.

When one moves closer to the source of supply, several things may happen. Those persons who have developed attachments to the social order, primarily through occupational or professional commitments, will tend to withdraw. The more diffuse and serious dangers of apprehension by the law for persons in this condition highlight the hazards. They know that their career would be irremediably compromised by a drug conviction or endangered by rumors that they were users. This is the kind of diffuse sanction that Nadel [2] speaks of in a discussion of social control in closely knit primitive societies. Presumably, the more closely people are tied to and dependent upon the legitimate order, the more damaging is public disclosure of a delinquent act. For some of our Colony members such controls are much more thorough than simple legal threats. For such people, of course, other considerations may enter in. They may feel uncomfortable trying to conduct a day's work while "high." It may become too much of a strain to have to segregate the legitimate workaday world so radically from one's leisure pursuit, which is necessary if drug use is that leisure pursuit. A small number of persons who confronted this situation did not withdraw completely but reinstituted the earlier arrangement of casual, occasional use within a group of friends. This is safe and does not involve regular use of or wide experimentation with drugs of various sorts.

An important turning point is reached when the person starts to have his own supply. This decision calls for risking whatever dangers are involved in favor of more systematic use. It usually entails some striking out on one's own. Sources of supply may be identified by friends who know them. A 21-year-old unemployed hard-core user described this development:

> Students many times, will get turned on and won't buy anything but will come over to my house or the friend's house and turn on and

[2] S. F. Nadel, "Social Control and Self Regulation," *Social Forces*, XXXI (1953), 265–73.

smoke a little now and then when they visit you. So it's much slower. Sooner or later, most of them end up buying for themselves because they realize it costs you money and most of them like it. Some people take a very long time. I know one that still hasn't really begun.

An important code is observed in obtaining drugs. Questions are not asked about sources of supply. The information may be volunteered, but participants feel it is better not to know. Questions asked about where the stuff comes from arouse suspicion. This is the kind of question a plant might ask. Or the person asking the question might be an informer. No matter how intimate relationships are, there is the general recognition that pressures can be exerted to compel people to inform. This is an extremely sensitive area and Colony members were reluctant to discuss it. Several articulate observers of the drug scene admitted that they could visualize conditions under which they would become informers. The more a person had to lose in terms of reputation, or separation from family or job by prosecution, the more likely he would be to cooperate with the police in some kind of "set up." The implications this has for social relationships within the Colony will be discussed later. A 21-year-old heavy user-dealer described some of the precautions he takes:

> The only problem is for a new person, like walking into town and make a friend in one day and ask him for some grass. You can't because that's the way all the busts are made and people are really suspicious of people they don't know asking about grass . . . I've had no fears of getting it for other people who I think are pretty straight, as long as I know them. I don't like to have them come and say, "well I have a friend who wants to get some marihuana, will you get some for him, or will you sell him some?" I'll say: "well, I can get some for you, and you can give it to him. I don't want to have anything to do with him." Because I don't, I trust my own judgment, but I don't trust the judgment of other people. And, I think, that's pretty much what people sort of do. But, you know, once you have a circle of friends, then the number of people that become available as possible contacts, you know, becomes fantastic.

The pattern of scoring from strangers seems relatively rare. It's considered too dangerous. It only occurs when you hit a new place and have not had time to develop friends who use.

The progression into more regular use seems to be confirmed at the point the user decides to turn someone else on. If the initial experience with marihuana is pleasant then there seems to be a general impulse to share it with others. It is usually not possible to introduce another to the experience unless one is closer to the source of supply than the novice is. Introducing someone else is usually not done thoughtlessly— there is a certain ritual character to it. It is usually thought of as a minor rite of passage. Turning someone else on usually signifies to the person doing it that he has now become a regular user. The person turned on is usually a close friend of the first user. One is not interested in introducing strangers to drugs at this point. As a person moves further into the drugs scene, he may turn someone else on who is not a friend but who is known by someone he trusts. The same respondent who reported her concerns about scoring from strangers reported how this may work:

> It was usually a thing of where the person ah . . . was accepted by us all. That's the important thing, I guess, and you thought they were good people and groovy people and they had good ideas and liberal. I mean, open-minded is perhaps a better word. And you say "Have you ever heard of harihuana and would you like to try it?" you know. And, usually the answer is "I'm willing to try anything once," you know. Sort of the existentialist experience view type thing . . . and they would do anything once. Not for kicks. Just to see what it was like and ah . . . to see if it did add to their life sequence and things like that. . . .

A 21-year-old part-time model and hard-core user described how she ascertains that someone is to be trusted:

> You gotta be careful with the come on. You can't just walk up to somebody, . . . and say "Here, you want some grass?" Because, you know, it's a bad trip, so you know, you find out about it. You find out if they groove the same way you do . . . [if] that's what they consider wild at all, you know, or if they're directly within the law type thing. You find out more or less their values in life. You know, that type of thing. And, then, you can just tell 'em, "All right, I have used it in the past." You can sorta say it that way at first, you know. And, then they say "Well, I'd like to try it sometime." And then a little while later you say: "Well, I had one yesterday" or something. And then they'd say: "Really, you should have called me."—that type of thing and then—"Well, next time I get some."

TURNING ON TO LSD

In the drug scene one will most likely have access to other drugs, primarily LSD. The initial use of LSD often ushers in a new approach to drug use if for no other reason than that it is a drug which is much harder to control than marihuana. The user cannot, while under its influence, very easily appear to be "normal" or control the information that he gives off to other persons. It is also a drug which definitely tampers with one's mental state. Its use is a testament of greater interest in the use of drugs, and acts as a message to this effect. Correspondingly, there are tales which deter some early users from experimenting with it. These tell of persons who were permanently altered (for the worse), who committed suicide, or who ended up in mental wards. For some, LSD becomes the line over which they will not step and, not doing so, they are apt to remain at a marginal position in drug use, not progressing any further into the drug scene. Colony members had read about LSD and discussed its effects at length. Those who tried it reported good experiences, beneficial experiences. The rationales for its use parallel those invoked for marihuana use with some important exceptions. There is no stigma associated with LSD as there has been with marihuana. LSD emerged out of a laboratory setting, it has been used experimentally, and the users have characteristically been students, professors, and middle-class professionals. The community's norms against its use are not as well developed and do not have as much history behind them. Despite the fact that the legal penalties against both are substantially the same, the moral indignation against LSD is not as strong. In short, there is no consensus on what its effects or significance are. Hence its status is somewhat ambiguous.

RATIONALES FOR USING LSD

The rationales for use usually focus on three main themes: It gives insight into the self and others; it dramatically opens up awareness by breaking down perceptual defenses—this helps one see relationships; and it provides spiritual experiences. Commenting on what it does for the self, one 20-year-old Colony member and heavy user said:

> . . . you can lose a lot of your insecurities, your feeling of paranoia and things. And lose them lastingly, little by little . . . you just work through different hang ups just hanging up your whole life.

A 26-year-old housewife reported:

> I have realized myself—my own façades, my own barriers, that I face the world with, that I face other people with and act. Although I consider myself a very real person and not at all phony . . . and I never put on acts specifically for other people. At least I thought I never did until I took LSD and then I realized that I was acting differently towards certain people. . . .

Other respondents emphasized what LSD can do for their perception. A 27-year-old male teacher, a recreational user, noted the more enduring effects:

> One extreme change that anybody can see is the increased visual enjoyment. I like colors better than I did. I am not indifferent to color at all now. Whereas before, I was working primarily with language. . . . I think LSD probably kicked me into a nonverbal orbit, more of a nonverbal orbit, certainly out of the black and white and into technicolor in my life.

He found that the enlarged awareness also functions in terms of other people and social reality generally:

> With the increased perception of LSD . . . you are extremely sensi-
> tive to the lineup of people. The roles that they play and the games
> they play . . . It's an intensifier . . . It sort of speeds you along,
> I think, in what you are going to do.

The description of social reality reveals the importance attached to the discovery of reality. There are two realities, both of which must be discovered: the *pseudo-reality* and the *real-reality*. The pseudo-reality refers to the façade, the performance, the roles, the games, the rules, the routine. These are phony superficial modes of being. And, more important, they are restricting, preventing the individual from realizing his true self, his whole self or the meaning and value of life. What is important is that one discover the faces, see them for what they are—dull, unconscious restrictions on the real self, impediments to development of consciousness, of awareness of self, of others, of the world. LSD is the tool to the discovery of *pseudo-reality*: A 32-year-old graduate student deeply involved in drug use reported:

> I was trying to relax, be silent, wait and see and so I began to under-
> stand some things of the LSD experience—all of a sudden I began
> hearing things and seeing things, possibilities, relationships that had
> never occurred to me before. . . . I felt I was a part of everything
> and I knew this wasn't hallucinations. I knew it was a legitimate ex-
> perience within experiences, more real than most. It made me realize
> that a lot of my thinking and a lot of my beliefs and notions were
> all based on unrealities. All of a sudden I saw, in the most real sense,
> that the nature of the universe is beyond the conception of the world,
> the concepts, the understanding. What they only understand in a way
> is self. I realized it was what I have been looking for all my life.
> Not LSD, but the state of being, or having being. LSD showed me
> that my sense of me-ness is just a habit.

The *real-reality* is discovered through LSD. It must replace *pseudo-reality*. Material gains, middle-class status, and the institutional means for gaining these ends are rejected. These goals are replaced by a new one: the experience of really being, or having being, which leads to an understanding of the true meaning of existence, to the truth of life, to the *real-reality*. The greater the variety of experiences one has the more open, the more skilled one is in understanding the meaning of one's own life and life around. One is enjoined to be alive, vital. Change, new experience, reflection of expanded awareness, these will lead to real meaning. Drugs are the tools inducing change, new experience. Man is a perceptual, intellectual, and emotional animal. He therefore should make every attempt to expand his capacity to feel, see, and understand. The goal of this expansion of consciousness is to experience one's true self, the true others, the reality of the world. The value attached to spontaneity, honesty, openness as important human qualities is an inevitable outgrowth of the belief in stripping away the façade and interacting as real persons.

The spiritual experiences that are used to justify LSD usually relate to one's sense of the presence of God, or love in the universe, or the profound unity between persons and all living things: A 21-year-old unemployed head characterized the experience this way:

> Indeed at the first part of the drug, the first part of the high, the universe around you comes upon you with such a blinding flash that it really seems . . . it gives you the opportunity to attain . . . say "divine presence," to use an ambiguous term.

> LSD accomplishes perhaps what the occult would accomplish in a man in Tibet, if he were genuinely interested in the occult and it's my way of escaping into this new realm which I'm sure Hume would call the collective unconscious . . . And, this is what happens with the peak experience of LSD. You see all the embodiments of people. You see your place among these people and most times you can pick out the qualities that you want to have in this normal society so that for me it's a very clarifying experience and gives me a profound sense of joy.

There seems to be a general caution about the use of LSD. Most Colony members who tried it do not take it often—from once every two weeks to once a month or less often. It is an intense experience which must be thought about. Furthermore, they will not aggressively proselytize—though they are eager to talk about it. Some feel that it can be dangerous, others that if someone is interested in trying it he will find it on his own. They will give it to friends if they are sure it will not hurt them and they are prepared for it. They are aware that the setting in which one uses LSD—or all drugs—is highly important and significant in relation to the effect of the drug. They tend to distinguish hallucinogens from other drugs, i.e., heroin, opiates and methedrine. A few have tried opiates, but reject them because "it's not a good trip; with them you're shut away, with LSD you open up." They are uninteresting.

To what extent can we speak of a commitment to use or a commitment to the drug scene among Colony members? It seems applicable to the hard-core user but not to the person whose use is very limited. As Becker[3] points out, the concept of commitment should account for the consistency of a person's behavior over a given period of time. To account for consistency in a hard-core drug scene the many diverse activities of the user must be linked to one goal, whether some kind of personal or occupational fulfillment. The hard-core users have described

[3] H. S. Becker, "Notes on the Concept of Commitment," *American Journal of Sociology*, July, 1960, pp. 32–40.

the "side bets" that give consistency to their action in the drug scene and assure their commitment to it. These side bets relate to dress, demeanor, education, and the world of work.

DRESS AND DEMEANOR

There was general recognition by community members that straight people were upset or offended by what they considered flouting of conventional middle-class norms in dress styles. Clothing was considered outrageous—too flamboyant, too colorful, too attention-getting. Men's hair was too long, beards contributed to a generally beat appearance. The casual attitude of young women about their hair style and their refusal to wear makeup also set them off from the all-American girl. Probably the attitude toward cleanliness among the hard-core user most grates upon the middle-class viewer. It symbolizes the corruption of "clean" values. A 24-year-old hard-core user tried to describe what the distinctive dress and demeanor represented:

> They're afraid of our corruption. They're afraid of our place. They're afraid of our divergence from their solid norm, because they're so afraid to step out of theirs. You know, they couldn't, they couldn't, they couldn't anymore go and turn around and grow a beard and wear dirty clothes and not wash for several days than some people I know would put on a tuxedo or something and dress up to the top—Ivy league to get something done that had to be done.

The refusal of heads to recognize status characteristics puts off persons with more conventional involvements. Heads seem to be interested, not in what a person has achieved or how much money he has or how old he is, but in how he thinks, how he relates to them. This makes any kind of structured interaction difficult. And to the extent that conventional people are aware of it they think it is either disrespectful or psychotic. In any case it is simply not "proper."

Whatever value the distinctive style of dress and demeanor may have in flouting general community norms, it has one inevitable result—it isolates the head from conventional people. The story of increasing involvement in the drug scene is characteristically one of increasing estrangement from straight friends. The pattern can be viewed as a kind of side bet generating a certain commitment to the drug scene and the social relationships surrounding it. Wearing certain kinds of clothing and acting in certain ways are part and parcel of being a certain kind of person. It emphasizes the values put on spontaneity, authenticity, and lack of regard for social proprieties. A person has ceased to be authentic if he conforms to society's rigid expectations in dress and behavior. Hence the person's reputation is very intimately involved in the way he dresses and conducts himself. To act straight is regarded as a betrayal to friends who are involved in the drug scene and to the open values represented by the scene itself. The clothing and behavior function as side bets in two ways: they isolate the head from conventional society and severely attenuate any relationship with that world or persons in it; and they symbolize a certain set of values the head espouses—symbols to oneself and to others. Essentially the dress and manner tell other heads that you are one of them and are trustworthy.

EDUCATION

A much more substantial side bet is placed in terms of education. The hard-core user is characteristically one who has ceased to "play the education game." He is usually the college drop-out. He is opposed, not to gaining knowledge or learning, but to the educational structure which dictates what chunks of knowledge shall be accumulated through this or that course or credit. The hard-core user may attend many lectures and do a considerable amount of reading—perhaps more than his college counterpart—but not with the intention of getting any kind of degree. The kind of accounting mentality that is required of a dedicated student (set so much time apart each day to study, plan your program well so you can graduate on time with just the right number of units) is completely foreign to him. He rejects it and with it the way of life for which it is a preparation. What is one to do at age 30 without a college education and no interest or talent in those jobs open to the unskilled labor pool or the lower middle class? The side bet placed in terms of dropping out of college has effectively closed off any feasible alternative to the way of life the hard-core user is now engaged in.

WORLD OF WORK

Closely connected with education is the world of work. As pointed out previously, some Colony members are only marginally related to the work world. They are dependent on others for their incomes, or they may work in low-level bureaucratic jobs episodically. They may be artists or craftsmen who work when the spirit moves them or they need money. This kind of job history is a difficult one to summarize in terms that a personnel manager could understand. From his administrative perspective the hard-core user is "unstable." He has done much job switching. He has shown no pattern of gradual advancement with age; quite the contrary, at times he seems to be downwardly mobile. There are large gaps in his work history. Where has he been? Was he in a mental institution, or possibly in jail? The refusal to meet the work world on its own terms in effect makes side bets for the hard-core user which, combined with his educational side bet, develop the commitment to the drug scene. The question can be asked—where else can he go?

SELLING DRUGS

The final stage of the process does not end with systematic and regular use. Persons involved in the drug scene who purchase their own supply invariably sell some of it at some point. At the lower levels the situation appears quite laissez-faire: I will sell next week to the person I bought from this week. By and large, however, the selling is not systematic. Occasionally such a person will make a trip to Mexico himself and bring back small amounts. He might be characterized as a small free-lance importer operating somewhat out of the main distribution system. There is a characteristic dash to Mexico and back to supply friends and acquaintances. Usually this occurs when there seems to be some malfunction of the distribution system so that a temporary shortage in marihuana occurs.

An enormous amount of traffic from nickel bags ($5.00) on down takes place through friends who are not making a living from pushing. Some users who hold steady jobs often buy in ½ pound or pound bulk, often in collaboration with several others to guarantee supply, minimize street dealing, and have enough to sell a little to two or three occasional users. The gain to the regular user is free smokes, and maybe a few dollars now and then. The trafficking usually occurs among such close friends that no one involved considers it illegal or risky. The user is doing friends a favor. He can be characterized as a part-time pusher at this point. He may gain prestige from his friends for being in closer to the "hip action." The infrequent user saves himself the task of dealing with someone he does not know very well. There are numerous part-time pushers who hold other jobs and push on the side. They tend to have a very small clientele. The profits are small, but the style of operation is not risky and consumes no time besides a conversation or two at coffee breaks. Pushing here can be considered a supplemental income.

Most pushers begin their work by drifting into it. They see the possibility of making "free smokes" and maybe a few dollars more with little effort. If successful at their initial ventures on a small scale—if they sell easily, quickly, at a profit, without getting paranoid about their graduated illegality—they will move up in the selling ranks.

SUMMARY

With 10,000–25,000 illegal drug users in and around the Colony, anyone who wishes to can easily try drugs, especially marihuana. If a person "looks right," marihuana and sometimes LSD will probably be offered to him.

Trying illegal drugs usually involves exhilaration, the discovery of a new "mind world," and initial paranoia due to fear of exposure and arrest. In a short while the initiate usually discovers that his experiences are easily comprehended by most Colony members and that the law is far from omnipresent. His chances of arrest, particularly if he uses drugs quietly, are very slim. Using drugs then becomes "natural." The user does not necessarily become a new person and he need not be paranoid every time he gets high. The likelihood of his identity changing is greater if he becomes a systematic and heavy user.

Not everyone progresses through these stages to become a hard-core user or head. Some move slowly into a pattern of limited use and remain there without going further. These are the recreational users, portrayed more fully in a later chapter. Others move to more systematic use according to the pattern we have described. Still others seem to be catapulted into the scene, moving very quickly through the early stages.

The sequence brings us from the initial stage of induction up to street-level pushing. The progress to pusher status will be described more fully in the next chapter.

4

Street Pushing in the Colony*

Prior to the mid-1960's, the standard version of drug use depicted two separate worlds: one the very small, criminal, desperate, paranoid world of drug use; and the other, abstention. In places like the Colony, however, a diagram of drug use would be diamond-shaped with the very bottom, the non-users, smaller than the mid-section, the very infrequent users. There is constant drug interaction between similar types of drug users, and with others in the structure just above and just below.

THE GIVE-AND-TAKE BARTERING SYSTEM

Living in a community where many consistently take illegal drugs, the user who comes to like them must decide how regularly he wants to use them and what he will go through to get them. Many merely sit back and wait, accepting gifts of drugs from friends. They choose not to go through what would be required to get drugs on their own nor do they choose to risk possession. Others buy small amounts from those who they know have the basic supplies at home. If an urge arises, the nonpossessing user will pay $5 for a capsule of LSD or several dollars for some joints without establishing any relations with a pusher.

There are many persons who take marihuana in small groups once a week or less often. They are not in the petty drug trafficking business because their needs are so minimal. A group of five or six might need only a single nickel bag between them for the weekend. A monthly purchase of an ounce for $10–$15 would hold this group for a month. They are not interested in increasing their usage and see no necessity for buying more than they will use, and there are enough contacts to buy small amounts in and around the Colony. To suggest to them that they buy in greater bulk and sell what they do not use would appear to them as out of character, profitless, and extremely risky.

The legal situation may drive users into situations where they might deal, the logic being: "Why constantly deal in very small quantities when you can pay less, avoid the nuisance of running out and have enough on

* With the assistance of Jerry Mandel.

68

hand for friends and special occasions by purchasing marihuana in slightly larger quantities?" The major risk is at the time of purchase and if this is done once a month instead of once a week the risk is cut down. The legal risk of holding an ounce of marihuana is exactly the same as holding several joints. Once friends decide to join for a bulk purchase, they generally have to buy considerably more than they could use in the immediate future because usually fixed amounts are sold. Marihuana, for instance, is generally sold on the West Coast by the ounce or the kilo. It is easier to get a kilo than half a pound.

There are many users in the Colony who have contacts with small pushers and buy their own, choosing not to combine with friends for bulk purchases. They buy in small quantities, about $5 for ⅕ of an ounce of marihuana and $10–$15 for an ounce, and $10–$20 for 2–5 capsules of LSD. The amount of money is not a problem; the major drawback from the point of view of the user is the risk of "holding" the drugs. Against the drawback of storing drugs, the user usually sees several benefits. The problem of obtaining drugs when you want them is eliminated; This seems especially important with LSD since relatively few persons have quantities at home. Another advantage of having one's own supply is that friends are not bothered, especially at odd hours of the night when the desire to take drugs often arises. And finally, instead of being dependent on friends, one becomes independent and capable of giving as well as receiving favors. The amount bought at any given time depends on how much money the user has to spend, how much he can reasonably expect to use in the near future, and how much he can get—which determines how much the buyer will store. Marihuana and LSD will keep for several months with reasonable storage precautions. An ounce of marihuana provides 50–60 cigarettes, normally, which will keep any but very heavy users at least a month or two. Since the prices are low, and inexpensive purchases will satisfy almost anyone's desires for a while, the real issue becomes "How much can one get?"; but this too is no problem as thousands of people can fulfill the demand of recreational users, and heads can easily get minimal supplies from numerous friends since "like knows like" and most heads have easy access to small quantities of marihuana and LSD. So there is actually no problem for a Colony member who wants to hold his own supplies of "basic" drugs.

Once a person holds, he gets asked periodically for very small quantities by friends, just as he had previously once asked them. The issue then becomes whether to hold more, or "how much of your supplies will probably be used, or requested, by friends?" This problem is faced by very infrequent users as well as by heads, only the level of purchase differs. A 22-year-old middle-range dealer reported:

> Everybody I know deals on some level . . . like if they have a friend and he will say "can you get me a lid" and you say, "Well, I don't

know—I'll ask around," and so you ask another friend, and they say, "Yeah, I know where I can get a lid," and they sell it to you and you to your friend with no price jack-up . . . and it's the same with acid . . . but in a sense it's dealing.

The holder must decide how friendly he will be, and at every level of usage some are friendlier than others. Some people are activists, organizers, and focal points of social interaction. These types, if they decide to hold, will naturally be asked frequently for drugs. These "outer-directed" persons are also the likeliest to hold in order to be in independent rather than dependent positions.

If a person holds and is amenable to giving or selling drugs to friends when asked, there will soon come a time when people "below him" ask to buy quantities almost up to what he has bought, and there will be friends "above him" in drug use who will be asking if he wants to buy more of the drugs he uses, or some new "exotic" drugs (like mescaline, peyote, methedrine crystal, etc.). A new set of decisions arises: "When asked by friends for drugs, does he give it away, sell at cost, or sell for a profit?" The decision is almost entirely in the hands of the holder as everyone expects to pay and there are informally fixed prices with mark-ups for very small quantity buys. The price, if any, will depend on the closeness of the friendship, the amount asked (joints will be given away, lids charged for), the number of times the friend has asked for the favor, and one's mood at the moment. When a friend asks for a small quantity, and makes an offer that is profitable to the seller, does he sell? Hardly anyone thinks of himself as crossing a line that makes him a pusher. Rather, that decision is based on the risk (which is virtually nil if selling to close friends), the inconvenience (based on how much he will have left after he sells, and how easy it is to buy more), and the amount of profit (which at these low levels of selling is minor, although present). If a person has already decided to hold more than he can reasonably expect to use soon, there is a strong chance that he will push. An 18-year-old top-level dealer described how he got started:

> My cousin turned me on, and about a week later I bought a lid from him . . . and a funny way to start dealing is I sold someone part of my lid because I didn't want the whole thing. At the time, it had no significance to me. I wasn't dealing—I was selling part of something I didn't really want.

Obviously, any holder can sell. Numerous people make free drugs by buying just enough over personal needs to provide enough small sales to cover expenses. So, for example, a user might buy an ounce for $10, sell two ¼ ounces for the generous price of $5 each, and have 25 free joints left. (Or, he may get a fairly good deal of 10 capsules of LSD for $35, expect to sell seven at the going rate of $5 each, and have three free LSD trips). One only needs two or three drug-using friends to operate like this. They may even pressure the holder for such amounts, and the free drugs are actually secondary to doing favors for friends, possibly to keep them out of the potential trouble arising from buying from "less than the closest friends." Small sales among close friends or relatives is not seen as pushing by any of the parties involved. No commitment of time is involved, and no one is living off the profits. Obviously, it is easy to "step up" and make extra money by simply buying a bit bigger and selling a little more.

SUMMARY

The process described—from curiosity, to trial, to initial stages of use, to the decision to use regularly, to holding for oneself, to being part of a give-and-take bartering system—can take a few years or a few days. It is likely to occur rapidly if the user finds drugs like marihuana and LSD very appealing, if his friends use regularly, if he likes the drug scene itself and his role close to the center in a number of petty friendly deals, if he has the time, and if he is willing to take the risk.

PROGRESSING TO PUSHER STATUS

Just about every moderately heavy drug user in the Colony, who has a little money, and holds, faces a decision to sell above the give-and-take barter level. Whether he does so or not depends on many factors. A 23-year-old ex-student, top-level dealer in marihuana and LSD, characterized the pusher's motivations: "Why do most street pushers start? Well, they may have $20 in their pockets instead of the usual $10." Because it is so inexpensive to become a pusher, many young people who are attracted to the Colony because it is a scene take to selling drugs, although they do so for very small profits. According to the ex-student:

> Some of these people who have to be connected with something— this time it happens to be drug-oriented—their life is directed around it. They don't work at all, but they don't make anything selling at all. They mostly stand around and bum coffee. All they do is run around. That's what they'd do if they didn't have any drugs. They don't do anything different except when somebody says "do you know where I could get a cap?" They say, "Yeah, let's go over to the head." They just happen to be bums with drugs in their pockets.
>
> They come and go every day. They get busted. That's where all your busts are. Mostly, it's somebody who gets high and thinks it's cool to get high, and thinks it's cool to say, "Yeah, I can get it for you," and mostly they end up losing money.

These are the most ostentatious pushers, and they probably sell a great deal to young, ostentatious, poor users. They make themselves noticeable, and persons interested in sensationalism will, naturally, notice them without recognizing their insignificance. This bottom-level pushing is often engaged in by young transients, selling to an even younger, more transient, market. They are rarely students, rarer still University of California students. As with friendly bartering, a lot of drugs are passed around to consumers on the Avenue, but again the larger regular users—and in this case, the bottom-level pushers—need their independent sources. Since most Colony members would not think of scoring from a stranger on the Avenue, the rest of this chapter will deal with more substantial operators.

THE TYPICAL STREET PUSHER

Almost all dealers, when asked to describe the "typical" street pusher, balk at answering. Standard answers are "There is none!" or "Me, you, you, and you, for example." *The street pusher resembles the market, and the market is becoming increasingly heterogeneous.* Accepting this variety, a summary statement can be made as to who might be likely to push above the barter, spare-time level. The person who decides to be a pusher will be free from responsibilities; not involved in other "bags" like school or work (not that a student or worker won't also deal, at least part-time, but he won't place dealing first and he won't risk the other bag); like the effects of the drugs he expects to push and like the drug-dealing scene (though the head and the hippie are not necessarily linked, and dropping-out of society's game-playing, if taken seriously, means staying out of pushing); value small amounts of money; be friendly; need the status approval of peers; like the center of action; require proof of a drug-centered identity; and be willing to violate the law by taking the risks and committing his time to surviving off illegal drug dealing. A 23-year-old researcher, occasional small pusher and past girl friend of 2 big dealers, depicted street pushers as follows:

> Most people who deal are lazy—they won't work. Dealing is the easiest thing for them to do . . . or they deal strictly to build up the ego. In the first place, they like being an in group—looked up to and respected and knowing what's going on in the scene. People sort of consider this a sign of extreme—a little more than normal intelligence . . . if someone deals. It's like any other ego boosting thing any other person would do. Why do boys brag to girls about, about what? He's an engineer and he tells his girl about this absolutely fascinating thing he did today—that's bragging too—it's absolutely the same thing in the drug scene. You're dealing, you're something more than somebody else.

In deciding to push, a combination of reasons will apply, though not necessarily all of the above. Money to some degree enters in. In almost every case, the career alternatives, at this stage in a pusher's life, not only do not exert a positive pull, but are downright discouraging. But in most instances of Colony pushing, the decision is not a desperate last-ditch effort to survive. *The pushers like what they are doing and where they are doing it.* When the decision to push is made, the anticipated customers are friends or friends-of-friends, so totally profit-oriented motives are rare. Small users who decide to push anticipate profiting from small sales to their friends. Heads will figure to sell to fellow heads, Hell's Angels to Hell's Angels, professors to professors. The ease of contact, the natural setting of contacts making for non-exposure and trust necessary to keep risk down, the friendliness of dealing, all make pushing to peers the typically anticipated manner of dealing. Friends are not expected to cheat by selling inferior merchandise or misrepresenting the quality of their drugs. For the pusher, friend-to-friend selling will regularize his dealing. Actually, pushers will be a bit above the customers in the extent of drug use. It is possibly nicer and safer to buy from someone who knows a bit more than you. So, in truth, professors buy from graduate students.

The motives for pushing, especially among young Colony members, are not very unusual. It is not necessary to be small, greasy, and pasty-faced to try your luck. It is easy to visualize the pusher jobs in the Colony: from nickel-bag, ounce (a cap to 5 caps of acid) to recreational users; a lid, several lids (a few to 10 caps of acid) to heads. In this free enterprise society, where there's a demand, the suppliers will rush in if the profits look good and the work pleasant. The pushers are obviously correct in their estimate of the demand—the question is have they correctly anticipated profits and working conditions?

The pusher most likely to get caught is the one whose dealings are most flamboyant. These persons are not usually indigenous to the Colony. Their convivial, easy-going, sloppy, free-wheeling style is conducive to arrest. Young pushers are constantly getting arrested because they forget, or never fully realize, that it is not an inconsequential game of cops and robbers they are playing. Most pushers who have been in the scene for a while and have moved up in the traffic, or who have stopped pushing, would agree that there are an assortment of problems connected with street pushing which are little appreciated by the beginner.

PROBLEMS OF STREET PUSHING

The pusher who regularly buys a kilo of marihuana and 50 caps of LSD is already fairly successful. He is probably at least $250 in the black or at least successful enough to have one or two people "front" the money for him. Seldom will a pusher buy more, although if he has acid-heads for his clientele, he might purchase slightly more LSD. Pushing a kilo of marihuana takes work, 35 one-ounce sales. Still, figuring a cost of $100 and an average sale price of slightly over $10, the pusher can anticipate $250 profit. If, in addition, he can sell 50 caps of LSD for $5 each, he might gross another $100 assuming he paid $3 per capsule. If he had a lot of friends, and many of them were running low, the pusher might figure to make the $350 in a few weeks time.

The only trouble is, it hardly ever works out that way! First, it is extremely difficult building the clientele much above twenty, especially if the pusher wants to deal primarily with persons he has good grounds for trusting. A 23-year-old ex-pusher said:

> When I do it again—which I think I will—I'm gonna do it differently . . . checking on the people I sold to for one thing—I wouldn't sell to as many people. I'd find the people who bought more in quantity rather than selling like one lid or 2 caps. I'll wait until I can sell to 'em, maybe a half or a third as many as before and, therefore, not have as many people to sell to—it's far less of a chance.

Low-level pushers in particular report an enormous amount of time spent turning-on with buyers. Low-level dealing is, after all, essentially a friendly business. If the pusher is businesslike and abrupt he may find himself minus a few customers. In thc Colony it is difficult being the only pusher on the block. Buyers who are not such good friends might want to turn on to overcome fears of illegality and to take some harshness out of the businesslike relation. Besides the social ritual, turning-on with the pusher is a way to test drugs. For the pusher, turning on is pleasant, but not a good way to run a business. He loses precious hours—one can't just get high and leave—and loses the mood for hustling. Driving may become more difficult and unpleasant. How many contacts can be made if the pusher turns on with every other customer? Two or four on good days?

With the soaring drug use in communities like the Colony, a pusher automatically finds his potential clientele growing. Unfortunately, as the increase reaches his particular social set, competition springs up, cutting into his market and driving prices down. So, for example, persons who entered pushing at the start of 1967 might have anticipated paying $3.50 an ounce for marihuana ($120–$125 a kilo) and receiving $15 a lid. By mid-year the prices had fallen to under $3 an ounce on the purchase end, but $10 a lid to the buyer. Net profits, to the pusher, had dipped over 50 per cent. If many customers start smoking more, it might mean more frequent sales and so more profits—but it also might mean that the customer will buy in greater bulk without providing much more profit, and the customer might start selling some marihuana himself. Young customers, inexperienced in drugs, are hardly dependable customers—but that's what most of the Colony buyers seem to be. If a pusher's customers are part of a close-knit group, the buyers may become partners in their purchases. It is difficult to sell separately to roommates or fraternity brothers or lovers. A 21-year-old nonstudent, ex-soldier and street-level pusher described such a situation:

> A friend of mine who used to deal, who I bought my first acid from, told me that he can't deal anymore because all his contacts know each other and there's no sense in dealing—in other words, everyone he knows who he gets his drugs from and they can get the drugs from them just the same as they can from him.

But even assuming a pusher builds up a clientele of twenty or twenty-five steady reliable customers who don't require the social ritual of turning on with their pusher, the merchandise seems to slip away before the profits come in. Vast leakage is almost always reported. Very close friends are not to be exploited, so pushers sell them drugs at cost. When a pusher has a kilo, he will give away nickel-bags to some people. Girl friends especially get free marihuana. Special occasions warrant gifts—like weddings, divorces, graduations, or getting classified 4-F. At Christmas time, pushers often can't resist playing Santa Claus. In addition, the pusher is usually a fairly heavy user. If he wasn't to begin with, he soon becomes that way. When marihuana is laying around all over the house, it's almost as easy and cheap to grab a joint as a regular cigarette. If the pusher is not careful, he gets sloppy.

A 23-year-old ex-student and top-level dealer in marihuana and LSD who had graduated from street pushing in the Colony reported:

> When you're breaking up a kilo into baggies, and a stem with a little pot on it falls on the floor, you know you're not going to pick it up and brush it off and clean it. You just kick it in the corner, and sweep it up when you're finished.

If a pusher is very gregarious, he may expand his market beyond even the good "friends-of-friends," and may even be able to judge perfectly whom he can trust and whom he can't. But a huge clientele brings new problems to the pusher. Even if he can trust people not to be agents or informers, he cannot establish friendly relations with too many persons. He is known to them as a pusher, and little else. Buyers are then likely to appear at the pusher's residence at all hours of the night. They will not take the precautions on the pusher's behalf which friends might take. They may make noise leaving the pad at 3 A.M., and appear obviously stoned entering and leaving. With persons in and out constantly, expenses such as telephone and food bills mount. Theft is an ever-increasing problem. The risk of holding soars as it becomes increasingly clear that something very unusual is going on in that little apartment. This type of "successful" pushing cannot last very long. Our top-level marihuana-LSD dealer continued:

> I had 35 or 40 lids and 10–100 capsules at my home, when I was dealing at that level. I'd reach into my bag here if someone asked for

a lid . . . Come on in, at 4 in the morning . . . bringing it right down from where you live to the Student Union or something like that . . . in your car you got 4 or 5 lids, in your pocket 5 or 6 caps, and a lot of people would come up to you. Some places in Berkeley you go up to them.

The type of leakage problem differs according to the drugs a pusher specializes in, but it seems to be everywhere, at least at the lower levels. Marihuana pushing seems loose all around. LSD pushers may less frequently give away free drugs, but when they do give it away, it's expensive. The LSD dealer might delight in sampling his merchandise, but that day can be scratched for doing business. A 21-year-old former soldier, now a Colony street pusher, observed:

I don't think I ever netted $100 a pound of grass. I should have—you're right—but I wasn't. I was making maybe $60 or $70. I was always high, mainly because whenever we broke up a pound we had a breaking up party and everyone sat around and smoked.

Methedrine pushers, like marihuana pushers, tend to lose track of things. They spill the crystal or forget where they put a "spoon" of it. Or they get unnecessarily paranoid and flush some down the toilet because of a false alarm.

Then too, there is overhead—which is seldom anticipated by beginning pushers. To obtain supplies of a kilo of marihuana or 50–100 capsules of LSD, the pusher often has to not only get over to the supplier's residence or hang-out, and guarantee that the drugs are actually available (which they often turn out not to be), but he periodically just has to wait around. Other times, with other suppliers, he may arrive at a meeting place only to be informed that the pick-up spot is someplace else again. This waiting, moving, and waiting increases considerably the larger the purchase. A 28-year-old graduate student in social science who sold marihuana and LSD to get free drugs for himself and a few friends described some of the difficulties.

We went over to pick up the kilo from Chuck. He didn't have any—he never keeps anything himself, but he almost always knows where to get about anything. So, he called Bill, who said to drop over in an hour and he'd have the kilo. So, we dropped over, meanwhile making an extra stop for Chuck, who's paranoid and doesn't like driving his own car to pick up smack. So, we get to Bill's, and he's not there but his partner is, and we sit around, and Chuck is nervous so he shoots up. Half hour later Bill calls to say he's having a bit of trouble, but will be along soon, and half an hour later he calls to say he scored, and he finally comes with the kilo, and then he and Chuck spend some more time making a little speed deal. By the time I dropped Chuck off it was already 11 at night, and the tail-light of my car doesn't work, and if I wasn't so tired I'd have really been paranoid.

Pushers who have been at it for a while probably have their purchases fairly regularized, although even dealers are not the most stable types. Today's supplier may be in another city next month, or may be dealing only LSD, or may have stopped dealing altogether. Even for pushers who usually don't have a waiting-time problem, situations do come up where quantity marihuana or LSD becomes hard to find. Most Colony pushers feel obligated to meet the demands of their clientele, and besides they fear if they are not reliable, a few customers may find someone else. In any event, without the drugs there is no business—only some overhead. So, the pushers try harder—they try secondary and tertiary sources, knowing that the probability of getting drugs is much lower and the wait will be much more than usual. Unusual risks are taken, both in whom the pusher deals with and in the willingness to lay out money before getting the drug. No beginning pusher figures in the dry periods when he anticipates profits—but it happens to the best.

The pusher, especially if he gets successful, discovers constant overhead expenses similar to that of any other active businessman. He finds himself with wining-and-dining costs. When he meets a buyer in a coffeeshop, it is the pusher who will probably pick up the tab. There is also a phone bill with mounting calls to San Francisco or southern California, especially if the pusher starts dealing regularly in multi-hundred dollar purchases. Travel costs eat away at profits, especially if there are difficulties at the purchase end.

Then there are special overhead costs due to the illegality. An active pusher, especially, should not keep his supplies on his person or residence, especially if customers stream in and out of his apartment. He should store his drugs someplace and, if it becomes too obvious, periodically move them. In practice, this is rarely done. A 23-year-old top-level dealer in marihuana and LSD described the problem:

> There ought to be precaution taken at every level, but there often isn't. What it turns out to be is, you got this dealing—it's a lotta hassle for me to walk down there, to the lot 2 blocks away for me to get a joint. I'm going to keep it in my house. The people who are involved in drugs mostly aren't interested in being involved in a hassle . . . and they don't want to walk down to the corner all the time, so after a while they do start getting sloppy. Somebody comes to the door, and "Well, I'll be back in 10 minutes."—It gets to be a drag. So you say, "nah. I'll just keep a few cans around the house."

At the very least, experienced pushers recommend an instant-disposal system whereby one can get rid of the drugs on hand if and when the police arrive. Some pushers have elaborate systems, but it is virtually impossible to do with marihuana because it is too bulky.

Two similar disasters for pushers—getting "burned" (paying for drugs and not getting any, or getting watered-down merchandise) and theft—

might be considered routine hazards. If someone wants to act illegally, no pusher can call the police. The risk of both increases considerably the higher up the distribution ladder the pusher goes and the more active he becomes. When selling to close friends for $10–$20, it is not worth the money to cheat "big." The buyer is, after all, your friend and he knows how to seek you out and make retribution. The little watering down of merchandise that might be done, especially with marihuana (LSD at street-pushing levels is already in capsule or tablet form, and nearly impossible to "cut"), is not worth either the effort or the risk of displeasing a customer, let alone a friend. But when a pusher has laid down $200 on the line, with a minor acquaintance, on the supplier's terrain, there is no guarantee that he will get anything but a swift farewell. Part of being a good pusher is to anticipate these situations and prevent them from happening—but the higher the dealing, the less control the pusher has. The problem of burns has, in mid-1967 in the Bay Area, suddenly increased considerably, because of a combination of market factors and the impact of LSD legislation and the growing sophistication of narcotics and drug agents. Theft is a constant problem, especially for active pushers at all levels. Drugs, if kept around one's apartment, periodically get plundered. Records get anonymously borrowed, but not anonymously returned. Small but valuable equipment, like hi-fi sets, tend to disappear. Who does it? A 23-year-old top-level dealer responded:

> A friend of mine. (He's still your friend?) Oh, sure. A friend, still. Maybe even a good friend. He's still my friend because I don't know who it is. I have several hunches, that's the trouble. And it hasn't happened once but a few times. I'll find out, I guess.

How does one figure into anticipated expenses the costs of arrest or near-arrest? When pushers start getting successful, they should start retaining lawyers, so some large dealers report. Even if this is not done, the costs of an arrest can mount. The police not only seize a pusher's drugs, including everything in his house, but they can confiscate money and even autos if drugs are found in them. A private lawyer can be expensive, especially if a pusher is pretty big; the enforcers know this and are trying to make the case solid and the penalty severe, and the pusher has been caught red-handed.

When profits of $150 a week are pretty sensational, it is easy to understand how a multi-hundred dollar burn here, a theft there, an unexplained $50 phone bill one month, a forced move and an extra residence for several months, a dead-week filled with traveling and hassling, and finally an arrest can keep the most active pushers living close to the bone. A 21-year-old non-student pusher explained why he stopped dealing temporarily:

(You say you were pushing 3 months. Why did you quit?) I ran out of money. This jail thing cost me $50 and I didn't have anything left to sell and my capital was gone, owing to different things. I did save money for a while. Then my style of life changed. I started doing like the Fillmore and Avalon Ballroom scenes, and all those places, and spending a fairly good amount on girls and things. . . . I sort of fell into that for being a dealer.

HOW TO SUCCEED IN PUSHING

Notwithstanding the difficulty of making good profits from pushing, the fact remains that good money is sometimes made. The pusher must be very active, he probably takes enormous risks without bothering much about them, and he must be lucky. A 23-year-old top-level dealer reported what was necessary to make a profit:

> When you're talking about dealing nickel-bags or lids or anything short of a pound, you're talking about an awful lot of discreet separate situations, in which I have to be present with another person and make a deal. So it turns out to take up a lot of time. If you really are going to do some volume, you are going to have to see a lot of people all the time at any hour they happen to have $10 . . . It is at least as hard as any other job. Certainly for the salary.

However, most Colony pushers do not like working so hard and so frantically. Most settle for less than decent wages. For example, the most organized street pushing that was described in dealer interviews was of a supplier who had four persons working for him, almost exclusively selling marihuana. Each pusher was sold six ounces every week or two for $50. The supplier's assumption, probably correct, was that each pusher could count on a 15–25 person clientele of nickel-bag and half-ounce buyers. Selling 1/5 ounce nickel-bags, the pusher could make 20 sales, grossing $60 profits every ten days or so. Assuming the normal leakage, (especially the pusher's smoking up the profits), it's reasonable to place the pusher's net at $25–$30 a week. Nineteen and 20-year-old Colony members will be content with these profits, especially since it requires only a few hours "work" a few days a week. Some pushers will be content with this level of income, except that periodically when they have a sure opportunity to score big they will round up the money for the purchase, and frantically hustle for maybe four or five days. That week they will net their $100–$150, and will then drop back into their typical semi-drift routine. Our 23-year-old top-level dealer characterized pushing at that level:

> The characteristic of that level is, you go in a house and there's nothing but dirt on the floor, and roaches—drugs all over the house and

people running in and out of doors that are never locked. Hi-fi always blaring.

To be successful, i.e., make good money, work few hours, with little hassle, and low risk, the pusher should follow a set of informal rules. Trust, regular transactions, caution, and deception are essential.

Trust: the pusher should deal with friends, or good friends-of-friends, or at least people he can trust. A 19-year-old top-level dealer described his rationale for not dealing with someone he didn't know:

> I make it a policy to never sell it to anybody I don't know . . . that's a groovy policy. Usually if someone you don't know comes in to make a buy, you can, unless it's a friend of a friend, you can make a pretty good assumption that he's the MAN so you don't talk to him.

He should recognize and understand the motives of his customers, and why they are buying. He should know something about the "history" of the customer—his past, his friends, his life style. A 28-year-old graduate student in social science who sold marihuana and LSD to get free drugs for himself and a few friends described one precaution he took:

> I figure if he's a friend of a friend of mine—I will pump the friend for information and then I will check it up—find out just who he is. So, if somebody comes up and says "Somebody I know sent him," I'd tell him to see me in two days.

The customer should be "vulnerable," at least to social disapproval. Otherwise, what is to prevent him from turning you in? It helps if the buyer is not the kind who constantly exposes himself to arrest by either looking outrageous or acting so as to constantly brush against and test the law. Someone who is on probation or who is known to the police as a heavy drug-user head is not a good customer. If he doesn't bring the police on his trail, he is vulnerable to police pressure. Our 28-year-old pusher also indicated that he rejected buyers occasionally:

> But I turn people down too. There's a lot of ways of checking up. I check on most people I know—reputation, burns, busts, the MAN, you know, how responsible they are, 'cause people have a reputation usually who have dealt, and usually you know some people they have dealt with. These people can find out, or already know.

But, for all that, pushers trust outrageous heads with narcotics records, even when they have only known them a short while. Trust is extremely difficult to define. But the successful pusher should be exceedingly careful because narcotics agents likewise are difficult to describe and spot, and informers often are very unlikely persons.

Regular Transactions: the main reason profits do not mount is that pushers spend so much "dead time" waiting, hassling, missing appointments, being stood up on sales and purchases, etc. Suppliers and customers come and go swiftly, and time is continually spent building trust and allaying fears. For street pushers, the profits on any single transaction are small. Decent money is only made by increasing volume—not necessarily the size of sales but the number of sales. Success, i.e., good money, requires a bureaucratic pusher. He should keep stable his suppliers and buyers, and repeat deals. A 23-year-old top-level dealer discussed the need for regular transactions:

> What it takes in this or any other business is a certain detachment from personal feelings and personalities—and I was always too wrapped up in other people, so I continually do things like somebody comes to my house and says, "I need a cap," so I give him a cap and he gives me $5 but that's the way you get busted. What you are interested in doing is the same thing the upper levels are doing—finding 5 or 10 people with whom you deal on a $200–300 basis every month.

He should buy regularly at fixed prices, and always be prepared, i.e., be prompt and have cash ready. If he can have his customers likewise responding promptly, and buying consistently, he can reduce the time spent in the social rituals surrounding street-level sales. This requires that the pusher does not operate so stoned that his efficiency sags. It should mean setting a routine and not deviating from it. If the pusher is buying kilos and selling lids, he should not squeeze out a few dollars more by shifting his orientation and style to meet the nickel-bag demand. If his profits are from numerous petty sales, he shouldn't attempt to parlay his contacts into a big purchase just to satisfy a customer or two.

Caution: if you are in an illegal occupation, it's only good business to take the necessary precautions. Pushers should not hold extra supplies on their presence or residence, and everything at home should be set up for instant disposal. Our top-level dealer continued:

> It's much easier to dump 900 caps of acid down the toilet than to try to get rid of a kilo—even 10 lids of grass. I try to keep nothing in my apartment—at least, nothing I can't flush down the toilet.

Marihuana, because it is so bulky, should never be kept at home.

> Keep almost anything around the house, if you want to make money, except grass. It's just too hard to handle. Too big—too gross. If you're going to sell grass—here on the West Coast at any rate—to make money, you're going to have a lot of grass passing through your hands over a long period of time. It's big. Man, an ounce is big enough that you have to have a special place to hide it, not like a little number 5 capsule.

Pushers should not get sloppy, particularly by leaving seeds, twigs, and roaches lying around. Phone calls should be guarded, deliveries should not be made in the middle of the night, contacts should not be made in public places subject to police and undercover agent surveillance. Loans or credit should not be extended. The same dealer summed it up:

> There are three basic rules in dealing: Don't front money; test all drugs before you buy; and don't front money!

Deception: the best pusher, just like the best agent, is one who you would never expect to be one. Ideally, the pusher is "uncool." He blends in with the crowd. Ideally, he has another job or a visible means of support. Besides "covering" his person, the successful pusher never lets his residence become a center for weird action. A 22-year-old ex-student and street-level pusher reported:

> I go on the Avenue once in a while, when I'm going someplace, or into Pepys for cigarettes . . . but otherwise I don't like it. See, I'm a dealer but also a college student, 22, married. I can't be defined as a dealer.

Obviously, there is a basic dichotomy between the informal rules for successful pushing and the motives of most Colony pushers. The format for success is to be a cold fish. The person who chooses to be a street pusher is about the least likely person to obey the rules. Frivolity and unseriousness pervade. Pushers choose their work because they reject businesslike jobs. A 23-year-old top-level dealer described why he wasn't as successful as he could be:

> I'm not a successful pusher because I don't have a vacuum-cleaner salesman's mentality. Sure, I made a lot of money, and have hundreds of friends who I've sold to, but I'm waiting to be sentenced and if it weren't for my friends, I'd owe my lawyer a few hundred dollars.

The reason the rules are so seldom obeyed is because of the low profit-margins in selling marihuana and (to a lesser extent) LSD. They are applicable, more or less, to heroin trafficking, where the parties to dealing are mirror-images to society (materially oriented, sensually-deadened, willing to treat others as objects, suspicious, etc.), where big money can be made, and where the clientele accepts a deadly cops-and-robbers routine surrounding drug use. The drugs used in and around the Colony are conducive to "love dealing." Drugs are sacraments and the heart of a new culture. One factor in the "take-off" of non-opiate drug use among young children of the middle class is that up to this point it has not been "hard" and "cold" criminals controlling the distribution apparatus. And, given the huge market, pushers can get away with recklessness. How many agents can there be "per capita user"? And how interested are agents in $10 or $20 purchases?

Not only are the "rules of success" antagonistic to the motives of most Colony pushers, but the pusher's way of life further estranges them from bureaucratic pushing. Being immersed in drugs that turn-on (rather than turn-off) people, the pusher tends frequently to get high. It is easy and inexpensive to do, and hard to avoid when everyone around you is high and happy, especially when the pusher is in contact with them. Pushers might begin in order to get high frequently and make halfway decent money. When the profits turn out less than expected, the decision as often as not is to benefit from pushing by *staying high* rather than working harder. A 21-year-old ex-soldier and non-student stated:

> The only thing I had to do was socialize, and I was high all the time —what I enjoy doing anyway, you know. The only thing was to stay around a lot of time . . . Yeah, to stay in touch with people . . . like on a Friday night—people would be coming around, you know, two o'clock in the morning . . . after a while I had to work pretty hard to keep myself covered, like I didn't have the people coming to my house anymore. . . .

Street pushing at its most typical is extremely risky. According to a few dealers who have been around drug traffic for several years, in several capacities, the arrest rate is highest among the lowest-level street pushers. Precisely the least "criminal" operators, the least profit-oriented and least paranoid, are those who fill the jails. "You either step-up or get busted," said one dealer (who, incidentally, did both). Or the pusher can quit. A 23-year-old top-level dealer explained why some quit:

> Selling drugs gives people like me some kind of pleasure. It's a way of making money, and mostly they don't like to work. And, they find themselves working much harder than they ever worked before, but possibly in something they enjoy. Most people at this low level don't stay in it. They end up quitting, because it turns out to be a 24-hour-a-day, 7-day-a-week job. . . . Mostly, they just get tired of the hassle and paranoia and start concentrating on school or get some sort of job or go to Mexico or Europe because they have maybe a thousand dollars.

None of these alternatives is considered very good. Colony pushers like what they are doing, so why get out? Although many leave, there is a constant drifting back into the action. Few actually want to get busted, but the consequences of their risk-taking seldom hit home until it's too late. If street pushers wanted to make good money as businessmen or in routine jobs, they would be better off at something else. Our 23-year-old dealer continued:

> I know I could make a lot more money if I went to school and got that piece of paper, because I need that—I recognize that intellectually, at least. Only I was not yet old enough—my glands and body hadn't calmed down enough—for me to go back to school, so I've been dealing for a year or so, and I think I'm ready to quit this too.

In many ways it makes sense to "step-up," though only a few actually do. Better money can be made and the actual work time is less. If security must be taken, it is clearly worth it at the higher levels. Paying for storage when you are netting $40 a week street pushing hardly seems worth the bother. For some pushers, the status accorded them gets flat after a while. They have come to use more drugs though their customers have not. Their new friends are higher in the drug traffic than their old ones (often their customers). Sophisticated, older, long-time, fairly heavy drug users may require pushers, may understand, empathize, and like them, but they often consider low-level pushers fools for incurring such risk and going through such hassle to make so little money. The more sophisticated market is unimpressed by anticipated profits on paper, and stories of "I have this plan, see, where if I can only get this, I can hustle here, and make that. . . ." Tales of "$125 I made last week" mean little to persons who once made this much and more—and decided to quit, or who make two or three times more in legitimate and decent jobs. There seem to be many who have been low-level street pushers for short periods. It may shock one's parents, and it may impress one's younger friends, but the glitter of any job dims if it gets repetitive. The only reason that low-level pushers would continue what they are doing for months is because they like where they are at, and it would be hard being in that place any other way. You may be poor but honest, and especially high.

Most of the Colony is not high all the time, at least not for most of the time. They may go through phases when a month or two is devoted primarily to LSD exploration (weekly trips, time spent trying to stay high when not on the drug, pursuing those aspects which were high-lighted on "trips"), or a few weeks of continual functioning "stoned" on marihuana but in the long run these are secondary. A professional in his mid-30's who deals part-time in marihuana but not for a profit reported:

> When I was out of work I hung around a few days always loaded. Then I decided I'd look for a job. Each morning I'd get up and turn-on. Instead of taking a dexamil I'd take a dexadrine and some pot. I was a tiger in the morning as I'd hit the agencies. Then by two I'd be wiped out, and I'd turn on again and hit the coffee shop. It was a gas, but after two weeks I decided I really needed a gig and being wasted every afternoon wasn't the way.

Older dealers higher in the distribution system report that the turnover among street pushers is very high. Either they step up their operations and move up in the distribution system or they decide to quit.

MOVING OUT

For some their career in pushing is relatively short-lived. It may last for several months, at which point there is a return to school or to some kind of regular job. But why would street pushers "go away" when they seem to have a low-risk, high-prestige, free-drug, constant-supply operation going? One major problem is that it takes a lot of time and petty hazards. The "kicks" of supplying petty amounts wears off. Supplying an infrequent user, who is a friend of yours, a nickel bag every three months can be viewed as a time-consuming drag, especially if the pusher has to deliver it to him. The friend will invite his supplier to light up, most probably, and after the first time or two the street pusher will consider the experimental user's handlings of the drug pretty inexperienced and dull. If the street pusher has been handling a moderate to large-sized clientele he might find people calling on him for supplies, where his original intention was just to have the drug-selling venture as a part-time "when I want to do it" venture. Some of these "callers" may be friends-of-friends, thus upping the risk more than he wants. Further, street pushers occasionally get burned, i.e., get inferior merchandise for their money. A street pusher reported one such incident as an example. He had a good deal to buy 25 capsules of LSD at $3 per capsule. He tested it and found it considerably weaker than the 500 micrograms he was promised. What to do then? He found it less difficult to sell it than return it. But, since he was selling only to good friends, he felt obliged for personal and business reasons to correctly identify his product. He scaled down his prices accordingly, and represented his capsules as containing "probably 350 only" and offered them at $3.50 per capsule. His profit margin dropped considerably, his reputation slipped as a consequence, and his discomfort and embarrassment increased.

Street pushing may be endemically a short-term proposition because it is virtually impossible to routinize the work so that it takes a minimum of time, is always as interesting and adventuresome as at the beginning, and returns a decent enough (if still very small) profit. Things never seem to work out for street pushers. They always give away, or sell virtually at cost—to good friends, girl friends, friendly initiates who they like to "get started" (because they like people to take drugs, not for pecuniary motives), to make up for past "bad deals" (such as selling weak acid or below-standard marihuana), or just because they are feeling particularly generous or are looking to liquidate and go out of business.

Like the laissez-faire drug traders among recreational users, the small pusher invariably finds himself in a "good deal" situation where he can buy in larger quantity at one moment, getting good price for one major risk. Often, however, the expenditure of energy and time on these "good deals" is enough to make him see that he is stuck with the nuisances and small profits of the small dealer unless he wishes to change his style of life and step up. The college student and those in the periphery of the university who have tried small dealing may often then cut-back their operations rather than expanding. Particularly is this so if the student seems to be advancing to a higher status or higher-paying position, or if academic demands begin to press. If exams are coming up, or if he has to maintain a B-average to guarantee draft-exempt status, or if he decides he really likes mathematics and wants to go on to graduate school, or for numerous other reasons, he may decide that the small risks are not worth the small profits. Besides, he now has a several months' supply of his own, and has numerous contacts for fairly good-sized purchases should he need them in the foreseeable future.

DIFFERENT STYLES OF
LOW-LEVEL PUSHING

Most pushers, in the face of several unsatisfactory alternatives, try to make compromises. If they won't commit themselves to bureaucratic pushing, and won't step-up, and won't hang around making little money for the hustling and risks of street pushing, they still won't surrender their involvement in the drug scene entirely, especially when they do have some fairly decent contacts "above" and some friends who depend on them "below." Several styles of compromise exist, where the long-run profits diminish along with the time and energy commitment, but the "pay per hour" and the reduction of risks are considerable improvements. Many pushers decide, often early in their careers, to be part-timers. They can either deal fairly regularly on a very small scale, or infrequently on a big scale. If one has a steady clientele of close friends numbering ten, or even fewer, and if these friends live stable lives and do not flit from drug to drug and mood to mood, the pusher might make small profits by always having supplies available. Assuming that each customer will make one or two purchases a month, he might be able to sell a kilo each month or two, plus a handful of LSD and maybe some other drugs.

SUPER HUSTLING FOLLOWED
BY SEMI-DRIFT PATTERN

More often, the part-time pusher will enter the field only when requests build up, especially for fairly large purchases. When four or five such requests have accumulated, he will foray among the contacts he has acquired, seeking a kilo or two from a few sources, maybe some LSD from others, possibly a spoon or gram of methedrine crystal. One customer may want a kilo of marihuana, another a pound, a third half a pound. The pusher offers each the possibility of getting some LSD. In the back of his mind, he knows there are two or three others he could probably sell ounces to if he approached them, and they too might be willing to buy some LSD. Two or three others may have made bulk purchases from him in the recent past. So the pusher—who has not dealt for a month—may call his former buyers and see if they would be interested in anything. In the process he may get another order for 20 caps of LSD. Then he sees his contacts, and places some orders. One may say that he can also get crystal; another that mescaline is available. The pusher returns home and contacts his customers to inform them of the possibility of getting some exotic drugs, and may return with another order or two. For two or three days the pusher is often on the go, sometimes waiting at home for return messages, other times cruising on the Avenue or other places where some of his suppliers hang out. The pusher is also rounding up money, some from his buyers whom he knows very well. His customers may front him money, but the suppliers will not extend credit. When the call comes, he must be ready. A kilo "comes in" from one source, another kilo and 50 caps of LSD from another, a third brings $30 of "speed." Maybe, all totalled, it means coming up with $350. He nets $25 as his mark-up from the kilo buyer, sells two half-pounds of marihuana for the price it cost him for the kilo, nets $30 from selling 3 lids of marihuana, nets $20 from a sale of 20 caps of LSD, nets $5 each from very small sales of LSD to two of the purchasers of lids, nets $5 each from his two sales of methedrine crystal. The $100 "net" actually does not yet register in his accounts, but the pusher still has 12 or 13 ounces of marihuana and 25 caps of LSD on hand. He uses some of this himself, and awaits a call which he knows will arrive every week or two. Then he will sell off much of his surplus and "bank" the profits. Then the pusher will forget about drugs for another month, or until the requests build up to make it worth his while to score big.

The above description is for a reasonable pusher. Super-hustlers may also try to sell quantity drugs without previously establishing that a need exists or waiting for demand to backlog. Such super-hustling often ends in arrest if done on anything beyond the very short run. A 23-year-old woman who pushed part-time described a super-hustling operation:

> I don't know anyone who's going to distribute it on a lid basis who's going to hold even a kilo. I know about a girl in Berkeley who just got rid of five ki's in five days . . . on a lid basis. She's dealing with a hundred people, at least—some people are just freaky. Her big thing was that the person who brought the five ki's to her said, "you're out of your mind—you'll never get rid of it," you know, and she said, "I can do it"—and that was an ego thing. . . . She didn't need the money. He stayed the whole five days just to see if she could do it. She did it, but the thing is she doesn't live in Berkeley. She's gone. She really got paranoid and split. She's simply lucky she didn't get busted.

Being a big pusher, but only sporadically, has its drawbacks. If too irregular, the pusher may lose his contacts or may be charged too high a price to make it worth his while. He also has to purchase in such large quantities (usually) that the risk of being burned increases. But these are minor drawbacks compared to the advantages of not getting overwhelmed by the work of pushing and not running the risks of holding or of having a continually active-looking residence.

SUPPLYING OUT-OF-AREA PUSHERS

There is another way to periodically up profits which, if it can be combined with a small clientele making infrequent fairly bulk purchases, makes part-time pushing worthwhile. Pushers in out-of-the-way areas will not be in touch with quantity suppliers, and will be in no position to spend the money and take the time to come to drug-dealing centers to make contacts and then hang around for the deals to be consummated. Numerous pushers in the Colony, because so many come from outlying areas and because so many have been at other universities or similar communities in other cities, often have one or two such contacts. One 29-year-old graduate student in biological science who made sporadic forays for huge deals in marihuana and LSD reported on his own operation:

> The first deal I ever made was when I was at the University of ———— and came to Berkeley because it was my first choice for graduate school. I was just visiting, but was asked to bring back 100 caps of acid and some pot, if I could. I was here a few days, and a friend from ———— introduced me to someone who got me the acid. I only made a few dollars, but when I came back to go to school at Berkeley, I made another big purchase and mailed back half of it and sold to a few friends here. Since then, I've been back twice, and another time another friend-of-a-friend from ———— came out here and bought 200 caps which I made about $50 on, just for getting it for him. I guess about every other time I buy a few hundred caps, a good part of it goes in one big deal back to ————. Dealing gets in the way of school, usually, unless someone wants me to get them 100 or 200 caps and they are willing to pay me as a contact.

Other times their customers may do two friends favors by putting the out-of-state pusher in touch with their Colony pusher. A multi-hundred-dollar LSD request every month or two, even if it only lasts for a few orders, makes periodic pushing seem worthwhile to the Colonyite who might otherwise seek other employment or sell his hi-fi set.

SELECTIVE RAIDS ON OUTLYING AREAS

Another style of part-time pushing (similar to the previously described occasional super-hustling interspersed among semi-drift operations) is to "raid" other territories when big scores are made. In this way outsiders cut into the Colony market, and Colony pushers bring in profits from outlying areas. This is something which can only be done infrequently, and must be carried off quickly. The pusher travels to an area where he expects there is heavy demand, buyers are paying fairly high prices, and he has a few friends. It helps if some sales actually take place in virtually public places—like the Haight-Ashbury, Sunset Strip, Berkeley's Telegraph Avenue, etc. The pusher arrives with his supply, and contacts his friends whom he informs of his intentions and asks to contact their friends. He will sell any quantity, so long as he feels the buyer can be trusted and so long as it is done quickly. A whirlwind of action is generated, even to the point of making contacts with friends-of-friends in bars, coffee-shops, university hang-outs, etc. The pusher takes enormous risks and virtually no precautions, but assumes that since he is a stranger in town no one (that means no informers or agents) will notice him, or if they do get wind of things, he will be sold-out and gone before they can set up a bust. A 24-year-old graduate student in social science who occasionally pushed marihuana in the Colony described one such pattern:

> I've had quite a few week-ends with over $100 worth of business, but that's mostly all that happened that week. For instance, a very safe way to deal would be to score in LA and go to Berkeley, because you can be—if you're not living in Berkeley—what is considered "uncool" 'cause you're not going to be there long enough for them to get a lot on you. You go up for the week-end and you can stand on the Avenue and sell dope, whereas you couldn't if you lived there—but then all the expenses involved . . . you don't hitch with a kilo, you fly.

THE TYPICAL COLONY PUSHER

In view of what has been said, is it possible then to portray the typical Colony pusher? Obviously not. There are some who work sixty hours a week and others six; a handful consistently net over $100 a week, but many more are happy to make half of this in a good week; there are straights and outrageous cowboys and Indians who push; adolescent drop-outs are plentiful among the low-level pushers, but graduate students in their late 20's are not unknown; there are pot-heads and acid-heads and sharp bureaucrats; there are kids out for kicks and action as well as spiritual types who view the drugs as almost sacred, their own roles as apprentice apostles, and their headier buyers as budding buddhas. The variety among pushers is enormous as would be expected given such a huge heterogenous market. With an estimated 10,000–25,000 users in the Colony and its peripheries and contact points within Berkeley, if half or more are supplied primarily through the barter-trade network, at least 5,000 probably buy mainly from pushers who more or less live off selling drugs. If an average pusher's clientele is twenty-five persons, and a few of these utilize more than one pusher, then there are probably at last 250 pushers in and around the Colony at any given moment. (Estimates vary considerably, but this is because there is no agreement as to how big an operator one must be to be considered a pusher or dealer. One knowledgeable interviewee estimated between 300 and 400 drug sellers in Berkeley in mid-1966, and a year later Berkeley's avowed acid-head candidate for mayor in 1967, Charlie Brown Artman, estimated there were only 50 dealers. Obviously, the Colony could not sustain 250 full-time pushers, handling 100 caps of acid and a kilo of pot every ten days or so. But it could provide work for perhaps 10–15 of these, perhaps 20–30 part-time "serious" pushers, and perhaps 200 who net anywhere from $10–$30 in an average week.) The turnover is huge, and probably several times this number flit in and out of the trade. Very few make a decent living, but that's not as important as the fact that many make some living off illegal work and they willingly try on this identity as an outlaw. A 22-year-old humanities senior and middle-level pusher put it this way:

> Hell, I don't know what I want to be. I know I don't have any, uh, image of myself as an adult pusher. I don't want to knock it. Like, it's a nice place to visit, even if I don't want to live there.

THE PUSHER'S COMMITMENT

The materials on those involved in drug trafficking are too meagre to account for whatever commitment they may have developed to their illegal careers. If we assume that all the pushers are heads, then we can note that their life style seems to be somewhat different. Since the pusher is not interested in calling attention to himself, he must not look too much like a head if he wants to sell to those who value discretion. His occupation requires him to be discreet. In this sense he might look like any hip young person. This mutes the emphasis on flamboyant dress and outrageous behavior. His occupation requires also that he be somewhat less trusting than his non-pushing head friends. At least it requires some calculation to participate in very risky activity without getting arrested.

For some who push, their career is extremely short-lived. It is an interesting activity in which one engages while on vacation or before going back to school or before beginning a professional career. For these persons there are few, if any, side bets placed that would sustain commitment to pushing.

For those who move up or get arrested there seems to be a deeper commitment. Why some move up is problematic. They may have become accustomed to a style of life that is not possible in any other kind of job—in terms of attachment to their customers and the amount of money they make. The longer they remain, the more isolated they become from traditional employment patterns. In this sense, they are in the same situation as their non-pushing head friends. Their employment record can't stand the critical scrutiny of an employer. For those who are arrested, their chances in more conventional occupations or professions are diminished. The impact of official action may be to insure a continuance of their illegal activity.

For others, it might provide the shock that removes them completely from the drug scene.

MYTHS AND REALITIES
ABOUT PUSHING

The version of the Colony pusher so far presented is basically contrary to the pusher myth presented by authorities and other "experts" for decades. The Colony pushers are in it for a little money and lots of pleasure. (Those who are pushing primarily for profits cannot make very much anyway.) The pusher is not selling non-opiate drugs in the hope that users will become addicts in a few years. The pushers themselves cannot wait that long. They are not very stable types, are generally experimenting with their pusher role, and tend to move up or out of the market in a few months time. The clientele also is not very stable, even for the most bureaucratic pushers. Rather than seeking to "hook" clients, the pushers like to sell the drugs they use.

The main reason for handling "heavier" drugs ("heavy" here used as a continuum going from marihuana to hashish to LSD—or peyote or mescaline—to STP to methedrine crystal to heroin) is for profits. For the same number of deals, the pusher can make more selling LSD than marihuana, and far more selling heroin than LSD. The mark-up at each level of the traffic increases the heavier the drug (although there are exceptions for very rarely used exotic drugs, where the mark-up is high because the pusher will probably have so much trouble selling it). Although most Colony pushers have their own drugs of preference, and have buyers who reflect these preferences, most pushers will try to purchase almost anything a customer requests. And many will plant suggestions about heavier and "exotic" drugs. Besides the profits, there is the high value placed on drug experimentation—especially among the heavier drug users which includes the pushers—though pushers draw the line between getting drugs for experimenting and supplying someone who is strung-out on methedrine or heroin. Also, the pusher justifies and improves upon his status as being "in" on the action and having good illegal contacts by meeting requests for and promising to obtain these harder-to-get drugs. By dealing in heavier drugs, the pusher also consolidates his reputation, and builds goodwill. If he cannot meet, or turns down, a request for heavier drugs, then he is demonstrably not a very worthwhile pusher. The buyer might consider switching all his business to one contact, who can get everything. Possibly an LSD pusher would not risk much loss of business by refusing to handle other drugs—and certainly the speed dealer could make his niche by specializing. The pusher who depends on marihuana sales for most of his profits cannot be so choosy, however. Changing marihuana pushers, for a Colonyite, is just slightly more difficult than changing brands of cigarettes. Still, the demand in the Colony is over-whelmingly for non-addictive sensory and consciousness-expanding drugs. The pusher generally trusts that his customers will not get hooked, and if the result of experimentation is a buyer's addiction, the pusher will prob-ably drop him if the buyer has not already parted company. A 22-year-old senior in humanities and middle-level dealer stated:

> If I sold someone a lot of methedrine—I'd get good money—but he'll also be likely to get caught . . . he'll also ruin his health. . . . I don't want somebody to do that, even if I could trust him.

Pushers are very similar to users, and not the intrinsically evil out-siders portrayed in the standard pusher myth. Colony pushers are not em-ployed by a "mob." On the contrary, Colony pushers embody some classic American values of independence and entrepreneurship. They do not deceive their buyers about drugs, especially those which a customer is thinking of using for the first time. A 28-year-old graduate student in social science who sold marihuana and LSD to get free drugs for himself and a few friends observed:

> Acid sometimes is impossible to cut, if it comes in tabs (LSD liquid smeared on tablets resembling aspirins). In caps, you can uncap them and cut it and recap it, but that's a drag. It takes time, you may lose a little anyway, and you could never get away with cutting it too much. Pot is pot, and there is no way really to cut it. You can add parsley or oregano, but that's more expensive than pot. I've known people add sugar, but that's usually to weight the kilos way back where they are packed in Mexico. Look, man, it's not worth it when you're deal-ing in such small quantity, and you'll never get away with it more than once. You want people to come back for more. You want your people to have the best stuff possible or at least you want them think-ing that. . . . Most of the people I know that are involved in drug traffic are fairly conscientious about the product they sell—they're just like druggists in a way. They like the product to be as pure as possible. Of course, like in any business, you'll have a few people who will sell fraudulent products. . . . There is generally a fairly tight control of people who are using drugs. They form their own sort of underground food and drug administration. They don't like to take bad stuff because it puts them on a bad trip.

The pusher, in fact, often wastes countless hours talking to customers about drugs. He is a pharmacological adviser, largely filling the void created by the sensational reports of those whose audience excludes the Colony and other areas of repeated drug use. Any pusher who made his sales by saying, "Here, try this funny new kind of pill; it'll give you a new kind of kick," would be lucky if the worst consequence would be the loss of his clientele.

Even some narcotics agents in the field recognize and accept this "new" version of the pusher. In practice, of course, agents have always faced reality in order to infiltrate the market. When masquerading as pushers, they do not put on pasty-faces or trench coats or shoulder holsters. Instead:

> The latest police undercover narcotics spy here [in San Francisco] . . . had been on the force only 10 months . . . Because of [Officer] Owens ability in poetry, they decided on his "cover"—he would pose as a Beatnik versifier . . . [with] a goatee . . . black turtleneck sweater, tight black pants and sandals. . . . Spouting his own made-up Beat blank verse, he infiltrated easily into the far-out crowd that uses narcotics. And they led him to their suppliers . . . 40,000 pep pills . . . 10 pounds of marihuana. . . .[2]

From coast-to-coast, the new undercover agent is the young student, the new informer, the fairly square co-ed. Recently, some narcotics officials have actually stated that the pusher reflects the market:

> The image of the man hanging around the high school in a black cloak and hat is wrong. Narcotics aren't sold that way today. You can't buy narcotics on every street corner . . . the user now has to be part of a scene—North Beach, the Fillmore . . . or Haight-Ashbury.[3]

If high profits, "crime," "the mob," etc., do exist in non-opiate drug traffic, they enter the picture above the street-pushing level—at least for the Colony. So far, the description of drug trafficking has concentrated on the pusher's relation to his buyers. At this level, pushing is strictly a *game* of cops-and-robbers, and everyone really interested in *criminal* law-violating is looking upward. The street pushers who really want to make money are trying to figure how to step up; the pushers in it for the thrill of brushing against the law and matching wits with "heavies" quickly become bored and disillusioned with the typical petty deals; the narcotics agents are interested in street pushers primarily to make inroads into the bailiwick of the "big guys." Most Colony members are curious about the levels above their pushers, but not otherwise involved. The pushers, of necessity, are to some extent involved. They have to interact with dealers, and some gravitate upward. The kind and extent of impact of these higher-level dealers on the Colony constitute another story. Without this contact, street pushing is usually child's play for child's pay, though, of course, it is a felony.

[2] *San Francisco Examiner*, October 23, 1966.
[3] Northern California Director, California Bureau of Narcotics Enforcement, quoted in *San Francisco Examiner, Chronicle*, December 11, 1966.

5

Middle- and Top-Level Dealing*

After a short while, a pusher is usually able to build up contacts with a few regular heavier purchasers and can step up his operations. He can buy more, and buy more regularly, and make his profits without having to make a large number of small sales. The most profitable, and least messy, way to "move up" as a pusher is to carry other drugs and then to emphasize their sale. Several former marihuana dealers carried marihuana as a sideline after only three or four months of dealing, much as they had a few pep pills and LSD capsules around as a service to their customers when they began dealing. So long as he avoids addictive drugs, the pusher does not increase his risks by handling other drugs. If caught, he will receive the same severe penalties that he would if he handled marihuana solely.

The demand for marihuana far exceeds the demand for other drugs, however, and there are many who push only marihuana. But the profits to be made on pushing LSD are well above those for marihuana. It is far easier to regularize LSD business operations to guarantee the profit, minimize the risk, and even minimize the hours of work, than to regularize marihuana operations at the parallel point in the distribution hierarchy. Further, the small bulk of LSD minimizes the risks of holding fairly large quantities. From the pusher's point of view, the following monetary comparisons are relevant. To net $300, the pusher must make 30 one-ounce sales of marihuana, but the LSD pusher at the same level who makes only 10 quantity sales grosses well over double this amount with fewer storage and travel costs. Five or six days a month he will be in no shape and no mood to deal; but, as he sees it, one of the major benefits of pushing is that it allows for trips of one kind or another. The pusher who is not a heavy user is, on the basis of this fact alone, likely to move up more rapidly in the distribution system since he is less involved in the total drug scene.

The demands of his market are such that the pusher finds it profitable to stock other drugs. If he can get marihuana, the chances are that he has

* With the assistance of Jerry Mandel.

the contacts to get LSD and methedrine. He can then make more money from the same number of contacts and also strengthen the ties to his customers by reducing the number of suppliers that they must contact. When the street pusher finds himself buying in bulk, storing a variety of drugs, and supplying someone under him who sells at the street level, he has moved into the middle strata of the distribution system. He is a dealer.

Because of the character of the demand, one would expect that all drug supplies would be consolidated in the hands of a single dealer. However, several factors prevent this from happening. First, the sources of supply are so diverse that the distribution systems diverge on top and only gradually come together at street levels. Second, since marihuana is so easily grown and so much in demand, there are relatively numerous contacts above and below anyone who might want to become a marihuana dealer. Being an LSD dealer is not so easy. Third, the bulkiness of marihuana makes its handling risky, and requires numerous precautions that a dealer in LSD (or methedrine or heroin) does not have to face. Marihuana must be concealed and made easily disposable; as this is impossible in one's residence, it really must be stored in some other place. This means extra work and time to pick some up whenever a sale is made. Fourth, the mark-up on marihuana at dealer levels is considerably under that for LSD (or heavier drugs). It makes sense for the marihuana dealer to try to stock LSD also (if he can), although the LSD dealer might be better off sticking to small-bulk drugs. In any event, there are tendencies for dealers to specialize in marihuana or LSD; the closer to the top of the distribution scheme, the greater the separation.

Those who deal to the Colony may also be regular or infrequent dealers, big or small. In this section, various types of dealers will be described, with the logic of the operation shown through "their eyes." For each type we will discuss the profits to be made, the amount and type of work involved, who that type of dealer might be, how many persons fill such roles in—or selling to—the Colony, and the possible impact of such deal-.ings on the Colony. The descriptions will begin with the least profitable, smallest dealer operations and work up.

UNUSUAL SOURCES OF SUPPLY

The manufacture of LSD requires an expensive chemical lab set-up, access to illegal chemicals (lysergic acid), and considerable skill. Therefore, it is only feasible to make in very large batches, and very few can enter its production. Its distribution requires a system which funnels drugs from the top down. With marihuana, however, it is possible either to grow Indian hemp at home or to import very small quantities. How important are such irregular operations to the Colony's supply of drugs?

The Green Thumb Gardener

The home-grower takes enormous risks because the mature Indian Hemp plant often grows over ten feet tall before it is time to harvest the top leaves. With marihuana so accessible and inexpensive, there is no financial reason to grow one's own and good security reasons for not doing so. An occasional Colony arrest because of home-grown marihuana is usually indicative of extreme "scientific" curiosity and experimentation. Only if grown on a farm can enough marihuana be harvested to make it profitable, but instances of this are rare. A 1967 arrest in Sonoma County (about 50 miles north of San Francisco) resulted in the arrest of four persons, including some San Franciscans, but there has been no rumor that such supplies drifted down to the Colony. The significance of domestically grown marihuana, which supplies little more than a handful of users, is that it acts as a potential check against prices skyrocketing. Short of that, it is not worth the investment and risks.

The Petty Importer

Petty importing of marihuana can be done by anyone who has $50, is in or near Mexico, is willing to make a low-level illegal Mexican contact, and risks brazening it past the border checks. Most petty importers bring over 1 or 2 kilos, usually costing slightly over $25 a kilo in Mexican border areas. For 2 kilos, the Colonyite stands to gross an extra $100 by importing, or $50 more than what he'd have to pay in Southern California. The risk is not so much getting stopped at the border (only a fraction of cars are searched on any busy day), but guaranteeing that the Mexican seller will not turn one in to the police. He stands to make as much in rewards as he stands to profit from the small sale. Obviously, for such low profits, it only pays to venture petty imports if one has other reasons for being in Mexico, such as studying or vacationing.

Petty importers do not stand to make much from their dealings, can make such purchases only occasionally, and, therefore, do not commit themselves either financially or timewise to importing and dealing. A few do get caught. A few, particularly the more respectable-looking, slightly older, and slightly wealthier persons on the fringe of the Colony, make it a fairly regular practice to import small quantities. One pusher told of a 30'ish professor who took his wife and children to Mexico for annual vacations, always returning with a few kilos. This is similar to a dealer described by nationally known police authority Thorvald Brown, in 1961:

> A San Francisco Bay Area dealer was known to make the trip to Tiajuana (sic) every week and taking his family, wife and small children, with him, but not just for their company. After making his contact in the Mexican border-town, the doting husband and father

would always contrive to return with the contraband on Sunday afternoon, reaching the border checking station at the peak of the returning weekend tourist traffic. When arrested in Oakland, he stated he had never been questioned or searched at the border on any of his main crossings. His family effectively allayed any suspicion.[1]

Petty importers are important to Colony drug traffic because a substantial minority of the marihuana supply is brought in this way. However, as the price of marihuana drops, the profitability of such ventures decreases. However, as the market increases, the feasibility of petty imports of 5–25 kilos increases. Anyone immersed in drug use in the Colony can easily and quickly sell a few kilos. A 25-year-old middle-level dealer, an ex-philosophy student, commented on the significance of petty importing:

> Sources for pot are mostly from Mexico. Mostly it comes from a student who kets a ki and sells it to all his friends. And people who have some investment money will try to get 5 or 10 ki's across. In Berkeley, maybe over half comes across like this, in the ghettos or freaky Haight-Ashbury places, probably over ¾ths of the pot is brought over by really big guys.

Many Mexican sellers will not contemplate small amounts. The possibility that one's Mexican contact might "tip off" the police is a constant problem. The rewards offered by Customs officials for being instrumental in the apprehension of a marihuana dealer far exceed the profit of a sale. The likelihood of being turned in is considerably less, however, if marihuana is imported in bulk and the transaction occurs regularly. Many hustlers in border cities will have a kilo or two to peddle, or maybe more if one is willing to pay prices close to those paid in Southern California. At discount prices, however, buyers must step up to at least 50–100 kilos. For the American purchaser, buying 5–25 kilos is extremely risky from the perspective both of hiding it while crossing the border and fearing the Mexican seller will inform on him. Getting more than 1 or 2 kilos takes one beyond "child's play" in the eyes of the courts. Since the risk and concealment problems are not much greater for 50 kilos than for 20 kilos, and the money is substantial but not overwhelming in either case, it makes sense to import big. Thus, the 5–25 kilo import category should be empty, but it still is tried by many Colonyites.

Unless the petty importing is regularized in substantial quantities, the dealer is probably in it for a "lark" or because he likes the action but has no better connections. Any self-respecting bureaucratic big dealer would not waste the time or take the risks for such small profits. That possibly two or three persons per month, on the average, do make such petty imports in the Colony only indicates that some part of the local market

[1] T. Brown, *The Enigma of Drug Addiction* (Springfield, Ill.: Chas. C Thomas. 1961), p. 137.

is supplied through noncriminal, virtually nonprofit, minor operations. As the market increases, and contacts for marihuana become easier at all levels of dealing and using, the need for and relevance of petty imports will decline.

INFREQUENT AND SMALL-SCALE DEALERS

The problem in dealing big seems to be having access to large supplies, regularly. The demand for small quantity marihuana and LSD seems to be fairly incessant. Some people have excellent contacts to quantity drugs, but for numerous reasons do not step up to dealing—except now and then. Usually, their contacts will be good but only for small quantities and only at fairly good prices. A 19-year-old top-level dealer, former university student, observed:

> When you're within a group of people who are using drugs—not necessarily a formal group—just friends in an area using drugs . . . most of 'em, aren't sellers, but on a large scale all of 'em sell . . . if you go up in buying quantity and you know these people, you can have them sell for you or sometimes they'll ask to buy quantity from you . . . because it's money for them and free drugs.

They may not be interested in working long hours and being fairly responsible to many persons, and they may not have enough contacts at the demand end for routine selling. The poor head who uses marihuana and LSD and maybe other drugs is likely to have poor friends who are in and out of money, but he is around drugs and constantly meets small sellers and occasionally big suppliers. If he wants to, and if pressured by a buyer or dealer, he could probably buy or sell small quantity drugs. If the head feels he needs the money, he might make a few deals. Mainly, the reason pushers don't step up to regular dealing is that they lack the capital. Our 19-year-old top-level dealer continued:

> One thing strikes me about selling drugs is how rigid the structure is that you cannot move up too easily. . . . It takes a lot of money and a lot of work and a lot of talking to people to move anywhere in the structure. To move up one notch, I'd have to be very rich or lucky.

To support his chosen way of life, the head who periodically deals might make but three or four sales a month, usually bunching his efforts as supply or demand requests stack up. This way, he works little, never holds, and therefore does not need a permanent residence, and does not get trapped in a "dealer bag." If poor, as most Colony heads seem to be, his infrequent deals will usually be substantially pre-financed by the ultimate buyers. No regular clients or suppliers depend on him. He chooses when, and how hard, he will work. The infrequent dealer can make six or seven deals in one week, and none for the next month or two. His major problem is managing bulk purchases and the time spent waiting for them, but by choosing to enter the distribution system only when he knows quantity drugs are available, he can guarantee that his dealing is always secondary to his other "life."

Averaging four deals a month, the infrequent dealer might make $100 and possibly a few free drugs. This may pay for some meals, his share of some rent, a new pair of pants, or some other minimal necessity. The psychological pay-off is that he demonstrates he is in on big action without getting the reputation of a dealer and without being known as a center of action himself. A 22-year-old unemployed ex-art student and head described one infrequent dealer:

> It's hard to say if he makes his money from dealing or shop-lifting. He's always on drugs, though he seldom pays for it. He's charming and manages never to eat too much or stay too long at one person's house. Once he became a big speed dealer and made $400 in a week, but then was burned for every penny on one deal. I don't think he's ever had more than $50 at a time since then. In a funny way I like getting kilos from him because $25 means a lot to him, and I figure if he didn't get it from me that way, sooner or later he'd get it from me some other way . . . probably borrowing it, and we know he'd forget it before he repaid it.

Probably most of the buyers of small quantity drugs in the Colony get them either from irregular supply sources (petty importers) or from small and infrequent dealers who perform no distribution function except for smoothing contacts. Although these persons do not replace the regular big dealers, many Colony members manage to survive or supplement their income by serving as go-betweens. Once they have bought small quantity drugs for themselves (or in partnership with others), they can do this for friends, and the more they do it the easier it is and the less it will cost to get small quantity. Naturally, pushers on the way up try quantity dealing infrequently; most of such transactions are done by persons with no intention of making this their business. They, too, like to provide drugs for friends, especially if there's a little money to be made and the connections appear extremely safe.

BIG DEALERS

A person can be characterized as a big dealer if he buys in bulk, stocks other drugs, and if the people he sells to sell at the street level. Although full-time dealing can be a very profitable occupation, there are some who work at it only part-time. Several different patterns of big dealing can be distinguished in the Colony: the All-Around Big Dealer, the

Episodic Marihuana Dealer, the Bureaucratic Kilo Dealer, and the Acid Dealer.

Given the large Colony market, there is room for regular dealers and others who sell in large quantities. The demand, excluding perhaps 15 kilos of marihuana brought in by petty importers and small dealers operating directly with manufacturers of LSD and importers of marihuana, comes to about a minimum of 35 pounds of marihuana per month and over 2,000 capsules of LSD.

How dealers operate depends largely on how their suppliers and customers sell and buy. For LSD, the suppliers like to sell grams or half-grams—there being 1,000 capsules of 500 micrograms per half-gram. The dealer usually mixes the pure LSD with an equal amount of baking soda, milk lactose or some other filling and then packs them in capsules. A 21-year-old middle-level dealer depicted this phase of the operation:

> LSD will stick to the skin and after a while capping can become ridiculous because everybody is loaded and work sort of falls to a standstill and everybody sits around and trips. Sometimes there are 5 people capping. Some people have to take over when other people are falling out of their chairs.

(Recently, some high-level operatives—either dealers or manufacturers or chemists at the top—have begun placing the LSD in tablets so that it becomes difficult for lower-level sellers to cut.) Because the top sellers prefer selling grams or half-grams, it is difficult to get odd lots, such as a 750-capsule purchase, unless one goes into partnership or buys through a top seller who has packaged his own LSD. The price to the dealer amounts to approximately $.85–$1.25 per capsule for purchases of enough for 1,000 capsules. The prices fluctuate but the mark-up remains fairly constant. The pushers who buy from dealers usually have little need for more than 100 capsules, since few of their customers buy more than 10 at a time, and most buy about 5. Pushing over 100 capsules means a fairly good-sized clientele or one that is predominantly acid-head. Most pushers do not have the money to buy over 100 capsules at a time at an average per capsule price of about $2.00. The dealer's profits are about $900, for 10–25 sales per 1,000 or 2,000 capsule purchases. A dealer with a regular set of customers—as most have—should easily sell these in a week or so, though he could not immediately negotiate another purchase and expect to sell out so quickly.

There are at least two distinct methods whereby dealers obtain kilos of marihuana. One version is that the major importers like to sell off their massive supply as quickly as possible in order to repeat big imports. Thus, the dealers buy small bulk. A 21-year-old middle-level dealer stated:

> 200 kilos will last an importer about a week . . . because the demand's so high. Mostly, they get rid of it to people they know—then

wait and go back a month later. Like somebody from San Francisco goes down and buys 50 kilos . . . some people buy 10, some 25. Maybe 10 people will buy this particular lot.

The other version is that importers prefer selling individual lots, even though they have hundreds, or thousands, of kilos on hand. A 23-year-old ex-Colony resident, an all-around middle-level dealer, described the other alternative:

> I guess if you look at it when you don't know anything about the situation, what else is an importer to do with 300 or 500 pounds—except get rid of it? The thing is, after you get out of Mexico, it takes an awful lot of bread for you to be buying things (like 20 or 50 pounds). There aren't many people who are able to do this. But nobody does it. None of the big guys want to sell like that. They figure they have this 2.2 pounds of marihuana in this little brick and it really looks nice, and "I'm just not giving it to anybody for $40 or $50. I'm just not doing it." The going price in Berkeley, say, is $125—you can get lower, but say it's $125. "Well, I'm not going there with my grass and giving people $50 kilos." There is, in fact, a going price. It varies with the part of the country, but in a given area everyone knows how much a kilo or a lid costs.

As the market has burgeoned the last year, the number of multi-kilo buys in the United States seems to have soared, even at small discounting below the single-kilo price. It is so easy to dispose of a few kilos that dealers will try for several kilos to cut down on travel time, and for the little extra money. The situation of holding bulk marihuana until the demand catches up with their supply no longer seems to prevail. A 25-year-old ex-philosophy student and middle-level dealer reported:

> Most people with a large market don't buy a ki of grass, they buy 5 or 10 at a time. It's much safer than to buy one a week every five weeks. I mean, I don't know anyone keeping the ki's in their house—that's silly—though I don't know where they store them. . . . Usually, if they have stuff they're keeping and want to get rid of it they'll tell somebody so people will know they want to get rid of it . . . and it won't last long.

However, multi-kilos buys require a lot of money, and most marihuana dealers do not have this. For instance, 10 kilos—which might sell for $90 each in the Bay Area—might cost $750 or more. Dealers rarely have customers who want more than a kilo or two at a time. How many ounces can a pusher sell in a few weeks? How much can a head or two keep at home? So, most marihuana is sold by representatives of big importers a kilo at a time at the going area price (say $90–$95 in the Bay Area), which provides a gross profit of probably $30 per sale to the dealer. If a major importer has 500 kilos and four regular agents in different areas, each may have access to over 100 kilos. Other dealers pay more per kilo, sell for the same price, but do not have to store, "hold," and conceal their supply nearly so long or thoroughly as the single-kilo, long-run dealer.

In the Colony, the demand is not big enough to support more than a handful of big dealers at any given moment. Regular dealers operate in San Francisco, usually, and Colony pushers often go there for supplies. There are several different styles of operations for big dealers, but not all of them have a bearing on Colony drug use.

THE ALL-AROUND BIG DEALER

The most useful dealer, from the pusher's perspective, is one who always tries to have on hand small quantity marihuana and LSD, and possibly a little amphetamine crystal too. These all-around big dealers perform the same function on the illegal market as drug suppliers do on the legal market—providing one-step shopping by the smallest bulk-purchasers. The all-around dealer probably has three or four sources for quantity purchases of either marihuana or LSD at any given time, and probably keeps $500 or more in cash on his person at all times to buy the 5–20 kilos of marihuana and 1,000 caps of LSD which make up his standard purchase. The all-around dealer has several enormous problems because it is so difficult to conceal his operations, especially in marihuana. A 24-year-old graduate student in social science and occasional kilo dealer commented on this problem:

> Here's this big—if you buy 1 kilo there's a package almost the size of a shoe-box—and you have to carry it along. And where you go to get it, it is obvious to everybody in the city what you're doing. There's no way to be cool about carrying kilos around, or having people walk out your house with kilos.

Like the big pusher, the all-around dealer has constant traffic in and out of his residence. Further, he has so much marihuana on hand that it is literally impossible to hide on his residence. This usually involves very sloppy relations between dealers and street pushers. A 23-year-old former Colony resident, an all-around middle-level dealer, talked about this problem:

> If you're dealing kilos you aren't able to be as careful about your customers as you might be with some other drugs because if you've got anything over a kilo in your possession it's gonna be known about all over, so you can't protect yourself from people knowing about you anyway—you just keep yourself in situations where you're never connected with drugs yourself—but you're still selling them.

A major motive for such dealing is the profits. Selling 15 kilos and 500 capsules of LSD each month (at gross profits of $25 per kilo and $.75

per cap) the dealer can gross $750. Overhead—particularly travel, waiting, and storage—can easily come to $150, but $600 net is substantial. Peripheral sales of amphetamines, etc., probably bring in a few more dollars. The pay may not be great, may not reach the levels expected of major drug traffickers, but such a dealer is a major Berkeley supplier. One such dealer was arrested during the course of this research. He sold 5 kilos of marihuana for $85 each, followed by an 8 kilo sale for $80 per to agents. At the time of arrest, police found possibly another kilo of marihuana and 1,000 capsules of suspected LSD. If we assume the dealer purchased 30 kilos a month and 1,000 capsules of LSD, his outlays would come to over $2,500 any given month, though profits could easily amount to over $1,500—enough for a two- or three-man partnership, each living fairly well. The pay for the time spent seems excellent, even figuring a few days of travel, a few more days of waiting, a few hours of negotiating and traveling for the stored marihuana whenever a big sale was made. How criminal is such a big all-around dealer? A professor described the student involved as follows:

——— is a bright kid from Los Angeles, about 20, nice but nothing very unusual or weird . . . until about a year ago when his eyes started changing. He really started looking beautiful, except now and then there'd be this far-away gaze. He spoke with me now and then about drugs, and wrote a paper on drug experimentation or something . . . that was fairly good. But who ever thought he was a pusher?

A similar type of operation, although around a college campus in Los Angeles, was described in an interview with a 23-year-old researcher, occasional pusher, and ex-girl friend of several dealers:

A 20 year old male used drugs for 4 years, started selling about 10 months ago—LSD to people on campus and to friends. Continually upped the amount he dealt, though he doesn't know why. His purchases were for $500–1,000 in acid, 15–20 kilos grass. He seldom holds, and has 3–6 sources for each drug (though each sells more than 1 drug). He buys whenever he needs it, from every week to every month. (Prices paid are $.85–1.25 per cap of acid, about $60 a kilo of grass). Sells to 30–40 people, the same people all the time.

THE EPISODIC DEALER IN MARIHUANA

Another type of big dealer is the sporadic purchaser of medium quantity marihuana. In the summer of 1967, Berkeley police made a record seizure of almost 80 pounds of marihuana. The purchase was, apparently, made in San Francisco. The newspaper reports indicate the major purchasers were very young: a 23-year-old psychedelic lighting technician, a 23-year-old self-employed agent, and one other. Also arrested were three others whose ages were given: a 22-year-old go-go dancer, a 21-year-old, and a 22-year-old musician. Because there was a temporary marihuana shortage, they paid probably $65 per kilo, and might expect to sell for gross profits of $35. Assuming only three partners, each stood to gross just over $400 for 12 kilos, and (given the shortage) they probably could each sell out in a day or two. Excellent money for the time involved, but it probably required an enormous amount of time buying, and would only be worthwhile in such quantity when the supply was bone dry. In any event, such bulk purchases could only be done infrequently—no more than once a month, assuming our estimate of Colony demand is very low and there is no other local competition. Although the purchase price for the 35 kilos was probably about $2,000, assuming three partners, and assuming each had several kilos pre-paid for, the dealers did not have to be very wealthy. The Colony has room for only one or possibly two such regular operatives, on anything like the level of 35 kilo purchases. One Colony middle-level dealer who was a graduate student in social science described a dealer he knew who occasionally supplied the Colony, periodically buying quantity marihuana. She was a San Franciscan, in her mid-20's, with contacts in Los Angeles. She'd been dealing over a year and was reported to periodically make over $1,000 per deal. However, she lived in a small apartment and apparently lived little better than most young Haight-Ashbury denizens. In describing her recent operations it was clear why she was not rich, and it illustrated the enormous expenditure of energy, anxiety, and high overhead involved.

> She was supposed to have a deal for 50 kilos or so in L.A., and she was always calling down, but it never seemed available. It was always "yeah, it looks like it's ok in another day or so," but the deals always went "poof." Last week she got a phone call that the pot could be had, so she went down with another guy, and two spades drove a car down, and they were to come back different ways—like she'd drive and the spades would fly. When she got there, the deal didn't come through, so they had to turn around and return everyone's money. It must have cost at least $150 when you figure it out, and that was all there was for 10 days of running around.

Obviously, she stands to make excellent money—if the deals come through—buying bulk, at L.A. prices, and selling in the Bay Area. Since many of her sales are pre-paid, she does not have to be very wealthy to deal. However, she takes enormous risks, with several others involved in transporting, many who already have paid her for drugs, others who have made requests, and yet others who are outside this particular deal but know it is going on. Whatever precautions she takes, scores of people must know that she deals, how she deals, and even when she deals. The only way for the sporadic marihuana dealer to regularly make good money is if he has a few excellent contacts for bulk supplies. A 23-year-old ex-Colony resident and all-around middle-level dealer underscored this point:

> I know of two dealers making, regularly, $250–400 a week. These happen to be the two best paid dealers—at this level—maybe in the whole country. Both are involved regularly, and they buy like 10 or 15 kilos at a time after they get some solid feelers from a few guys. They have a friend, not in Mexico, who's doing them a favor. They'll buy them for $60 apiece and sell them for $80 or $85, or if they're ambitious, drive north and sell them fore $100 or $120. These guys are tied in with the "organization" of the top-rung—the importers.

THE BUREAUCRATIC KILO DEALER

Most kilos of marihuana are sold through regular bureaucratic kilo dealers, who sell one or two kilos to a customer at the set price. They are linked to a stable distribution system, and they need a major importer or two as their sources, but once they are set up they do not have to work for supplies. A major importer, with 400–1,000 pounds of marihuana to unload, can keep a few bureaucratic dealers stocked for months. The Bureaucratic dealer has an enormous stake in the game, and almost necessarily takes great storage precautions. He must operate like a criminal, as if the police know him and are trying to catch him. Given the fact that his existence becomes public knowledge among numerous pushers once he starts dealing kilos in an area, his assumption is probably correct. With what the importer has at stake, it figures for him to choose a very dependable agent who takes maximum precautions when dealing. The profits are considerable, the bureaucratic dealer grossing (probably) $25 per kilo. Making seven or eight sales per week (maybe 10 kilos) he can gross $250 per week for a few months, possibly netting almost $200. Though such big bureaucratic marihuana dealers might sell to many Colony pushers, the Berkeley market is too small for them to operate in, at least regularly, though they may place an agent there for a while. The bureaucratic marihuana dealer also sells other drugs, but relies on his excellent source of two (the importers) and the continually large demand for marihuana. He may not go out looking for additional drugs, but periodically a good offer for a small trade might come up (say 200 caps of LSD for 3 kilos) which works out well for all parties. Still, the profits from marihuana are his stock-in-trade.

ACID DEALERS

Acid dealers especially, if their supply contacts are good enough, have profit motives for specializing. However, unlike the pot dealer who is probably allotted 15–20 kilos at a time by the importer (or his representative), the acid dealer must have substantial money to enter the trade—a minimum of about $1,000. A 19-year-old top-level dealer discussed the amount of money required:

> You don't have to buy the acid connection, but you have to run in the circle of heads so to speak, be involved in money and involved in these big dealing things. Their parents are rich and they have had money all their lives, and they are used to having money. And, they get high, and having this money background naturally get into big deals.

Sometimes, less wealthy smaller operators can go into partnership for large buys, but even they must have their hands on a few hundred dollars each. Therefore, street pushers cannot just step up when they hear of a contact. A 23-year-old researcher, occasional pusher, and ex-girl friend of several dealers described several people involved in buying LSD:

> There were four people involved in this $2,000 acid deal, but only 1 met the person selling. These four pooled their money and it ran from $400 to $1,000, depending on the person. . . . Of the four, one's been dealing for quite a while on a smaller scale—anywhere from 100 caps to 1–10 for friends. Pot the same way. Been at it 4 or 5 years. Then there was this pretty chick from San Francisco, who broke off from an acid-head group. She's wiggy, flipped out. Tremendously confused but functions. A third, a kid from a good home who admitted doing it totally for the excitement. Maybe 21, living at home with his parents—maybe in the acid scene for 8 months. I guess his father is the type gave his kids savings bonds, and he had an account of maybe $1,000. He only dressed the acid-head now and then, but always dressed upper middle class. He, like everyone, only sells to his own strata. The fourth I'd classify as lazy more than anything else . . . 21, married, a kid 4 months old. . . .

Acid dealers do not have the enormous storage problems of bureaucratic pot dealers. They only need to hide, rather than store, their bulk purchase. Acid dealers usually buy grams or half-grams (at approximately $1 per 500 micrograms, or $1,000 a half-gram), and cap the drugs themselves (after mixing with filler). They can cut the drugs, but usually do not—at least not much. The major risk in operations of this level is getting inferior merchandise, or having your money stolen. The best check against this is regularized dealings with reliable sources. In the cases we interviewed, or heard about, the acid dealers always performed tests à la an informal FDA. The major means was the "taste test"—the dealer with an acid-head friend or two would actually try the drugs before selling. A 19-year-old top-level dealer described such a test:

> You taste the acid caps before you sell 'em. Someone came up here with liquid acid once at the time acid was very scarce . . . and

wanted to sell it to me at $2 a cap. We were gonna cap it here—I didn't want to take any so I had a friend of mine take some—aaahhh—no response—mild—very mild—so I said, "no deal."

One dealer actually tested 4 of 16 bulk purchases in chemistry labs at a university where he had friends. Although the demand for LSD is far lower than for marihuana, the acid dealer could make more profits on fewer sales if he bought 2,000 capsules per month, made 25 sales (probably to 20 or fewer customers) at an average of just under 100 capsules to each. Net profits could easily be $1,500. Assuming a major burn or theft of $1,000 every 4–6 months, the acid dealer still appears capable of making substantial profits. Our 19-year-old top-level dealer also commented on the profits to be made:

> Well, considering burns—considering people losing—being picked up—I have made $1,000 in a month, for a while . . . but that's like only 3 months I've been dealing. I've lost money. I've lost $1,500 in a month. 'Course, I'm still after the person who burned me—and, aah,—eventually, well, he's going to jail, but eventually he'll come out and I'll get my money back.

Even the big acid dealer must work hard to make good money. However, his style of work and the hours he puts in differ from the lower-level pushers in several ways. First, the dealer must always be ready to do business and must be alert, but most of the time he is either between transactions or in preliminary sparring with his sellers and buyers. Our top-level dealer continued:

> You can make a lot of money—it's hard because it's gotta be a full-time thing . . . You always have to be available to deal . . . to go into a deal. You always have to have money available to buy something, and it's almost impossible to do two things at once—to be a dealer and to have a job or go to school, or even to be a dealer and be married.

Certain things that are wise for the pusher are imperative for the big dealer—such as limiting his clientele to a few regular trustworthy persons and not having any drugs in his home that cannot be easily disposed of. Also, the dealer can cash in heavily on his supply contacts, whereas the pusher ups his profits by expanding his clientele or selecting bigger buyers for customers.

> I know a lot of people—maybe 3 or 4—who need more big customers —$1,000 at a time . . . and I know some more persons who want, say, $300 or $400 of acid. So, if I just put together the two I can get myself an awful lot of free acid.

Naturally, the acid dealer is very wary of the "MAN" (enforcement agents) because he has so much to lose. The temptation to make a small sale is not there, as it is with pushers or even kilo-dealers. The big money lies in the big deals, and these take a few days (usually) to consummate, which allows the acid dealer time to check on his newer customers. Where the pusher strives to reduce the risks and consequences of arrest by looking uncool or regularizing his transactions and the people he deals with, the big dealer (particularly in LSD) strives to create a situation where it's impossible to be arrested, even if apprehended.

> I can't get caught. The only possible way would be by the police raiding my apartment in the isolated times I have something here, and it's so easy to get rid of—at a loss, a fantastic loss—but not as much a loss as going to jail. I don't carry on the street, don't carry around, don't keep things in my apartment. I don't even use drugs that much, and when I use I certainly don't sell. . . . With dealing pot it's different from acid as there's no way to hide that you're dealing. The idea is to keep yourself in situations that you're not gonna get busted . . . you're never connected with the drug itself, but you're still selling it but you don't make the kinds of sales we might make by selling a lid or something like that. They gotta be personal recommendations.

If you work very hard for excellent money, it figures to take that extra precaution. If caught, the law will show little mercy to the big dealer.

What does the big acid dealer look like? Mass media reports drawn from police records and interviews offer several examples. One incident involved 5 persons with a reported $10,000 cache of LSD, which actually was only 2,000–3,000 LSD capsules probably costing the arrestees one-fourth the estimated value and worth to them probably only one-half the estimate. Still, these were big dealers. The alleged major peddler was 22 years old; the others 17, 18, 19 and 24. They had $1,600 in cash with them—typical of acid dealers buying grams or so.[2]

Another example reported in an interview with a 23-year-old researcher, and a ex-girl friend of several dealers, is as follows:

> Male, 22 years old. Been using drugs under 1 year, dealing about 6 months. Had 3 or more sources at all times, and a clientele of 10–30, almost all "regulars." Bought in lots of 1,000–3,000 capsules averaging about $1 per capsule, sold in 100 capsule lots for $300–350 (except 3–5 capsules to friends). Took very few concealment or storage precautions but quit dealing when the law went into effect—a few thousand dollars to the good. From an upper middle-class family, dislikes working, liked dealing because he was "looked up to and respected" by his customers. Dresses like a student and has short hair.

[2] Berkeley's first reported "Mr. Big" of acid dealing was a 22-year-old student who was arrested for making a deal to sell to local police $10,000 worth of hallucinatory drugs. The deal never came off, and it is unclear from press reports if the $10,000 is "Mr. Big's" sales price or the retail value. In any event, a year later this Mr. Big was a medical student at a midwestern university.

This is not the usual portrait of the heavy criminal although since enactment of the laws the picture may be changing.

Obviously, one of the main problems a dealer faces is that his operations become too public. For precaution, many dealers frequently change residence, and even locale. If the dealer has a few excellent sources of supplies, and if he is interested in making extremely good money, he will set up bases of operations in a few places, which enables him to constantly be operating, but only sporadically in any single place. Rather than having 25 or 30 customers in a single place, he may have 15 customers in three separate places, all of whom come to rely on his periodic visits. One good part-time locale is, naturally, the Colony. An interviewee, a 25-year-old social worker, described the biggest dealer she knew as follows:

> ———, when I knew him was just in his first few months of dealing, mainly in Berkeley. He was from LA, or at least had been working there as an auto mechanic for a few years. When he came to Berkeley, he had maybe $50,000 put away from work and from investments on money he had inherited, I think. He went into big dealing almost immediately and was making a deal for $1,000 or $1,500 every 2 weeks, about . . . mainly acid, but he also tried a very big pot deal once, and he periodically bought a few kilos. Once he even bought some stolen pills—a whole satchel full—which caused a lot of trouble. He kept carrying around this satchel which he couldn't figure out how to sell.
>
> After a few months, he was working out of LA and Berkeley. He'd fly up at least once a week, regularly. I hear he also now is working someplace in the East, and I hear he has a guy in Florida he deals with.
>
> (Can you describe who he is?) ——— is about 28, lives in a small apartment that is really furnished great. He has terrific hi-fi and tape equipment, which has been stolen from him at least twice that I know of. He drives a good car, although these have also been "borrowed," and once he found it 3 days later piled up. Naturally, he had to pay the repair bills. He must make a thousand a month, at least, when he's operating, although he's gone over a month without a deal. Once he borrowed $150 from me, and I was supposed to get it back quick with a kilo interest, and it was months before I got paid back . . . without the kilo.

In the few years that upper-middle-class youngsters could easily become big dealers, there has been a tendency toward quitting the trade after a few months. A few quit when the LSD laws went into effect in 1966— or at least toned down their operations. A few were reported to be fed up with the enormous hassle and paranoia which accompanied big dealing. They never figured such excitement would demand such hard work. Others became disappointed with the profits, as the thefts, burns, leaks, and other profit reducers simply would not slacken. Some had earned enough. Others were growing into other pursuits more typical of upper-middle-class persons in their mid-20's. Hardly any, however, seem to regret the experience, for almost all entered big dealing because they liked to see people using the drugs they sold, and liked to see people get a fairly good deal. There are, of course, exceptions—and they seem to be noticeably increasing—but the rule is exemplified by this statement of one of the largest dealers in the Colony, a 19-year-old ex-student:

> . . . I don't want the people I sell to hurting people. If I find out they are watering lids down or cheating or burning people, I'll try to do something about it . . . again, I'm a dealer but I'm also a human being. There's some people who don't give a damn—they're in it for the money—they'll do anything. I won't. Some drug users—they'll steal anything—papers, candy, cigarettes . . . and it's like "I'm a criminal anyway, why not go all the way, you know." It's a very little thing, but I'll pay for it and maybe they'll look down on me . . . but luckily the majority of people have compassion for others.

There are probably several other styles of operation, but unless the demand in Berkeley has been grossly underestimated, several of the most relevant dealer operations have been described. How many of each type could work in the Colony? Maybe one or two all-around dealers, occasionally a big marihuana dealer and a big acid dealer, maybe one large multi-kilo marihuana purchase every month or so. In all, maybe 5 or 6 big dealers in any given month, maybe 25 over the entire year. Several times this number operate in San Francisco and are tapped by Colony pushers, a few other big dealers are tapped in Southern California (primarily for multi-kilo pot buys). Since Berkeley is a funnel for drugs to outlying areas, especially other campus communities, there may be room for one or two more local dealers. Possibly, a part-time dealer or two who operate out of several locales can be added to the Colony total.

THE DEALER AS CRIMINAL

How criminal are they? Generally, not very. Most are fairly young, in their early 20's. The two or three bigger operators are in their late 20's or early 30's. Almost all, at least those who live and operate in the Colony, are from that milieu or fit easily into it. Generally they are from upper-middle-class families, usually inheriting the money necessary to become big dealers. The presence of outside hoods or small pushers who work hard and accumulate money and connections to enter dealing and live the high life is rare. Those pushers who step up generally do so very quickly, and have several hundred or thousand dollars available in addition to profits scrimped from small drug trafficking. All we know of take the drugs they sell—at least the basic marihuana and LSD. They all like these drugs, and have no moral problems involved knowing that immature or "weird" people will take their drugs—even LSD. Some won't sell to those they consider "freaky," but this is usually just good business. Most, however, will sell to anyone so long as that person seems trust-worthy vis-à-vis the law. One of the largest dealers in the Colony, a 19-year-old head, commented:

> I refuse to sell to people I think are cops, uncool or will flip out . . .
> I think it's both good and moral to deal. So, if I trust a person I'll
> never refuse to sell it to him. After that, it's their own responsibility.

Probably those dealers we interviewed, heard reports of, or read about in newspapers are not representative of dealers all over. Still, these cases apparently service a good part of the Berkeley market. The "typical dealer" is probably changing some since late 1966 and 1967 (when most of our information was accumulated), because of changes in the laws and law enforcement.

That big dealers in, and to, the Colony tend to be young and "look like" Colony members serves several functions from the view point of Colony pushers and drug users, and also those who supply the dealers. It insulates the lower levels of trafficking and use from having to deal with "heavier" and "hoodier" elements. By approximating a situation where friends deal with friends it also protects the top levels from exposing themselves to the public view of rank amateurs who are un-reliable from top-level perspectives. A 19-year-old top-level dealer de-scribed how this worked:

> People are connected to people and there's a line. I could talk to a
> person one step above me and one step below me, but I can't talk to
> a person two steps above me—unless I move up a step. I can't talk
> right now to a chemist—I can talk to a chemist's helper. . . . I don't
> know nothing about square middle-class scenes on the Peninsula who
> use drugs, and nothing about high school scenes, though I know they
> use a lot. I don't really want to know, just the same as I don't want
> them to know who I am. The more people you know, different peo-
> ple, the more chance you're gonna get busted eventually.

The big dealers routinize drug trafficking a bit. They and pushers have ongoing relations which benefit them both financially, time-wise, and in reducing risk. By definition, such routinization makes the drug operations criminal but this, obviously, is a mixed bag. Still, up to now, big deal-ing is not that special bureaucratic criminal operation which only the heavies can break into. On the contrary, the rise of Colony dealers has almost always been extremely swift. Apparently, as the market burgeoned, persons from out of the new group of users came forth to assume dealer positions. Our 19-year-old top-level dealer continued:

> I have maybe 4 or 5 connections for acid deals. You come up with
> new connections all the time, you know. I first got in touch with them

by wanting to do a big deal, and you tell someone who can't do the big deal himself, but who can get in touch with this other person . . . because they do it—I know a lot of people who need more customers—big customers—$1,000 at a time.

The prevalence of friends-dealing-with-friends tends to improve reliability. A dealer will not sell inferior merchandise to a steady customer whom he happens to know and like. If the merchandise is bad, some informal method of making up the bad deal can be worked out. By having dealers from within the Colony, the money is also kept within, and insofar as the dealers live well, they tend to support local Colony institutions (coffee-shops, rock dances, local clothes shops, record and book stores, in several cases the University itself). By having Colony dealers, there is less difficulty for pushers who can easily "run across" their contacts when their need arises. This saves time and travel, and cuts down the risk for all concerned.

The myth of pushing—seedy outsiders, selling to addict-pushers who seduce the users, huge profits, controlled by a syndicate, etc.—seems irrelevant even at big dealer levels in the Colony. The profits, though good, are not that exceptional. A steady net income of over $1,000 a month is a rarity—most big dealers in (or near) the Colony average half this or slightly more. The profits should not be judged by the "good months" and the "good deals." There are dry months and bum deals, burns and thefts, obviously costly arrests and seizures, costly and necessary overhead, and the need to drastically shift residence, locale, and even styles of dealing. If there is an all-controlling syndicate, it does not seem very evident. Dealers always report 3–6 sources for each drug, unless there is a direct tie to a very big and regular operative (such as a 1,000-pound marihuana importer). But, even though the dealers may not have the socioeconomic characteristics of criminals, and may not dress, look, and act like "hoods," they characteristically take the precautions of criminals, with an eye and ear constantly attuned to narcotics agents. Sometimes, however, this is not done. Our 19-year-old top-level dealer discussed the difficulties in taking extensive precautions:

> I do a lot of my things over the phone—which is bad—because I think my phone is tapped—but it's very hard not to talk on the phone, to go to a phone booth every time is a trouble. You get a call in here and you say "wait a minute, and I'll call you back," and go to the local phone booth—like at 12 at night—it's impractical. So you take your chances.

The precautions are more extensive, the bigger the operation of the dealer, and the greater the impact of the anti-drug laws and their enforcement. To see this clearly, it is necessary to describe traffic above the dealer levels, and then to discuss the relation of drugs and organized crime.

THE CHEMIST

Above the dealer levels, the channels for non-opiate drugs are almost always distinct. LSD is either smuggled in from overseas or manufactured illegally by a highly skilled chemist. (In mid-1966 a large amount of LSD was smuggled in, predominantly bearing the Sandoz label. Sandoz had already recently stopped manufacturing it, but several persons reported that there were still vast quantities available. By mid-1967, this may no longer be true). Not everyone can manufacture LSD. Besides the skill, it requires an expensive laboratory set-up (estimated at anywhere from a few thousand to $10,000) and generally access to lysergic acid. Making low-quality acid by some less expensive process does not seem to be worth the trouble and expense to anyone from top-to-bottom of the traffic. Lysergic acid seems to be essential.

There are, according to our informants, six or seven chemists in California, at least half in the Bay Area, who manufacture LSD. California, supposedly, is the leading state in the nation in the manufacture (as well as use) of LSD. Each chemist probably makes enough LSD for 10,000–20,000 capsules per month, the current rumor being that 80,000 to 100,000 capsules are distributed through the Bay Area each month.[3] Almost always, the chemist is a specialist whose job is over when he leaves the laboratory. He is too valuable to risk in other operations, and probably doesn't have the skills for it. Our 19-year-old top-level dealer commented on the risks the chemist takes in making LSD:

> That's something I'll never be able to produce. It takes a lot of technical skill. It costs the chemist about $.10 to produce—and it's no trouble . . . he won't get caught either. It's hard to catch chemists. You don't know where he is. You don't know where he's selling from or where he makes it and you gotta catch him just at the right time when it's happening—because until then it just isn't acid.

The chemist's salary is reported to be approximately 10 cents a capsule—or $1,000–$2,000 per month. Excellent pay, but he is obviously a treasured talent.

THE TOP MEN

It may be appropriate to end our description of the illegal careers available to Colony members with middle-size dealing since only a few of the top dealers come out of the Colony, though a few more may live there occasionally. The theoretical possibility exists, however, that a

---

[3] The 80,000–100,000 rumor came from the middle-size dealers. A big dealer who was about to enter the manufacturing of LSD at the time of the interview estimated that the figure is closer to one million.

Colony member can aim for the top and may make it. His achievement invariably takes him out of the Colony into a larger world of illegal drug dealing. Because the career possibility exists it may be helpful to describe briefly the character of jobs available at the top.

The man-behind-the-chemist is the biggest investor, and stands to make the highest profits from LSD. Selling grams or half-grams to dealers for an average price just above $1 a 500-microgram capsule provides the Mr. Big of acid traffic a gross profit of possibly $.90 per capsule, or $10,000–$20,000 a month. Minus the cost of lysergic acid and laboratory costs, the Mr. Big should take but two or three months to clear his major expenses for the year, and then his overhead is merely precautionary. The Mr. Big obviously needs but one motivation—*money*. Obviously, he must operate as a criminal, hiding his raw materials, his finished product, his laboratory, and even his chemist. Mr. Big—knowing how good the money is—may even have agents working for him in his sales to dealers. Dealers, despite a willingness to talk about their own operations, are extremely reluctant to describe their suppliers—as is everyone in the traffic. They do report that buying from the top suppliers usually involves enormous difficulties and a complicated game of hide-and-seek. Most dealers complain that the runaround is really far more than necessary, but—given the money at stake—possibly it makes sense for the suppliers. The usual thumbnail description of the top acid dealers portrays them as in the playboy image—sharp, mid-20's to early 30's, not acid-heads in the least, and very materially oriented. A 23-year-old former Colonyite, all-around middle-level dealer, depicted top LSD dealers as follows:

> They like to drive nice cars, always dress nicely. They're always hustling girls, mostly they are not in a marriage or any kind of scene where they are tied down at all. They are very wrapped up in *things* and how the *things* can affect their lives—rather than the poorer class of acid-heads around who are continually screaming how they are *not* interested in *things*. . . . Caucasion, upper middle-class. Most, in fact, are unemployed, which is one reason they have to change residences so often. What many of them do is work occasionally—like an extra in the acting field, or a jazz musician who plays only an occasional gig. And they seldom spend their money on permanent types of things that can be seen by anyone, like their own big house. And a lot of them even rent their cars. They deliberately make it hard to see what kind of income they have.

Occasionally, descriptions are of more traditionally "gangster" types, including a Chicagoan involved in a multi-gram transaction who from the moment he disembarked from the airplane until the moment he returned to the airport, hardly uttered a word but led his client on a merry chase—shifting cars, getting out, meeting in another place, etc., etc.

MR. BIG OF MARIHUANA

The Mr. Bigs of marihuana trafficking are usually of a qualitatively different kind. Several dealers describe major importers as often being wealthy youth on a profit-making lark. With several thousand dollars in allowances and inheritances, they ventured to Mexico with some contacts and managed to swing the smuggling of several hundred kilos. Another report was of a dealer, just peripheral to the Colony, who expanded his operations by importing several hundred kilos. Several different stories have rumored that major Mexican contact points were in a city's jailhouse or police station or courthouse, so—at least according to rumor—the contacts may not be that difficult to make. Another, and possibly the dominant, "type" is the businessman or ex-professional, in his 30's or 40's.[4] Still another type, though the least typical, is significant because of the quantity of marihuana he brings in. Those described by dealers did not emerge out of the Colony, but were based in Southern California. Their operation did not seem to be relevant to Colony use. They resemble more closely the official version of the top man in marihuana traffic. They tend to be more organized and look like criminals.[5]

For each type of marihuana importer, the overhead is enormous. Primary cost is making, consolidating, and overseeing the Mexican contact. Apart from the purchase, this consumes several weeks time and an enormous amount of money. The danger is also probably greatest at this level, particularly as (in most cases) the importer is operating in a foreign country. The Mexicans can simply steal the money, or give too little marihuana, or sell the marihuana and immediately inform the local narcotics agents. The reward, to the Mexicans, is reported to be at least

[4] In Spring, 1967, there were two major Bay Area arrests of this type: one of the "phantom flyer," a 43-year-old ex-electrical engineer and pilot, arrested trying to sell agents 275 pounds of marihuana; the other, a pizza parlor operator who was seized with 1,400 pounds of pot. The "phantom flyer," at least, seemed obviously a regular at making such deals.

[5] The largest operation that U.S. agents have caught is the "Bono Ring." In March, 1967, agents followed a 51-year-old dealer to a suburban area outside Los Angeles. There, agents confiscated 2,156 pounds of marihuana in addition to 100 kilos from the older dealer. Two months later, two border guards were shot, and in the following few weeks there were several more seizures, a confession by two others and the arrest of the alleged ring leader (Bono) and one other. Those arrested and several of those alleged to have sheltered them all had Spanish surnames. Besides the ton of marihuana seized in March, agents picked up another 400 pounds in a raid on Bono's home and 2,900 pounds when his camper bus was captured in Guadalajara. The two confessors claimed they were running 400 kilos across the border when accosted by the border guards. In all, 5,700 pounds of marihuana were captured and anywhere from 480–880 pounds were outstanding. Additionally, in the raid on Bono's home, police confiscated numerous weapons. The ring seemed to be a large-scale organization clearly willing to resort to weaponry.

15 per cent of the value of the marihuana and the car being used—and probably considerably more if it is a big operation. Other overhead involves paying for transportation to the United States (most importers will not carry it over themselves), and at least one storage point. The "up-front" costs prior to getting the marihuana across the border has been estimated at well over a thousand dollars, at least the first time or two. This is in addition to the cost of the marihuana. Travel costs amount to possibly $100 or so, the drivers often being paid 5 or 6 kilos for 200 or so kilos brought over. Storage costs are a small apartment or two, periodically shifted, for the few months it normally has to take to unload. Additionally, there are domestic costs, often involving hundreds of dollars of phone, travel, motel, and wine-and-dine expenses. Even the best operatives face the problem of burns; witness this statement by the Phantom Flyer at the time of his arrest:

> Gee, this is tough. I guess the only tougher thing was when I was back in New York with the airplane and made a big sale. I was paid with a .45—the person who made the purchase just beat it.[6]

For all the problems and expenses, if the importer gets his hands on the merchandise in the United States, the chances are his profits are fairly good—but nothing like the Mr. Big in LSD. Mexican prices for 200 or more kilos of marihuana are probably under $10 per pound. FBN agents a few years ago paid $7.50 per pound for 1,500 pounds of marihuana delivered in Mexico. One all-around middle-level dealer, age 23, reports that even this was too high a price:

> There is no price for pot in Mexico. If someone pays over $2,500 for 1,000 pounds they're crazy. Places all over Mexico charge 3½, 5, 8 dollars for a single kilo. In Oaxaca the natives give it away and think you're crazy for using anything but the mushroom.

Whether federal agents were paying an extremely high price is difficult to determine, but in any event, even the officials pay considerably under the going U.S. price. Assuming an import of 200 kilos, at $20 per kilo, with additional expenses of $2,000, the importer can easily net $30 per kilo selling through his agents primarily in the Bay Area. That, however, is about maximum for this scale of operation. To get much above the $6,000 level, the importer must start dealing in thousands of pounds. If 2,000 or 10,000 kilos are imported, then the profits start mounting, but the purchase price also becomes enormous. Many persons can accumulate $5,000 but $25,000 is prohibitive—and extremely dangerous. One must know his Mexican contacts extremely well.

The profits in importing marihuana are, obviously, too low for a thoroughly organized, fairly large operation (say, even six or seven persons). The Bono Ring, the only known importing operation making tens

[6] Quoted in *San Francisco Examiner*, March 28, 1967.

of thousands of dollars, seemed too disorganized to be a "mafia-like" operation, although it is possible that there was a financier or two behind them. (Cutting even $150,000 profits ten ways, at least, doesn't make any single operative a millionaire by any stretch of the imagination). But even if every part of the importing forces the Mr. Big to act as if he is a criminal, by the time the marihuana gets dispensed by agents of his at $90 a kilo, the profits on an individual transaction are too low to warrant gun-play. There are enough other large importers to handle local needs, besides the occasional petty importers from the Colony. So, the heavy importer is not a major Colony supplier. The numerous importers apparently have separate distribution channels, though a few may inter-lock at the dealer level.

The portraits of top-level LSD and marihuana traffic may, however, be in the process of changing. Our respondents reported enough rumors of "Mafia" and "heavies," and enough indications of tampering with the normal "non-criminal" operations to warrant closer scrutiny.

THE IMPACT OF THE LSD LEGISLATION ON COLONY TRAFFIC

In the standard myths, organized crime has always controlled drug trafficking. Especially has this been true of marihuana, which, in much of the early (1930's) literature about it, also led to crime and violence because it supposedly removed civilizing inhibitions, and made the user subject to the suggestions of an evil mastermind. Since marihuana use was banned in the 1930's it has been criminal not only because its mere use is a felony, but because the middle-class user has had to have lower-class contacts where usage was concentrated. The description developed here indicates that the Colony user has virtually no self-concept of himself as a criminal, and virtually no contacts with criminals in obtaining his supplies. This is especially so regarding marihuana, which is to be found almost everywhere. An occasional nonprofit pusher, and graduate student in his early 30's, stated:

> If the laws about "entering a house where you have reason to suspect there is marihuana" were ever seriously enforced, the local jail would be bigger than the University. No milk-man or Fuller-brush man would dare set foot in a house on South Campus.

The pushers and dealers usually resemble their customers, like the drugs they are selling, work for very low wages considering the risk, seldom cheat their customers, and hardly ever resort to violence.

Many persons accept the essentially non-criminal description of Colony drug use and low-level selling, but still worry about the ultimate "control" of organized crime. The Mafia, so some think, handles all drugs, using the non-addictive ones to build a market of potential addicts. But since there is no evidence that a hard-drug market is being created in communities like the Colony, any "syndicate" must be in it for the money derived from non-opiate drugs alone. Until recently, the market for marihuana and LSD (except in a few ghetto areas, for marihuana) was too small to make large profits.

In many ways LSD seems a natural for criminals to attempt to control. The profits, as pointed out, are very high for big dealers and especially for the top levels. The bulk is small enough to conceal, and its manufacture requires a skill that few possess, excellent connections (for the lysergic acid), and considerable money to finance a good laboratory. In many ways, the situation resembles heroin, although the drug is non-addictive and the effects of the drug, and hence the character of the user, are different. LSD traffic was perceived as non-criminal initially, because of the essentially middle-class market, the small demand, and the fact that it was fairly easy to obtain or make. Quantity lysergic acid could easily be obtained by chemists with the simplest subterfuges. Since there were no laws against it, dealers could operate fairly openly—at least until 1966. Controlling production and distribution was thus extremely difficult, and in the absence of a very large demand, it was hardly worthwhile. When the demand started increasing, the chemists and their sponsor-helpers seemed to be satisfied with making the "good money" from 10,000 –20,000 capsules of LSD each month. Our 19-year-old top-level dealer reported:

> There's not that competition between chemists in producing acid— there's always people who'll buy it—there's so much money floating around. I could call five people right now and get $4,000 to buy acid with . . . the biggest guy right here, right now, has hung up the ten people he sells to because he has enough money right now and doesn't want to take the trouble of going to his stash of 5,000 caps and getting them out and giving them to his helper—just wasn't worth the trouble to him.

The introduction of laws and the sharply curtailed manufacture and overt distribution of LSD and lysergic acid changed the situation. As soon as the California legislation was passed, a few dealers quit. If the law is effectively enforced, several things can be expected to happen: the top men will become more cautious in their dealing. At the top level, some organization may begin. The profits are too high and the risk too great not to formalize operations, regularize distribution networks and distributors, compare information on middle-range distributors as a reliability check, and so on. One dealer reported that communication has already begun at the top level in the Bay Area, primarily to create a list of buyers so as to minimize the information obtainable by agents and informers. The goal was to tighten up the distribution network and remove some of its open character.

There have been reports from dealers that LSD has become increasingly unreliable. New suppliers are reportedly appearing in and adjacent to the Colony. Increasingly, methedrine and other relatively cheap drugs have been added to LSD to give the impression of a "bang" while the LSD has been drastically cut. Colony pushers and dealers report an increase of "deals" that have fallen through. This suggests the entry of more criminal elements into Colony trafficking. The increasing organization at the top level due to the legislation, however, should change the character of the top men. They may look more and more like those dealers at the upper echelon of the heroin traffic or will conform more to the respectable white-collar criminal. In short, what little mixture of business and appreciation of the "acid scene" currently exists will disappear. Even before the law went into effect, the major traffickers could be characterized as sharp and hardheaded. They took the usual precautions of criminals. That the distribution channels beneath them were not heavy suggests that changes at the top might not affect lower levels of distribution—and hence the Colony scene—very much.

Marihuana is a different story, even if there may be strains toward linking the control of the traffic in both. Marihuana is too profitless to warrant the entry of major criminal elements—or at least this was true until the demand so expanded that it became feasible to regularly import literally tons of marihuana. It still is virtually impossible to control production and importing of marihuana at anything resembling the possibilities in LSD. When the demand was small, the petty imports could fill a sizeable enough portion of the demand so that big profits could not be realized. The existence of several major importers virtually guaranteed a fairly nonorganized traffic, even at the top. Once the demand soars to several hundred thousand pounds in the United States, the situation changes. If an "organization" can import 50,000 pounds annually, netting only $10 per pound before surrendering the marihuana to dealers, the profits are obviously enormous. A hundred petty importers per month, bringing in a thousand kilos, can be easily tolerated. These unstoppable imports get instantly devoured by the enormous market. What can be limited seems to be major competition (particularly in a given area) and possibly major bulk sales in Mexico. Partially controlling the supply guarantees the market for the enormous imports of something like a large marihuana ring. Partial control could also force up the prices. If dealers are willing to pay $5 more per kilo, a major ring stands to profit an extra $100,000 or so. Though there is some kind of logic in attempting to limit marihuana importing, there is little evidence that this has occurred.

All of the above is not to say that the Mafia, organized criminals, or even anything more than an occasional lone thug has moved in on the non-opiate drug traffic—only that the supply and demand conditions are ripe for attempted control of certain markets because huge profits can now be made. The conditions would not, however, be such if it were not for the law and its enforcement. These drive up the prices and profits at every level, increase the risks considerably, and force the drug-trafficking and using worlds to develop their own sets of rules and regulations outside the formal legal system. The mere entrance of gun-toters in the drug traffic forces others at the level being threatened to respond in kind. No one calls the police. The law and enforcers compel traffickers to act like criminals to avoid arrest. The conditions would also not be ripe for criminal involvement were it not for the enormous demand. With usage resembling the days of prohibition, it should not be surprising if the distribution begins to resemble it.

Insofar as criminals come to influence and control parts of the top-level LSD or marihuana trafficking, the major effect will probably be an increase in prices. The situation with LSD may parallel that of heroin forty or fifty years ago. Federal legislation banning opiates was passed in 1914 although enforcement did not really step up until the 1920's. Both are valuable chemicals, not easy to produce, strongly desired by many, very inexpensive to produce but capable of commanding a high price. The effect of stringent laws and enforcement on heroin traffic was the influx of criminals, especially at top levels of selling, and a skyrocketing price.

An organization controlling LSD might, however, be a mixed blessing to the consumers. Poor fly-by-night chemists would probably no longer enter the trade; the LSD would probably be fairly reliable—at least, when it got down to the hands of dealers and possibly lower. It seems reasonable to assume that "big crime" would bureaucratize their operations, and would not tolerate petty hoods tampering with the distribution system. There is, and will be, too much at stake in regular operations to permit serious tampering at low levels. An organization might also routinize sales to dealers, thereby making their lives a lot easier. There might even be fewer middle-level dealers, thereby guaranteeing each good money but demanding hard sober work and precautions.

The impact on the Colony of criminal control over non-opiate drug traffic seems fairly minimal. The pushing system, chaotic as it is, seems to work very well. Drugs are very easily obtained, through friends, and the pushers take a very small profit considering everything. No organization could hire such poorly paid pushers. Similarly the dealers seem to do a fairly good job, only the biggest making very good money. If dealers were backed up by a "force," it might simultaneously limit the unscrupulous dealings of a handful of middle-level operatives and also restrain some of those who currently take a good part of almost every dealer's profits. The system works, and only the most outrageous and unreliable types seem a potential threat to any organization. The obvious change in style for the dealer would be that he would be less free to choose between suppliers, he would have to buy from a criminal, and he would have to act more "criminally"—which merely means more efficiently and with greater precautions. Whether this is any worse than the current situation where dealers have several suppliers and are constantly trying to guarantee that they are not stolen from or sold inferior merchandise is problematic.

For all the public fears, and the recent rash of newspaper stories, the Colony pusher does not seem affected by criminals except insofar as he is losing money because he cannot get much marihuana and his LSD gradually become less reliable. The same pushers are operating as before the rash of stories—the same style of operation continues, although some are willing to take more risks (contact secondary sources, maybe even front a bit of money) to get the treasured marihuana. If "crime" was really moving in to control most of the distribution apparatus, there would probably be a wholesale exit of pushers. One 22-year-old middle-level pusher, a college senior, reported:

> I haven't seen any criminals. Look, I'm not in it so much for the money as the drugs. I figure if I can deal, then I can get whatever drugs I want, as much as I want, and it won't cost me anything. If I had to deal with criminals, I'd get out. It doesn't mean that much to me.

Occasionally, it appears that the only ones concerned and worried about "gangster control" are the participants in the non-opiate culture—the users and sellers in places like the Colony. If nothing else, this should indicate that the motives for using and selling drugs are not to emulate gangsters because this is the extreme form of rebellion. What the future pattern of organization in drug trafficking will be is hard to predict—but the current pattern indicates that selling drugs is one of the few occupations open to Colonyites where they feel they are performing a service to the community, enjoying themselves, earning a living and yet not overcharging their customers—their friends. If marihuana and LSD were legal, a lot of the excitement and money flowing through the Colony might disappear—but the level of drug usage would probably remain the same.

The user-dealers who function within the drug distribution system and supply the needs of Colony members are central to any discussion of this college-related drug scene. They are, however, only one part of the Colony, although a significant one. The bulk of the Colony is made up of a much larger group of persons who do not deal. Their drug needs may be quite minimal or fairly substantial. The following two chapters will explore the life style and values of the bulk of the drug-using population in the Colony. It is their pattern of living which gives the Colony its distinctive atmosphere.

6

A Portrait of the Recreational User

Recreational users are a difficult group to characterize. One might be describing the student population generally. They constitute a larger proportion of those who use drugs than do the heads. It might be easier to describe them by indicating what they are not: they are not part of that large group in and around a campus community who have at one time or another experimented with marihuana and stopped. This is how they got started to be sure: marihuana was available and they decided to see what it was all about. But the recreational users continued their use in a fairly regular way. This would differentiate them from, let us say, the sorority-fraternity group. Their use requires privacy and some kind of association with others who are involved in the drug scene, and they are not students who live at home. This distinguishes them from the commuters. They are also decidedly different from students in the professional schools: engineering, agriculture, education, social welfare, criminology, business administration. They are more likely to be found in the college of letters and sciences, or majoring in one of the social sciences or humanities. They see themselves as liberals or radicals politically, and most of them have participated in political action of one kind or another during the past year. They are different from the heads, whom they regard as too dependent on drugs and too outrageous. They consider themselves as critical, open-minded, sensitive, and aware. A 19-year-old student described his own circle of friends:

> The people I've found who use drugs, the people I've found that I like who are open minded and all these good kind of things most of them do use drugs because they are open enough to try to find that it has a very good purpose, and know it's not gonna kill you or nothing like that and that you've gotta make a decision, you can't always go by society's values. And sometimes you can't obey every aspect of the law you know. . . . I'm pretty sensitive. I can read people pretty well. As far as deep, I don't know. I go as deep as I have to, sometimes it's pretty deep. Depth is a thing. It's cold. I gotta get warm at least up to my skin.

122

Recreational users see themselves also as intellectually oriented and anticipate that their future profession will be in university or college teaching fields or in the creative arts. They see themselves as preparing for a career and part of their free time might be taken up in a career-related interest. The role drugs play in their lives is a relatively minor one compared with the heads. A 20-year-old student revealed the role drugs play in his life in discussing the future:

> I'm gonna have to get a place that's somehow isolated. Have a wife and kids. Have to have at least two or three, because I want some. Possibly teach or write, do something, in some kind of academic work. That's sort of my fantasy for the future. A number of acres 35 miles away from the college where I teach. Possibly I'll build, you know, some kind of ranch. . . . But as far as ever stopping the use of drugs, I doubt I ever will. Possibly I could be in a situation where it would become too dangerous. If I'm in a very tight scene where it's hard to get drugs or associate with drug people then I may have to quit.

STYLE OF USE

Marihuana is considered appropriate for movies, concerts, and parties with a small number of intimate friends. Preparation is usually made for it, and it's considered a special occasion. One 19-year-old student described a situation in which several friends had gone to watch fireworks in San Francisco as an appropriate occasion.

> I unfortunately didn't think of it [marihuana] until we were already there in line with all the other cars ready to watch and I said, "boy could I sure use some grass now." But these situations only come up, you know, Fourth of July is once a year.

Marihuana particularly is felt to be a drug that not only produces a different state of mind but one which improves upon one's chances to enjoy certain kinds of activities. For example, greater enjoyment is taken from listening to music or eating an onion-cucumber sour cream sandwich. Consequently, it finds a special place in leisure-time activities, parties, and weekend entertainment. Some recreational users actually referred to themselves as "weekenders."

A typical situation in which marihuana is used is at a party with some of the following properties. In the first place the party is often planned some days in advance so that the event can be staged appropriately. There will be an unwritten guest list which will include those persons with whom one desires or dares to turn on. People who would react unfavorably or who are thought to be untrustworthy will be excluded. Special food is apt to be prepared in advance, the kind of food one would particularly enjoy while high. Similarly, phonograph recordings are selected which are felt to be the sort of music to be enjoyed while high. One 19-year-old student described the staging of a party given by a couple:

> The way you would turn on would be you'd go down at 11:00 in the morning sometimes and you would sit around until 10:00 or 11:00 at night and you would do things like ah . . . we went to these people's house one time ah . . . we had ah . . . a breakfast that was served that consisted of sliced cantaloupes, Thompson grapes, sliced peaches and strawberries with a mound of powdered sugar in the center of the plate. And we turned on and we ate these and then we had Canadian bacon, scrambled eggs. After that two of us went down on my scooter to the liquor store. We bought 11 bottles of beer for something like . . . there was about 8 of us. It was enough for two good swallows. The beer was from Malaysia, Scotland, England, Greece, ah. . . . Israel, all over. And we charted out our course and we went across the world with beer.

Very often, and unlike a large cocktail party, there will be a common activity. Persons will compare their feelings about their high in relation to whatever is present such as the music, the food, or innumerable other things that might be commented upon. It is a group activity. As such it is also a leveler in the same way that drinking in bars is. Persons who are smoking marihuana are, for the moment at least, equals. This is one element of the camaraderie found among persons who use drugs together. Barriers of class, attainment, and the like tend to be broken and the commonly shared activity of the party becomes more relevant.

Such a party has other features which make it a bond between persons. It is a state of mind, shared with a few people for a short time, which is radically sealed off from outsiders. It may even take place behind locked doors and drawn shades with no one going out or coming in. It is a shared trip experienced only by those privy to it and, as an isolated event in time and space, can never be duplicated again but can be talked about for a great while. Because it has no connection with the outside, it is a creation of those present and felt to be just that. A less pleasant side of this privacy is the fear that it may be violated by the wrong persons—the police or others who might be upset. This is an aspect of the "paranoia" that many users talk about as a "bad trip" which is to be avoided if possible. A 20-year-old student in response to a question about turning on with straight persons present said:

> No, that ah . . . unless you know the person is very liberal and they don't have to worry about it. But otherwise everything would absolutely freeze up and stop. But it has happened occasionally. If another person is cool—don't worry about it.

The party gives the basic handle by which recreational drug use can be grasped, but it is certainly not the only sort of situation which elicits use. Recreational users will go into certain sorts of public surroundings but they are largely confined to the kind that don't require interaction with others who are in no position to share the high state. It is common to go to movies or a concert, both of which require only the most perfunctory relationships with the straight world. Recreational users are not likely to use alone. A 22-year-old woman, a student, emphasized the social character of marihuana:

> I rarely take pot alone. Very little happened to me when I took it alone. I think that was because I was afraid of taking it alone and I reacted against it, but usually it's just with maybe, oh another girl.

If they go out into public, it will be with someone who is likewise high with whom they can share experiences. This unwillingness to interact with the straight world is not so much a matter of fear at being found out as it is the feeling that one is alienated while under the influence, that one cannot share the experience with people who are straight, and that one must guard one's behavior.

Marihuana is clearly the recreational user's drug, the one that he feels most comfortable in using. The only reason that is given for not using marihuana is the brute fact that it is illegal and can lead to nasty consequences. This style of use makes it extremely unlikely that one would be high every day. It would be like getting drunk every day. Some recreational users stated that they used marihuana as a kind of cocktail—at the end of the workday and before eating. Others used it as a nightcap. No one spoke of going to school or work while loaded. Marihuana can be inserted into one's daily round of life with the least amount of interference or hassle. It does not require a major shift in orientation for recreational users to use it nor do the imperatives surrounding the acquistion of the drug drastically affect their life style.

The recreational user's views of other drugs are more helpful as a means of articulating his feelings and thoughts about the part drugs do and should play. This amounts in the main to a list of reasons why other drugs are not particularly good to use.

Many recreational users have tried other drugs, particularly LSD, but few use them with any regularity. While occasions for the use of marihuana may occur once a week, month or even year, there is almost no occasion for which LSD or heroin is felt to be appropriate. A 24-year-old professional person characterized a common view:

> I'd stay away from all the big stuff . . . heroin, cocaine, morphine, anything that you shoot; and I wouldn't mess around with any of the pills, the up and down pills. I just don't feel I have the need for it . . . to come up or down.

It is not so much the use or experimentation with methedrine and heroin that is frowned upon but the addiction that is felt to go along with them. There seems to be some symbolic significance in the needle. Persons who would shoot a drug are addicted. A 20-year-old student reported his fears of addiction:

> Addiction just isn't my scene. As long as I've got the things going for me or half or a quarter of the things I have going for me now—addicted means losing all the advantages of drugs, and not gaining anything. . . . With marihuana it's one thing. But with other drugs there's the addiction.

A 26-year-old housewife expressed similar concerns:

> I myself know what I would depend on and what I wouldn't and I keep away from things that I could depend on too easily. As I said I would never let [drugs] become such a part of my life that I would change anything. I never want it to be a thing, a need. I never want it to be anything more than a pleasure and a nice experience and when it stops being a nice experience for me, and it would if I saw myself becoming dependent.

The main theme emerging from the interviews among recreational users was that powerful drugs are capable of *victimizing* the user. They act upon the user in such a way that he cannot control what is happening to him.

LSD is approached very gingerly. The feeling is that it is extraordinarily powerful and can be quite dangerous since it dissolves the boundaries of the ego. A 23-year-old woman, a student, reported her concern about LSD:

> LSD is something that they don't know about yet, enough to know what kind of people it can just murder, you know, it just really do bad things to their mind. . . . I always worry about the indecisive reaction that I've seen. That people who suddenly can't make decisions and who sort of walk back and forth between things for hours and can't exactly make a decision. And if I felt that LSD could have affected me as far as making me indecisive I'd be afraid.

It is from the recreational users that stories can be elicited about the damaging effects of LSD. Our 23-year-old respondent continued:

> This boy that I was going with when I was in New York ah . . . told me immediately that he'd had a bad trip with LSD. He's flipped out temporarily.

The theme of "losing control" comes on different levels. First, there is fear that moment-by-moment behavior is not manageable under the influence of a drug like LSD, that it is going to get out of hand and some unexpected, and presumably unpleasant event will occur. A 22-year-old female student alluded to the theme of losing control:

> With LSD you have a feeling that maybe you're not in control. There are some very scary moments when you just don't know what's going to happen next or what you're going to create next. So I prefer pot.

A variation of this is the fear of a bad trip, which may last for minutes, hours, or days. Persons, some in the Colony, reported very nightmarish experiences under the influence of LSD which were enough to deter them forever from using the drug. A 25-year-old graduate student in the humanities, a woman, reported that such experiences recurred long after the initial experience while using the drug.

> I just went off into a catatonic whatever it is and just lay on the bed for a long period of time and then tried to cry and wouldn't understand why I was crying. I would stop just as abruptly as I started. I didn't want to eat, I didn't want to get up. I knew where I was and what I was but I had just gone so far away, like up and up and up and was way away and just didn't want to come back down again. . . . I, thank God, was there and realized what had happened and helped me come back. It took about a week. I started going out into the street and did a thing to bring me back which was a very good thing to do. The one about pick something out in the room and look at it, touch it and tell me if it's solid. I just didn't know if a lot of things were solid or not. . . .

Only one person among our respondents required medical attention which was attributed to LSD. There are any number of thirdhand tales which present this as a serious possibility. "Flipping out" is a concern of recreational users who contemplate using such drugs. It reflects the fear that the drug can do something to them which is beyond their control.

There are milder forms of the victimization theme attributed to the drug. Character changes can occur which, while undesirable, are not so severe as insanity. The drug is said to incapacitate one for customary activities like taking a job seriously, graduating from college, and so on. Some persons state that they will not try to work, or go to work, when stoned or high. Nor will they try to study. The perceived effects are such that the kind of attention and discipline needed to do these things is impaired. Others speak about becoming "hung up" on the LSD trip, meaning an over-concern with flowers, birds, and innumerable other features of the world which are irrelevant to conduct required in conventional relationships and activities. Fascination with the color of a candy bar wrapper is not relevant to actually buying or eating it. This kind of preoccupation is said to take the form of indecisiveness, an inability to sort out the customarily relevant objects of attention and respond to them in a consistent, effective fashion. Such accounts provide acceptable reasons in the minds of recreational users for not using LSD or using it charily.

For recreational users the victimization theme most certainly extends to their thinking about opiates such as heroin. They are definitely opposed to use of such drugs and for conventional reasons. They see the opiates as drugs that a person can become "hooked on," a state where the drug makes uncontrollable demands on the user. They do not think of marihuana in this way. Only a few remarked that marihuana caused them to lose control momentarily; most felt that the drug is easily manageable compared to alcohol.

Recreational users tend to think of marihuana and alcohol in the same terms. They are not anti-alcohol with the same intensity as are hard-core users. A 26-year-old housewife compared the two drugs:

> [Marihuana] is not so different than liquor or any other form of relaxation. It really doesn't make you feel that different. It's very pleasant and I think a lot of people are curious about it.

One would use marihuana for the same reasons he would use liquor: to get high. A 20-year-old male student stated:

> I think most people use drugs because they get high. You know they could get high on alcohol. A lot of the time getting high is you can't get high on other things, when you can't get satisfaction from those things so you get it in other ways for awhile.

A 24-year-old male student expressed the same sentiments:

> Marihuana, to me, is not ah . . . an involvement. It's more or less of a kick. I like to keep it at that. Because it—if it becomes an involvement, it loses for me, it loses its purpose. It becomes damaging. I use it the same way I use alcohol. Just to get high.

Views of drugs are essentially an extension of attitudes about alcohol. One takes drugs primarily for relaxation or for "kicks." If some aspects of the drug experience are not pleasurable, then it is not considered a good trip. It should be avoided if it doesn't make one happy. This is the key to the LSD reaction. Why should one risk schizophrenia or insanity for a high or a kick? It's simply not worth it.

The recreational user's style of use can be characterized as a disciplined one. There are certain occasions appropriate for use, certain preparations which one must make, and certain rituals which accompany use. A 28-year-old laboratory technician who characterized himself as a "reformed head" described the ritual:

> There's a lot of little etiquettes and social customs, and I think that a lot of pot smokers, one of the appeals is that they like to, they like the little ceremony. Where frequently a lot of people sit around in a room and, and if, usually the way I've run into it is that somebody has some, pot, then it's sort of everybody's that's around. And it's not a kind of thing where some guy runs off into the next room and smokes some pot and then goes back into the group. And if you ask for some pot he'll take it out and roll some joints or something, and pass it around. And there are little bits of etiquette, little customs . . . it's kind of appealing, because somebody will roll a joint and being very careful to do it just right, and get a nice clean joint, and then light it up and take a few drags, and, and, drag some more on it and passes it to the next person, and if somebody doesn't want any,

then they shake their head or say "no" or just pass it on to the next person.

LSD is used instrumentally. Since it is a difficult drug to domesticate, it cannot be taken at any time. Preferred times are on long weekends or perhaps between semesters in case something untoward happens. It is not seen primarily for its significance in broadening perception or evoking some kind of religious experience. It is rather to be used for developing self-insight—the kind of self-insight that will make one a better person—more sincere, productive, authentic, and possibly for some, more successful. There is a considerable amount of interest in the promise that hallucinogens will make a person more creative or more intelligent. If one is enabled to pass difficult courses or write "A" papers, then certainly LSD-type drugs are a contribution. Finally, an ideal experience is one where self-control is not lost. A 25-year-old woman, a graduate student in the humanities, stressed the importance of exercising control:

> I'm beginning to understand about the reality of choice in any psychedelic situation and that the drug does not run away with you. But in order to take it one must exercise control and choice over what's going on. You make your own trip. You make what is happening happen.

STYLE OF LIFE

Recreational users' lives are very much patterned by their student status. They are concerned about what is happening to them in school, and the rhythm of their lives reflect this. Weekends are usually for parties, going to movies, dating, etc. The period before examinations is spent in rather spartan fashion. Vacations are spent visiting families and summers usually involve some kind of temporary job. Intellectual and creative ability and accomplishment are valued, for they directly determine one's success within the formal institution and thereby confer status on the individual. Many recreational users bring an attitude supportive of intellectual and creative endeavors to the academic environment to match what the university has to offer. This distinguishes them from those within the university milieu who never develop a deep attachment to self-enrichment and expression to the extent that it molds and determines their lives.

Their interests and concerns outside of their major activity as students include reading, listening to music, playing a musical instrument, writing poetry or prose, drama and film, painting and dancing. A 19-year-old junior college student described his interests:

> I play in a symphony besides school, which is a very good thing. Occasionally I play high and it's lots of fun. . . . Music is my entire life. . . . Music and school.

A 20-year-old student of drama reported his major activities:

> Right now, I'm on, my schedule is going to be very very full, besides
> going to school. I'm working on a play starting tonight which will
> probably start taking up, like three, four, even more hours. . . . In-
> terest besides theater, I enjoy a lot of things. Theater is the thing that's
> really involving me now. Like right now I'm taking a sculpting course
> which I really enjoy. I read plays, novels, poetry. Some non-fiction.
> I go to movies, art flicks, foreign movies. I enjoy working in the
> theater.

Their interests are heavily weighted in the field of creative arts in terms
of attendance as well as participation. A typical recreational user might go
to two or sometimes three movies a week. He is likely to read a book
or more a week, usually contemporary fiction like Kesey's *One Flew Over
the Cuckoo's Nest*. He is interested in the theater but "it's too expensive
and too far away." His interest in the theater would be twentieth-century
modern. He would also like the "theatre of the absurd" but not be "hung
up" on it. He would listen to a lot of folk rock music on local radio stations
and might have quite a collection of 45's and LP's. He would have a
moderate interest in Pop Art and Op Art. He would not spend a lot of
time in local hangouts. A 24-year-old laboratory technician described what
he did after work in the evening:

> (Do you spend much time in the local hangouts?) No, mostly in
> people's houses . . . especially since I've been working. I often just
> go by somebody's house after work, and then they come up to
> dinner, and maybe go see a movie, or go see some other people, or
> listen to music, about half, at least half of the time, I guess, roll up a
> few joints. . . . When I say come up for dinner, it's not like going
> out to dinner or anything, I cook spaghetti and she pays for half of
> it, something like that, you know. Very casual things.

RELATIONSHIP TO THE STRAIGHT WORLD

As reported earlier, recreational users were quite disillusioned with the
larger society, but were not prepared, as were their hard-core counterparts,
to want out. However critical their stance vis-à-vis the straight world, they
still saw themselves as essentially involved in it. As one 20-year-old student
put it:

> It's got a lot of room in it for people, got enough room for me. I got
> myself sort of carved out a pretty good niche in society and I figure
> people could if they want it, without getting too hung up by it. It's
> morality? I don't see how anybody can do things that happen in Viet
> Nam. I don't know if it's the morality of it or just the nature of it.
> Something's wrong, something has to change. And then segregation
> which just doesn't make it.

Or as a 28-year-old woman, a professional, put it:

> I really don't like to think of it like that [sharp separation between user and straight people], you know, because part of me is straight. I mean I do perform, I do function, and I can communicate with people that don't take drugs, therefore part of me is there.

Recreational users are in fields that will not, in all probability, lead them to institutionalized or bureaucratic careers (except as employees of universities or colleges), but rather are training in areas of study which will, and perhaps do now, require individual talent and creativity, independence, and initiative. Their "in training" status and expectation of future achievement are very much part of their thinking and discussions with one another. Recreational users define themselves in terms of a professional career. A 24-year-old student depicted his own response to work:

> I mean I'm from a very money oriented background . . . And I probably have some of it in my blood. I mean having been brought up in this atmosphere. I hate retail business from what contacts I've had with it, and I'd like to get into a profession. Working to me is not a waste of time because it keeps me busy for one thing, 'cause boredom is probably the greatest defeater, the easiest way to self-destruction, and if you can't order yourself and discipline yourself to make wise use of your time you might as well have a job and be forced to.

When discussing their perceptions of themselves, recreational users employed terms like "rebel"—meaning dissatisfied with the way things are, "interested" in changing social arrangements and self, moderately "ambitious," "growing," "productive," and "successful" in terms of where they find themselves now. Their identity is constructed in terms of themes related to self-enrichment and expression. Those things that recreational users would like to change about themselves relate to lack of ambition, lack of organization, lack of dicipline, or laziness. A 22-year-old female student focused on her own lack of organization:

> (Is there anything you would like to change in your life?) Just organizing my life, personal habits that I have that I know have to be rectified some time: neatness, punctuality, that kind of thing, that I am very bad at. . . . (Are you happy with your self?) Yeah, pretty much. Cope with things that bug me, lack of discipline a little bit, more satisfactions and my discipline increases, more real satisfaction.

The people recreational users like are perceived to have the same characteristics as they do. They too are intellectually oriented, open to change, interested in finding out about themselves, and discreet in dress and behavior. They reserved their most serious criticism for the "heads" or "hippies." A 26-year-old housewife reported her own reaction to hippies:

> Berkeley's hippies are outrageous. I know almost all of them. And I don't consider myself one of them. They're idlers, the real downtown

hippies in Berkeley are pretty freaky. I consider myself very hip, like I know about most of the things that are happening, doesn't mean I'm a part of it, and it doesn't mean that I'm one of them, but I know what's happening, I know the different scenes, I know what parties are where, who's going to them. I consider a person hip by the way they think. I consider a person a hippy by what they do. And most of the hippies hang out, lot of 'em play guitars and take dope, but most of them hang out and I really don't think they're that cool.

The criticism of hippies is essentially the criticism the straight world invokes. They are lazy, unambitious, and take undeserved pride in knowing where the action is; any knowledgeable, sensitive person can be aware of that. But most important, the hippies just hang around *killing time*. Statements such as these pinpoint one essential difference between recreational users and heads: their attitudes toward time. Recreational users believe that time should be used productively, not wasted. Heads believe the preoccupation with the use of time stifles spontaneity and self-discovery. The only reason a recreational user can envision for hanging out is to cope with boredom. Our housewife continued:

In Berkeley you hang out because you've got nothing else to do. Hang out and watch people go by and I have too much to do to do that really, when I'm bored I'll do it, when I'm bored I'll go up to Telegraph or something or hang out around the campus.

From the point of view of the recreational user the hippie is everything that he is not. A 24-year-old student observed:

I think it's hygienically horrible. I mean it's just filthy. For what I'm interested in it proves nothing. I mean it's just a form of rebellion which sort of turns me off. I don't really care for it. I like to have my hair long, I don't like brush cuts or anything like that, but shoulder length hair is sort of ridiculous as far as I'm concerned. I mean it just doesn't do anything for you. It casts more suspicion on you for one thing. I think it's more or less sort of a faddist type dress, and it's a form of rebellion probably. Also it stereotypes you, and this is the type of thing that these type of people are trying to get away from. They're so far out that they're in a group. They are a group. It's sort of taken away from individualism.

This is not to say that the attire of the recreational user would not be distinctive. He, like his head counterpart, is interested in color and texture. One 20-year-old college dropout when asked how he would identify a user replied:

Well, you can tell mainly, or at least the initial idea is from attire, it's unconventional. Very seldom is it a straight suit, black tie and so on.

To the initiated, attire would communicate that the wearer knew what was happening and where the action was. But the indication has to be ever so subtle: a dash of color on a tie, a certain kind of shirt or collar, style of shoe or jewelry. If the presentation is too explicit, then it might be communicating to the wrong people—namely, the police!

The recreational user is closely tied to the straight world in terms of friendships he has with straight people. It is very important to have these relationships. Several persons reported dismay at discovering that straight friendships gradually withered as they became more involved in the drug scene. This had the effect of reducing their drug-related activities. If one has no straight friends, then he has isolated himself from the society, he has missed an opportunity to be heard, to change people's minds about drugs and other things. The straight world will not listen to someone who is defined as "too far out." A 25-year-old married graduate student, a woman, gave her rationale as follows:

> I like to preserve a façade of elegance and straightness which makes it possible for me to have some kind of exchange with them [straight friends]. When I expose my bohemianism to them, for example, at times they consider it a manifestation of my wildness but they kind of excuse it because they know that basically I'm all right and really I'm responsible. I do keep my daughter clean and fed and don't leave her alone at night and have always gotten good grades and entertain. All the things that are superficially comprehensible to them make me acceptable, despite the fact that we disagree basically on lots of things.

VALUES

The person who has managed to be part of the society yet be critical of it, to be involved in drug use yet feel comfortable with straight friends, to be committed to a career but one that allows some independence, is defined as being "cool." A central value for the recreational user is being cool, behaving in a cool way or being able to maintain one's cool. A person who is cool does not identify himself as a user to persons he does not know. He is wary of unknown persons who show up at pot parties, because he knows that others might not have the same stake in the conventional order he has and consequently not be able to maintain information control. A 19-year-old student when asked if he identified himself to users as a fellow user replied:

> Not anymore. When I first started I used to think that all people who took drugs were cool, but I really don't think that distinction has any validity anymore. I've met some very indiscriminate people who try to turn on everybody that they meet. I managed to stay away from people like this.

Someone who is cool is cautious about appearing in public high, or going to school or work while stoned. The dangers are too great. It calls attention to one's self and might lead to rumors among straight people about one's using. This could seriously damage a person's reputation. Being cool in terms of behavior is only part of what the term means. It also involves dress and hair styling. The cool person does not dress or act outrageously. A 26-year-old housewife explained:

> I'm clean I dress more neatly than 80% of the people in Berkeley no matter how wasted I was or what I did. Even when I'm loaded I'm straighter looking anyway than most people walking down the street. And I know my potential, I know my capabilities, and I know, for instance, LSD is something I would not want to be running around the streets because if I felt like singing or skipping I want to be able to do it, it would not be wise. When we take a trip on LSD we like to go up in to the country and dig the animals. I wouldn't want to offend anybody and I wouldn't want to put me up tight.

The cool person is one who does not give himself away to those who might not understand or actually might harm him. On the surface he appears detached, not engaged. He gives the impression of being disengaged, not really caring, not able to be hurt by what others can do to him. He is not overly emotional, or garrulous, impulsive or undisciplined.

Very closely linked with being cool is the discretion a person exercises. This is more directly related to the precautions one must take when involved in illegal activity. Sometimes the preoccupation with discretion becomes too intense. If someone becomes overly concerned with being "found out" he is characterized as being paranoid. An 18-year-old student described the precautions he takes:

> As far as drugs go, I'm pretty paranoid. I feel that being picked up would be a real threat, really shake me up so that I try to keep real cool in public. Don't like to show that I'm high in public or on the street, don't hold on the street unless I have to. I'll take enough for transit if there's grass anywhere, I won't even take any home . . . I try to discourage friends from bringing marihuana by because I have had dealings with LSD and I don't want any felony drugs around the house. (I've) . . . had dreams about it occasionally being busted, socially ostracized and things like that. I realized that there are consequences and that there is a certain amount of risk involved and a certain amount of care has to be taken when you are smoking— discretion.

The person who is discreet acts in such a way that he does not take unusual risks in buying or selling drugs, does not hold around his house or apartment and does not put himself in a "situation of suspicion" or "act suspiciously." A situation of suspicion is defined as one which brings you to the attention of police as a possible user. Regular relationships with persons who had been arrested or were known to the police as users or dealers would bring suspicion on oneself. Acting suspiciously usually refers to being on the streets while high: They were very aware of the phenomenon that sociologists call the labeling process. A 23-year-old student who had pushed marihuana at the street level described what he thought was the process of graduating to "hard drugs":

> I find that a great part of the ah . . . people's involvement with, in particular the heavier narcotics that comes through, at least partially through, traumatic experiences with institutional authority such as being beaten by the cops, ah, or the things of this order in which a person, ah, obtains a fixation on this particular relationship to the rest of the world such that the rest of their life they will play a game of cops and robbers. They have a vested interest in the game. These people pay attention to them. They're involved with them. It's the sort of thing where even if you're involved in ah, you tend to feel more intimate or more related to that person for having gone through that experience.

Recreational users seemed to have a fairly realistic perspective on the police. They were aware that the likelihood of being subjected to harassment was very slim unless they were defined as a "suspicious" person— i.e., someone from the wrong race or social class, in the wrong place at the wrong time, and dressed in such a way as to arouse police concern. A 22-year-old student worried about the police when he was high—

> Going into the straight world when high—it's terrible. I get paranoid, and I'm always worried about the police, and you know like people who know that I'm high because it's so hard to keep straight because people are so ridiculous you want to laugh all the time.

Some recreational users described various strategies to hide the fact that they were high. One 24-year-old student reported what he did:

> Somebody, you know, especially to see you in the daylight when you're supposed to be normal and alert and, you know, situation where you haven't had anything to put you in a sort of strange appearance. I don't like to go places where I have to do thinking, definite thinking and be stoned. You know, like I can always, if I'm stoned, I always have at least one or two beers or something with it so that I have some sort of, you know, people are aware that I've had a drink or two and they'll say "you're drunk or something?" And this is sort of a defensive way of covering it up.

The precautions taken in maintaining secrecy about use are designed to protect the recreational user from society's disapproval of his use. This is not an abstract consideration. The concern is quite specific—it relates to the police, being found out by them or getting arrested.

SIGNIFICANCE OF THE POLICE
IN TERMS OF VALUES

Recreational users seemed to have a regard for the law and the necessity of maintaining social order. But they were also critical of prevailing law and order and would break the law under specific conditions. Initial use of marihuana may have been generated by rebellious motives but it did not seem to account for continued use. Consequently they seemed quite uncomfortable with the fact that it was illegal. To be sure they thought that it should not be against the law but they were acutely aware of the consequences of getting arrested. Since they were people with foresight they knew what the effect of an arrest could do to a later career, they knew what the results of becoming known to the police were in terms of becoming a "regular customer." Their academic success, they knew, boded well for later professional advancement. It also gave them a general education in how bureaucracies function, and in the significance of a record in a society of secondary contacts. This seemed to account for an almost pathological fear of getting caught. A 20-year-old student who had been involved in a marihuana give-and-take bartering system diagnosed the possibilities of getting caught:

> The police aren't going to bother me as long as I keep my cool and don't start dealing outrageously. You know they're, they're too much trouble. Some of the people around here don't get busted even when the cops—I'm sure they know about 'em . . . it just isn't worth their while, you know. I'm not hurting society ah . . . and it's too much trouble, I think, for them to want to hurt me . . . a long time before they'd be busting me they'd be busting a lot of people.

The authority which the police represent is not called into question. Recreational users accept the fact that the police are necessary and they must perform their job. Police authority intimidates them to a certain extent. This might be very much a function of their "probationary" status as students, the fact that they have not quite achieved full adult citizenship. A 22-year-old ex-student reported how she felt during an interrogation session with the police after being stopped while high:

> Well I got all giggly inside and I felt like I was about four years old and had—I had stuck the stuff in my pants because I didn't know where to put it. . . . meanwhile I'm thinking this is my father standing there and he's questioning me the same way my father used to when he knew I was guilty, and he just wanted me to confess. And all of a sudden I felt like saying, "I've got it, here it is, right here. I'm guilty—here are my hands, would you please cuff me and take me away?"

Recreational users' reactions to the police seem to affect their social relationships. Knowledge of their use is shared with only a small group of intimates. They are suspicious of strangers, and are less open with them than they would be if they were not involved in the drug scene. A 27-year-old teacher stated:

> Unfortunately I am afraid of the aspect of law enforcement and it makes for a great deal of façade, fabrication and so on, on the part of

many people with relation to discussing the subject of drugs. Because obviously you can't tell a person who feels that this is the most evil thing that you can do, you can't tell this person that you use drugs because you endanger yourself.

Because of their conventional commitments recreational users felt they had a great deal to lose if they were found out. Some reported that if they felt the stakes were getting too high they would stop using drugs. Our 27-year-old teacher discussed, at another point, how the danger of using would affect his future use:

> Well, it all depends on its availability and if the legal danger, the danger of being busted isn't too high, then I'll suppose I'll just continue to use, on special occasions.

Because of their vulnerability recreational users are unusually susceptible to police pressure for help. They are more likely to assist the police in some kind of "set up" than are the heads, because in their view much of the drug scene is pretty unpleasant to start with. It's not as if they were informing on close friends who were mature and responsible. Some of our respondents reported that police seemed to have a working knowledge of the recreational user's susceptibility to inform and part of the strategy of enforcement was built upon it. A 22-year-old student described this working knowledge in reporting an approach used by a state narcotic agent:

> Somebody knocks on his door (a friend next door) and says: "all right we know you are a known user of marihuana. . . . I'm from the State Bureau of Investigation." And I don't know how it happened, some kind of fluke, I guess, but anyway the guy was, you know, was trying to, he said, "we don't want you, we don't want your sorts we want you to help us" and all that kind of stuff, and we were scared man, I mean Jesus, we had just talked about it and our hands were slapped, you know. So it was a long time before anybody, you know we thought Jesus, you know, the walls have ears and everything, so forget it.

The police role in relation to the recreational user's values is a symbolic one. They give a concrete meaning to the notion of being cool or playing it cool. They sharpen the user's perception of what the future means to him and what he must do to hold on to it. They deepen the solidarity of the small intimate friendship group standing against the outside world. And by their enforcement strategy the police provide a way for the recreational user to differentiate himself dramatically from the "degenerate" head.

POLITICAL VIEWS

Most of the recreational users were not active in any political organization at the time they were interviewed. A number of them had been active in the Free Speech Movement and had gradually become disillusioned with the response the university had made to it. They seemed to feel that no real concessions were made and the dazzling maneuvers executed by a politically sophisticated university administration had taken much steam out of student politics. A 21-year-old ex-student, formerly a recreational user, now a head, observed:

> It seems very hard to work within the system as shown by FSM. I think considering what happened the accomplishments of FSM have been minimal compared to the damage that's been done to a lot of people's lives so I really am in kind of a dilemma.

This does not mean that they had given up hope that the situation could be changed. Their political views were instrumental: the social order could be so rearranged that some of its more obvious injustices could be remedied. Only a few had concluded that the structure was beyond correction. This usually coincided with their deeper involvement in the drug scene. A 23-year-old female student reported how her own political orientation had shifted:

> I am interested in political rights, in the sense that I think we should have them, but in the sense of participating in such a way as to make these things possible. I don't have any specific convictions in that direction, simply because I think the structure has gotten so far beyond the possibility of political correction, that too many people who are concerned politically are already so involved in the structure that they don't realize their own involvement and dependency on certain structures and forms that exist.

The focus of political action was likely to be around the peace issue, civil rights, or student rights. A 22-year-old female student depicted her own political activities:

> Anything that I would do that would be extra-curricular would be political: The FSM, civil rights picketing. I went to Viet Nam meetings just out of interest. I'm not a member and I haven't done any demonstrating for them but I did go to the meeting just to hear what they were talking about. I've only been arrested once for FSM.

The war in Viet Nam seemed to crystallize their reactions to America. Here was a huge, powerful country trying to destroy a small nation and one whose people happened to be a different color from ours. There was no idealism in the war—self-serving interests were thinly concealed by talk about "stopping the communists." The response to the war was in terms of the hypocrisy of the larger society and its unjust character. It was not in terms of pacifism. They could conceive of some situations where violence would be appropriate. In this sense they differed sharply from their hard-core counterparts who disavowed the violence theme in American culture completely. A 24-year-old married graduate student characterized their attitude:

> I don't like war, right, but if someone attacks me I'm going to fight back. If someone attacks my house I'm going to fight back. But I won't go along with encouraging war, with encouraging fighting and all this. But when you get me right down to it, there are some aspects that I've got to admit. At a certain point you can't let people destroy your way of life, and somehow that point gets pushed out so far that I find myself having to follow my logical argument and condoning attacking whichever, North or South Viet Nam that we're attacking because of someone else's infringement on someone else. I feel like somehow there's gotta be a compromise.

The recreational user's attitude toward war could be characterized as situational nonviolence. He was not against all wars, just this one. What gave a more acid note to his criticism was the possibility of his own involvement through the draft.

The recreational user saw his participation in political activities as antithetical to using drugs. The political groups themselves discouraged it because they feared the general disapproval of their cause by linking it with drug use, and they felt that continued use made a participant undependable and undisciplined. A 21-year-old ex-student formerly a recreational user and now a head, reported how a political club warned him about using drugs:

> (Did the club rap on you about using drugs?) Oh yeah. They were very paranoid about it because it was illegal and besides they're [the larger society] trying to tie up, you know the use of drugs with the left wing.

But apart from the organizational point of view there seemed to be a general recognition that politics and drug use just didn't mix. A 24-year-old married graduate student said:

> But when the political stuff started in September I stopped [turning on]. I couldn't do both—the Berkeley uprising. (How much were you involved?) Anything I could do. It was a full time job for a semester for a lot of people. There were probably about 100 people who spent full time—I mean 40 hours a week. . . . One thing about pot, it doesn't mix with some things, like revolutionizing, if you're doing it full time.

Recreational users felt that most people active in liberal or left political activities had at least experimented with marihuana. One 27-year-old male involved in various temporary jobs put it this way:

> You can't make a generalization like everyone who's in the political, civil rights scene, liberal types, ah is a drug user. I'd say that the

majority of them have tried it. I think they all have a completely tolerant attitude towards it. I think this is one of the characteristics that I was talking about before where they're broadminded, they're open to ah . . . to trying new things, to looking at new things, to accepting a whole lot of new things. It's sort just part of being liberal.

The feeling generally seemed to be that political activity should preclude drug use. The person who would continue to use while participating in some political organization was not being cool. He was being quite indiscreet. One 24-year-old student concluded:

When you involve yourself in politics you leave yourself open for verbal attacks and close scrutiny and things like that are very much against my nature.

The recreational user's views of political activity fit in with his general style of life and values. There is the conviction that one must work through conventional structures to accomplish meaningful change. Political groups must not be "too far out" otherwise their effectiveness is diminished. The recreational user's stance is rational and pragmatic. One does not confront the laws on marihuana directly, let us say with a "smoke in," because it would not be effective. The purpose of various political strategies is to win unconvinced people to your side. Hence you don't outrage the people you are trying to convince by doing something unacceptable to them. Some felt that the ideal arrangement would be to work within traditional political structures. One 24-year-old graduate student described an admired friend who did just this:

He dresses fairly conservatively, I mean you see him walking down the street, he usually wears slacks and button down shirt . . . he's, you know, in the main stream of the Democratic party, he, I think he's more liberal than the Democratic party, but he sees that through the party system is the only way to bring about liberal reforms. And so he's probably the most squared away person I know, in terms of knowing what he's after, and what compromises he has to make to get it, and is really a pretty healthy sort of a person. He, of course, in terms of drugs, can't be high all the time because of his job. Likes to, you know, cut loose on weekends, and wear Levis and sweat shirt. Mainly, politically though, if you made a generalization, or a composite picture, I mean there'd be more than a liberal but not quite a radical, very much get out of Viet Nam, very much for federal aid to education, medicare, you know, all for most democratic reforms, but just thinks that it's not enough being done. And very much down on Birchers and thought Goldwater was insane, thinks that Johnson is the greatest phoney that has ever come around, and you know, just the general picture, I think that is very common around Berkeley.

All of our respondents tried to account for the presence of laws making drugs such as marihuana and LSD illegal. This concern, perhaps due to their status as law violators, leads them to scrutinize the warrants used by legislators and others to argue for the presence of these laws. Recreational users react to these warrants in a rather standardized fashion. Marihuana, for them, is only illegal. There is no acceptable warrant for outlawing its use. It is not physically debilitating, addicting or unmanageable. The LaGuardia Report (called by one of our interviewees: "The Recreational User's Bible") is the most frequently cited work. In response to the statement of proponents of the law that "marihuana is dangerous therefore it must be outlawed," their reaction is: "It is not dangerous." A 23-year-old female student put it this way:

> I will defend the fact that drugs such as marihuana should be legal. I think that before [turning on] I sort of felt like the laws had to be, because in general, they were best for society, even though some of them were a little bit peculiar—the whole was good for society. I sort of believed that. I don't know if drugs was the first aspect of the law that I challenged but it certainly was the one that succeeded in making me believe that not all drugs are illegal.

Not all drugs should be illegal but possibly some should be. Reactions to the warrants for stringent regulation of LSD are ambivalent. On the one hand they are certain the drug is extremely powerful and should only be used by persons who are "stable" enough to keep themselves together under the impact. That is, they see it as a potentially dangerous drug which should be controlled in some fashion. However, they do not take seriously the attempts of the police and legislators to brand the drug a tremendous danger to public health and morality. They are not about to argue for the presence of laws which make use a crime but support a model of controlled access much in line with what the AMA would recommend—the drug by prescription with checks on its production and on the setting in which it is used. Our 23-year-old student continued:

> I think it should be administered to people who are ready for it. Oh, maybe once every two weeks, in some kind of church or something I think it should be, I think it should be used by people who are prepared for it. I think somebody who has had experience with it, some good guy, some good Guru ought to nurse a person along in his initial trip. I really think that's a necessary thing, if it's going to be a good thing, because, you know, like if it's disseminated any old place to anybody, no matter what age, or what their preparation or what their mental makeup, then it can be bad, too, it can be very bad. Just like anything else that is very intense.

Not all recreational users are willing to give control of the drug to the medical profession. Some suggested churches, universities, or other kinds of professional personnel to administer LSD and regulate its use.

These users are also in accord with most liberal thinking on the opiates. These are surely dangerous drugs that must be controlled, but present means of control are too punitive. Most commonly the so-called British system is recommended as a way of handling the social problems surrounding the opiates. Some recreational user's views differed not at all from what they perceived to be the informed public. A 26-year-old housewife was characteristic:

> Hard drugs that are addicting, that have been proven harmful should be outlawed and there should be a penalty if you get caught with them, like jail. But there are some that aren't harmful.

The recreational user's view of drugs, then, involves both the idea that persons can be victimized by some drugs and that they should be helped. Outside control must be substituted for internal, personal checks when these dangerous drugs are in question. They will object to the way these controls are being exercised but not about the necessity to have some controls.

Commonly, the presence of contemporary laws regulating use are seen to be the consequence of ignorance and occasionally vested interests. The recreational user's emphasis on the value of rationality leads him to conclude that an absence of knowledge is the key problem in drug legislation. Society disapproves because it does not understand. A 23-year-old student in response to the question "why does the straight world disapprove of drugs?" replied:

> Ignorance. Well, no, no, it's because they think they can do harm to you which—like anything too much will do harm. But basically they aren't harmful and aren't habit forming, but most of the public thinks that all forms of narcotics and stimulants are habit forming and they think of it as stuff that you shoot into the arm or having the same kind of consequences, and they have an ugly picture of it.

Another 22-year-old student concurred:

> 'Cause they don't know about them. All they can know is what they hear, you know as built up stories.

A 22-year-old computer operator also agreed:

> An uninformed view. They haven't contemplated it, they don't want to contemplate it.

The public at large is seen as unknowledgeable as far as drugs are concerned. Partly this is because of the misinformation which agencies like the Federal Bureau of Narcotics has spread for the past thirty years. The remedy for the problem of the kinds of laws that are required is education. Where knowledge is lacking, supply it, to the general public and to legislators.

While all emphasized lack of information as the problem, some were inclined to give more weight to other kinds of interests. They felt that "liquor interests" and others were lending support which prevents reform. A 23-year-old female student commented on the role of vested interests:

And then, there are a whole lot of people who make a lot of money on illegal drug rackets who are in very high places which is, of course what I've heard about and never seen. . . . And the entire liquor industry, for instance—they would not like to see drugs legalized. 'Cause they sort of got a corner on the "flipping out" market, you know. It's the only way to escape.

Their manner of contending with what is seen as a maze of bad laws supported by ignorance and dishonesty is to give face compliance to the law. They are not apt to call attention to themselves as potential drug users by dressing flagrantly or behaving in any particularly noticeable way or by appearing in public in a state of psychic undress due to drugs. They are very interested in regulating who knows that they use and because of this were difficult to interview, because of distrust of our affiliations. For example, cash reimbursement was often given to those queried. On one occasion a respondent petulantly refused this money because it was necessary for him to sign a receipt in order to receive it. In the same vein they are concerned about being "clean," not carrying drugs on their person or keeping them in obvious locations in their lodgings. In short, they are very concerned about the possibility of detection by authorities through indiscretions of their own or by the lack of cool on the part of those around them.

Their orientation toward drugs is intricately bound up with a notion of being "reasonable." This conception is a way of balancing the effect of the drug, it's value as a high or in more long-range terms, against the various perils which go along with use. Many people feel that the euphoria produced by marihuana is not worth the risk taken to use it. Others feel that the benefits of LSD have to be weighed against the possible drawbacks such as flipping out or going on a bad trip. Being reasonable, then, is to accept certain possibilities as persuasive deterrents and these are listed as reasons why a person might refuse to use some or all drugs.

There are others who are very obvious in the social world they inhabit who clearly do not abide by the deterrents which recreational users take into serious account. Recreational users see these people as deviants, persons who must be given account of. Many of these "deviants" are flagrant in their refusal to be secretive, and they are termed "outrageous" —which from a recreational user is a term of opprobrium. Such persons are accounted for in a manner which attacks their claim to sanity. This, of course, is a traditional way of accounting for people who do not abide by conventionally authorized deterrents. A 22-year-old student contended:

. . . in other words they're not so much socially motivated. They get their money where they can, borrow, beg, steal it—very few morals, very few values. The values they do have are not rigidly defined. The only values that are really strong to them are the brotherhood, the brotherhood of drug user, which is very interesting. No experience by themselves on anything, everything is the group experience. I mean, like they're helpless alone. These type of people, and I don't like it—they're psychopaths, they're pathological liars, they're psychotics.

This is a very strong statement of the manner in which recreational users try to account for behavior unlike their own. Less severe terms are generally used to convey the same message. For example, being "outrageous" is often attributed to a psychological compulsion to be different or to "rebel." Another common tack is to see "outrageous" users as being "unstable" and having personal needs which can only be met by making a spectacle or drawing punishment.

The situation which seems to surround persons who are using drugs on more than an occasional basis is also an affront to the sensibilities of recreational users, who have a great concern with secrecy and discretion. There is a strong tendency for implication in such drug use to go along with an extreme breakdown of information control. Persons come to be known by reputation upon entering social circles where drugs are very common. As mentioned earlier, instead of being known to a small circle of trusted friends, one becomes *known about* by a much larger number of persons. Recreational users find this disquieting. Those who are going to explore drugs more thoroughly are almost forced to accept this as part of the life.

The situation becomes one in which it is hard to keep secrets. This combines to deter many recreational users from further entry into drug-using circles beyond their own circle of friends.

The recreational user is not, then, challenging the right of the law or of established authority to regulate his behavior in any serious way. His style is very quiet circumvention of the law on narrowly defined occasions with a very narrow repertoire of illegal activities. That is, he will stay almost exclusively a user of marihuana and will not compound that offense by trying to make money selling drugs. If he moves to an area where drugs are not easily come by, he is not apt to go hunting for them. This is compounded situational use: use on defined occasions and in the general situation where drugs are readily available. Perhaps the most apt summary of the recreational user was given by a 23-year-old male student:

I should say I probably live an outstandingly conventional life in many respects. I know for a fact, with certain exceptions such as my involvement with drugs and my appearance with which I consider minor aspects of my life, with the exception of those things I should say I lead a surprisingly conventional life due to habit, you know, due to the fact that I was raised in terms of the structure and so on. . . .

7

A Portrait of the Head

Another orientation to drugs will be considered in this chapter. The persons holding its view and style of life commonly call themselves "heads" and so they will be called here. The face meaning of the term "head" indicates considerable frequency and variety in drug use, though they have much more in common than such a position on a quantitative index of use. The term "head" highlights the significance of the mind or the brain in living. Perceptual organs are extremely important in the head's scheme of things. The center of the self is not the heart nor the face but the *head*. Colony members describe heads as more free and open, particularly in relation to others, not hung up on rituals or on roles: more spontaneous, more natural. They have a greater awareness, consciousness of self, of others and the world. They are searching; they believe in change. They are more tolerant. They are not oriented toward material gains. A 21-year-old part-time artist, part-time street pusher, described them as follows:

> They [heads] are people who are searching. Straight people are usually people who think they have found. You know, there's an old Chinese proverb that says: "Follow the man that searches for truth, but beware of he who has found it."

> (Can you pick out a head on the street?) His eyes are usually much more vivid and full of life. And he, himself, is much more, has much more character in his face. And, you can tell also by his hands, and the way his hands move. And, his type of dress . . . much more colorful as a rule.

Drugs mean something different to heads than to recreational users, which accounts for a number of seeming peculiarities. Heads are very stubborn about using drugs and about disregarding the deterrents that the police present. On the other hand they make very little effort to be secretive, making clear by their dress and behavior that they are legitimate suspects. Drugs are important in their lives and have a specific place in their daily round. To make sense of this kind of information it will be necessary to describe the views and values that heads support and in the context of these broader views try to see the specific value attached to drug use.

STYLE OF USE

It was noted that clearly delimited situations elicit use for recreational users. This is not the case for heads since so many situations are appropriate for use, in their eyes, that it is easier to describe those that are not. Drugs like marihuana may be used as something to smoke with breakfast coffee or as a mild sleeping potion. The only situation that would universally inhibit use is one that offers immediate dangers such as arrest; thus, some would not smoke marihuana in front of their parents or in public places where the police are known to be present. This is not to say that heads would not be high in such situations; only that they would not be open enough to offer grounds for arrest.

There is great casualness in the use of drugs, particularly marihuana, that does much to destroy the party atmosphere noted among recreational users. The ceremonies are curtailed and one seldom talks about the high or volunteers whatever peculiar things are happening to their sensations. There is no planning of occasions for using drugs except possibly for LSD, which is powerful enough to command respect. In the case of LSD preparation is sometimes made to see that outside disturbances will not interfere with the person when he is actually under the influence of the drug. This preparation is not to make sure that the police will be kept out, only to ensure that the experience will not be dampened by interferences such as ringing phones. In these circles it is not considered proper to be greatly worried about the possible intervention of the law, and those who do so are considered paranoid or "up tight" indicating that they are not free of bias which has been ingrained since childhood.

Frequency of use is variable, depending on the drug in question and the supply. Heads in the Colony would use marihuana every day or several times a day if there was enough to sustain this rate of consumption. Use of LSD is more spaced. The LSD experience is not likely to occur more than once a week if the dose is in the region of 250 micrograms. Only one or two of the respondents broke a "cap" to get a smaller dosage to be used, perhaps, daily. Also the cost of LSD on the black market inhibits frequent use, running from $2 to $5 a cap depending on the source and state of the market. Five dollars is a substantial sum of money for these people. The amphetamines, particularly methedrine, are cautiously used by some of our respondents and not at all by others. They have a reputation for being physically debilitating, and causing loss of weight and jitteriness after any considerable period of use. It is held that a person can become "strung out" on it and suffer withdrawal symptoms. Consequently, while most of the heads had used them, sometimes for long periods of time, they were reluctant to recommend it as a drug for regular use.

Marihuana is seen by heads as a friendly drug which is a companion that one can live with, use regularly, and experience only favorable effects. A 27-year-old divorcee described the friendly feeling she had toward marihuana:

> Yes, I recommend grass on all occasions. There isn't anything that I really dig as much as I do grass. I think that's because it really doesn't hang me up. . . . And, grass feels like the next door neighbor or your friend, yeah.

Nothing special is made of it beyond this. It is a mild drug and does not get in the way of most forms of activity, though some would not use it if they had to work on their tax forms or go on a job interview that threatened to be unpleasant. It is seen as leading to a relaxed mode of behavior and easy conversation but not as a drug that promises tremendous experiences. Because it raises no, or few, management problems it can fit nicely into the day's activities. If not present, it is missed much like one might miss a friend if he were out of town. Unlike recreational users, no head would ever mention the possibiilty of being "strung out" on marihuana.

LSD is seen differently because, in the first place, our respondents do not think that it is possible to be "loaded" on the drug and conduct daily business. It cannot fit into daily life as comfortably as marihuana for this reason alone. Secondly, many heads see LSD as an avenue for very profound, sometimes religious, experiences that should not be played with as one plays with marihuana. It can be a serious business. The drug dramatically expands awareness of oneself and the nature of the world, providing an instrument for seeing and coming to terms with the world. Thus some respondents felt that using LSD to "trip out on" is a mistake. It should be used for serious purposes, not as a means of getting a high.

Some respondents saw the world under the influence of LSD as reality rather than as a distortion. Unlike the bulk of the recreational users and most heads, these people see the world when straight as a distortion of what is really there and apprehended under the influence of LSD. This view is best expressed in writings with a religious bent.[1] Some heads follow this general line of thinking without taking every word that Huxley writes as gospel.

A main thrust of their thinking about either LSD or marihuana is to view them as private experiences. They feel that their experiences are very hard to communicate and they only circuitously have an effect on others. Drugs offer ways of finding solutions to personal problems and

---

[1] See, for example, A. Huxley, *The Doors of Perception* (New York: Harper & Row, Publishers, 1954) and *Heaven and Hell* (Harper & Row, Publishers, 1956).

hang-ups by forcing unbiased or less conventionally structured perceptions. They allow the person to avoid routine ways of misperceiving by jolting him loose from a screen of preconceptions. LSD does this on a grand scale, marihuana much less, but they are both highly personal events that only affect one person's psyche and nothing else. A 27-year-old married woman employed as a research technician observed:

> Drugs, generally, I see as a tool through which you can achieve greater understanding. LSD and grass are very much the same sort of thing, though grass is very, very inferior, if you want to look at it in those terms.

Other drugs are sometimes mentioned. Heroin is rejected though a number of head respondents had tried it. It is not rejected through any great fear of becoming an addict but because, for some, the experience is found wanting. Heads seem not to be looking for drugs that provide a profound calm but those that "rub your eyes in the world." A 22-year-old computer operator characterized a common viewpoint:

> I'd stay away from heroin because ah . . . let me see, how shall I put it? It's—I don't feel like becoming a junkie, you know, and all that it implies. I just don't want to be in a position where my only connection with the outside world is that shot of heroin. Because I really dig what's going on and I don't want to just sit and contemplate my own high.

They are not hostile toward other drugs and think they understand how a person could come to like the experience but simply do not like it for themselves. Others do not like the sordidness of the scramble for the drug, the constant involvement with the police, and the generally unsavory world that they feel is associated with its use. A 21-year-old part-time carpenter stated this view:

> I can't—couldn't get up the energy of going out and hustling the bread to make it $20, or $30 or $40 a day habit. Man that's a lot of work! And for one thing—and, well, I can spend $10 a week on psychedelics or weed, and really enjoy it, you know, and not have to move off my front porch.

Though many smoke, tobacco is seen as an unpleasant drug, one without benefits even though it is possible to become "strung out" on it. Alcohol is almost universally frowned on in these circles. It is said to be a drug with almost no benefits and many drawbacks: hangovers, truculent behavior, loss of sensitivity, and so on. A 26-year-old housewife explained her reactions to alcohol:

> I don't enjoy being drunk at all. You lose your sense of balance. You lose your sense of perspective. You say things you might not want to. I know girls who have done things they don't want to because of liquor. I've seen guys that I really respected and really liked make

fools of themselves because of liquor . . . and so I decided that if there was another form of relaxation and getting high at a party besides booze, I would try it and so I tried it and ah—I never said anything that I didn't want to say, or was embarrassed in any way.

There are many other drugs, such as cocaine and peyote, that are highly regarded though a bit difficult to procure; some like belladonna, ether, and nutmeg are said to offer something but are hardly used because of the superiority and ready availability of LSD and marihuana.

STYLE OF LIFE

Heads have only minimal attachments to the customary institutions of society. This state of affairs is desired, and there are many signs that express their attitudes. Sometimes these signs are spectacular: shoulder-length hair, flowing beards, bizarre and striking clothes. Sometimes it is a much more subtle style of presentation—a gesture, a nod, a stance—but the message is conveyed that the person is not caught up in the straight world of jobs and mortgages. These public signs of estrangement are also sources of commitment to their style of life since persons who present themselves in this fashion are not likely to be acceptable members of conventional goings-on; they are not, for example, going to be hired by an insurance company. From the point of view of the conventional world these signs are stigmata, albeit deliberately worn.

Expressions of estrangement show a disdain for membership in a society composed of adults and those who want to be like today's adults. In this regard not using liquor is a sign of estrangement because that intoxicant is seen to be the traditional one for straight adults. It is suited to them, in the minds of the young heads, because it emphasizes what adults are like underneath it all. Namely, it is a drug of violence and insensitivity, sloppiness and lack of awareness. It is a drug that provides "hung up" people with a way to knock themselves out, to forget what ugly people they are. Liquor does not go hand in hand with a desire to know oneself but with the desire to escape such knowledge. Rejection of liquor is a very pointed rejection of what is seen as the dominant characteristics of adults in this society.

Out of this style of life some sort of identity is, presumably, being created, but its nature is not altogether clear. It is not one that can be adopted by persons engaged in more customary pursuits and it cannot come from attachment to kinship units. In fact, the more striking personal characteristics of this population are not sources of identity but ways of disclaiming membership in conventional institutions that are sources of identity. Peculiarities of dress are not merely "role distancing" devices but expressions of estrangement from any possibility of being associated with conventional roles.

Along with this rejection of conventional sources of identity is the strong feeling that this form of labeling is stultifying. It is a procedure which makes robots of people which their expressive disclaimers do something to confound. This is, of course, not entirely the way the disclaimers work out in practice, because the public, especially through the press, is quite able to label people who go to extremes to avoid easy labeling with the introduction of such terms as "beatnik," "kook," or "hippie" which seem to evolve as rapidly as do means of making labeling difficult. However, in face-to-face contacts such confounding tactics work well enough even if they run afoul of journalists and radio commentators. It is very difficult to say just how one is expected to react to a person even if the term "beatnik" is deemed appropriate. There is not enough substance in such a quasi-role to structure interaction.

In face-to-face interaction expressive disclaimers occur in some form. One form is the "put on." It can be used in the sense of deliberately misleading a person into a false encounter and suddenly pulling the rug out from under him, but it is also used in the sense of provoking telling reactions. How a person reacts to a girl with a vintage 1940's hat on her head says something about himself. If he reacts by trying to label (e.g., beatnik) he has tipped his hand. If he doesn't notice, that is an expression of blindness to detail. A 22-year-old computer operator reported how a friend of his provoked telling reactions:

> Yeah, I know a chick with a most beautiful collection of 1940's hats you could possibly imagine. They are really works of art. I don't know how she got them but they are outrageous in terms of contemporary fashion. They are finely made hats and occasionally she'll wear one and it doesn't fit, it doesn't always draw stares but a person will notice it and his head will snap.

Thus such signs say a good deal about what the person is not, but when taken as a sign of what the person is they tend to be very ambiguous, providing a lay Rorschach Test, a classic form of "put on." Our computer operator continued:

> A put on is when something outrageous or insane is placed before you with great equanimity as though it was very straight and ah . . . this gives you a very enjoyable jolt of discovery . . . for the same reason that a person tells a joke at a party.

The importance of drug use for this population must be judged within the rather shifting network of disclaimers and preoccupations. For example, many of our respondents would term themselves heads if asked directly but very few would volunteer this information as though it were a major source of indentification for them. It is another preoccupation which is not, per se, integral to their character. It can act as a means of sounding out others, much like bizarre dress, for there can be more or less veiled allusions to use, which if detected say something about the person detecting. A 21-year-old episodically employed male and part-time student reported how he identified like-minded persons:

> If I walk up and meet a person, I'll throw out certain leads to him. I'll use a word in the dope scene. I began using words—"hip" and "straight," in a sense that would be connected with dope and just throwing out this vernacular, and if he comes back with it, I'll throw him a little more and pretty soon it's relatively established, without mentioning dope at all, that we're heads and we'll start talking about it. It's relatively easy. Sometimes I can even see it in their eyes. They don't have to be high—there are subjects that remain in the realm of the dope scene, sometimes you can catch it when they talk about the apartment they have and the weird things which usually a head will have, or he'll groove on creative ideas, and he most often is very liberal thinking too . . . he'll go out of the way to not put me in [a strain] and he possesses a greater amount of subtlety than is normally seen. He's more objective. He's right on top of something. . . . He'll catch very subtle things. Sometimes, to play around with them, I'll become very subtle and throw them out and if he catches it, which most of them do because they have a sense of involvement which is greater than most people. They listen very carefully to what you're saying and catch it on many more levels. Sometimes I speak on several levels at once and he'll catch it.

There is one way in which an identity may be made out of this drug world but only rarely and for a limited period. Namely, there are a few who manage to support themselves by selling drugs, by working at it something like full time. There are some deeply preoccupied with drugs though this does not seem to be frequent or long-lasting. Such people are constantly experimenting and seem to be constantly loaded on one drug or another. Nonetheless, compared with information we have on heroin users building identities out of their drug use, heads are not as involved with drugs regardless of whether they think them to be important parts of their lives or not.

Instead of occupations which provide sources of identity, there are numerous preoccupations that do not. These run the gamut from drug use to music, with many in this population being amateur musicians, actors, and so on. Almost none, however, if asked for their identity would answer "musician" or "actor." There are, in short, no ready-made identities for them, not even "in training" identities that can be trotted out. By style of life and, to an extent, by drug use, the usual mode of fixing identity is incapacitated. Even their daily round tends to support this avoidance of ready labeling and the necessity to abide by those applied by other people. For example, they seldom put themselves in a position where others can insist upon deference by dint of institutional office, sex, age, or any of the things that roles are usually grounded on. There are few persons who can claim to command respect by "being something." These persons are equalitarian in the sense that they make irrelevant personal attributes that might be binding elsewhere. It is not coincidental that heads are usually hostile to such institutions as the army and the draft, to employment agencies and other officially constituted bodies. Such institutions are built around principles contrary to those upon which they want to construct their lives. A 27-year-old married woman employed as a research technician explained her own denial of conventional status structures:

> The trouble with all of this—and this is the reason that we have found ourselves more and more and more in a world of heads is because it is impossible to exist in the other world, and to practice these things. It really is. Because age does matter in that world. Age doesn't matter in our subculture because of the people that make up the subculture. . . . Certainly what I have learned as a head has helped me to manipulate myself within the straight world, but I can't live in that world any more. Because I can't be me in that world. And I'm not willing to accept the prices they impose. (What are the prices?) The whole status structure.

There is general recognition that not all straight people are equally involved in playing status games. Occasionally one is likely to run into them. Old people and children seem free of this kind of preoccupation and some heads feel they can relate to them much better: A 21-year-old part-time carpenter described what he saw to be the freedom of older people and children:

> I dig old women and I just get, and old ladies. I just get these little old ladies in black with a big red flower on their hat. They can see you coming down the street smiling and I'm sure they don't know anything about dope or anything, you know, but they see someone smiling and there's that happy vibration of happiness and they smile back and say "hi" and they know you're happy, you know. They know you're high, they know that you are pleasant and at peace with the world because most old people are. They just sort of sit and watch it man and enjoy it, and children do and heads do and those other people are in-between growing up, you know (laughter).

One way of relating to straight people where status doesn't become a problem is in hitchhiking. Some heads feel that other aspects of the self are permitted to surface while one is driving. The hidden self of the straight person can be engaged and status ascriptions lose their meaning. As a result hitchhiking is quite popular among members of the Colony who are heads: something interesting can even happen while waiting for a ride.

The policeman is one person who enters into the lives of heads and tends to disrupt attempts to free themselves from deference-tainted relationships. He is by occupation and law the one who can claim access to them and demand deference and respect for his position. Consequently the police become a symbol for what the ordinary citizen is like. It is strongly suspected that the average American would like to demand attention on the basis of his institutional connections, be it doctor or housewife, but is fortunately not empowered to do so. Some citizens, of course, try to do this anyway by berating exotic-looking young people on the streets with moral lectures and the like which reinforce attitudes which already comprehend this kind of activity.

Since the most obvious signs worn by these respondents are not claims to identity but rather disclaimers of conventional sources of identity, some notion of the materials that are used to construct identities in the absence of more conventional ones should be given. In short, these people are trying to construct identities on the basis of very personal characteristics of style and moral character.

DAILY ROUND

The term "hanging out" is used to depict this round. Usually there is no set time schedule that necessitates getting up, so the day commonly begins in late morning or early afternoon. A 21-year-old former student who lived in a house commune reported his own daily activities:

> Sometimes I sleep all day. Sometimes, you know if I'm up during the day, I ah . . . usually the first thing I get up ah . . . usually go out and sit on the front porch for awhile. Look at the morning, you know. If it's in the morning. Sometimes I sleep up on the roof, so I can watch the city at night kind of thing. Ah, ah . . . I'll sort of look around the house and see if anybody else is up, you know, and if somebody else is we usually have breakfast and ah if I feel like writing maybe I'll sit down to the typewriter for awhile or I'll just sort of wait around the house, you know, looking at things. Or maybe go out and take some fog or something and then as the day goes on . . . just usually anything that happens around the house, you know it's easy to get involved if somebody is doing something. . . . Sometimes go for a walk just to look at the sidewalk—patterns or something and just walk about for about 2 hours, just digging it.—And then, you know the patterns in the sidewalk.

There is usually nothing to demand being anywhere at any particular time since regular jobs are the exception. Most heads are not regularly employed, perhaps getting necessary money from odd jobs, from parents, or from the sale of drugs. The latter provided enough for a number of our respondents to make ends meet. Similarly, most heads are not students and not subject to whatever discipline exists in that life. The freedom that lack of commitment in the conventional order permits is highly valued. A 21-year-old part-time carpenter stated:

A lot of my straight friends . . . are on a time schedule thing. Where they have to ah . . . they, you know, have so many requirements a day that they have to meet. And ah, whereas I, if I want to go to Big Sur for two or three days, I'll go. If I want to go anywhere I'll just split and the people that usually go with me or who can go with me are my friends, who are my head friends. Because they also don't have a time schedule or a requirement page kind of thing, so the people I spend most of my time with are my head friends because they are always available, for anything—you just say "hey, do you want to go?" and I usually do. Whereas the other people are ah . . . they don't have the time for it.

Heads seem to have a distinctive attitude toward time. The focus of interest is on the present, which should be enjoyed, not some future good. A 27-year-old married woman, a research technician, captured the distinctive attitude of heads toward times:

You have to live for right now because if you live in terms of what might happen to you, what you expect will happen to you X number of years from now, you end up doing nothing but anticipating. I used to invest a great deal in anticipation . . . I thought you could make more of an occasion by going through a long period of anticipation. What usually happens in a case like that—ok you're a kid in high school and someone groovy has asked you to a dance and you spend 2 weeks in a state of excitement about this dance, you go through a whole scene and the dance is a drag. It always is a drag. Or a party. You invest far too much in it and expect far more than you can ever get from it. If you just take it for what it is—you're not going to be disappointed.

The mind has to be really free of plans and calculations if one is to enjoy the present. Heads don't usually make dates for something that is to happen even in the immediate future. A 21-year-old former student who lived in a house commune put it this way:

. . . if I make [a date] Monday night for Friday night—all right by Friday night I won't be for it. Because I'll be involved in something. I might be in Los Angeles. I might be in New York, you know, cause things happen that way. But it's always, but you're always falling into scenes kind of thing. You walk out of the house, you just got tired writing or something so you decide to go to Berkeley to have some coffee and maybe see some people and on the way you run into somebody and somebody else and it just keeps happening that way, you know but it's so hard to schedule. I have no long range plans. I don't know what I'm going to do the end of this week.

The attitude toward time is intimately connected with the disavowal of ambition. Ambition which keeps people working for some future status and ignoring the present is rejected. A 27-year-old female research technician reported that using drugs had helped her free herself of this kind of status striving:

> I no longer have any desire to set my life off in this particular way. You know, in X number of years, I expect to have achieved X position on the ladder . . . (Do you ever worry about falling off the ladder?) No, that ladder is "theirs" it belongs to "them" you know and it's they can paste me up there if they want to, but it has very little to do with me in my life. Because in fact, where my husband and I stand on the ladder. For I'm sure the overwhelming majority of people who are on the same rung with us, they would find our way of life just appalling.

Housing is very irregular and a substantial number of our respondents had no fixed address. Even the identity that came from an address is eschewed. There are ways of finding a place to sleep without paying rent: sleeping on the floor of a friend's apartment, in a garage that someone has opened for use. When an apartment is rented, a number of persons are apt to share the cost. There is a strong emphasis on mutual aid. A 21-year-old ex-student who lived in such a situation discussed the mutual aid emphasis:

> One nice thing about being a head is that usually no matter where you go it's not very long before the other heads in the area ah . . . see you and sort of take you under their wing. It works that way. Like if I'm walking around and I see a cat man coming into town with a big bag on his shoulder and just wigging into town and he's been on the road for two weeks and he's dirty but he's just walking into town and smiling—say I'll pick him up and take him home and he can stay as long as he wants. . . . Sort of—you take care of your own kind— of thing.

Mutual aid flows from the fact that identity is not developed in terms of the possessions a person has nor the property he owns. Our computer operator continued:

> To anyone who is . . . ah . . . holds on to anything rigidly ah . . . and derives their identity from something, whether it be a pose they maintain or an article of furniture they hold particularly dear ah . . . (the drug exp.) poses a threat, it shatters their identity.

A 27-year-old married woman, a research technician, when asked, "How do you feel about material possessions as compared to how you used to?" replied:

> Well, they're nice. They're also expensive—to keep as well as to get. Oh I used to think that they were everything. Not everything, I wasn't in quite that bad shape. I knew there was more than that. Material possessions are the way in which you display your wealth

and prestige. I still think that material possessions are groovy things but not as something to display your affluence.

Property, food, and drugs are shared but the relationship is not expected to be one way for a long period of time. You can't mooch off people for too long. If you're to use a drug fairly regularly, you must have a supply of your own.

Hanging out is used to describe the round of life of heads. It may involve a search for thrills, excitement, and stimulation much as it is with lower-class youth.[2] The phenomenon may involve engaging in interesting conversations, improvising word games (a counterpart to lower-class "doing the dozens") or getting involved in risky situations, e.g., trying to score from a stranger who may be a police plant, goading or testing official authorities like the police or merchants on the street, picking up girls, petty thievery and joy riding. One 22-year-old unemployed respondent described word games that are played:

> We'll throw phrases to one another . . . Ah, you know, strange, well strange, yeah in a wild kind of speech pattern, ah—almost improvisational ah—kind of way. We'll be cooking something and we'll say, as they say "jibe on what's cooking." We'll start making comments about it. And, you know, because we're so in . . . we get involved in this and we start really thinking about, you know, things to say and pretty soon it turns into a riff, I said and somebody says the line that somehow or another ends it. It always ends all of a sudden. Making a kind of piece, you know.

Whereas the "excitement" theme among these persons and lower-class youth might be quite similar, their reaction to boredom is not. In the lower-class community life often involves monotonous and dull routines in the home, on the job and in just hanging around. As with disadvantaged or outcast populations generally this generates a certain capacity to "do dead time." Hence the youngsters can be quite ingenious and creative in killing time. For the Colony member who is a head empty time is partly filled with excitement and partly filled with *waiting*. Waiting for what? Waiting for the happening. The happening is an episode, an occurrence or an event which generally originates outside onself. It may involve conversation which reveals insight about oneself, the world or the political order. It may entail encountering "beautiful" people, that are spiritually attractive, loving people. It may refer to the giving and receiving of love. One 21-year-old part-time carpenter described meeting a certain kind of person as a happening:

> They have a cool and the—the right size beard and all—and they bop up the street and ask you "what do you think of the nature of the universe" and some other absurd question. And you say "it's a nice

[2] W. B. Miller, "Lower Class Culture as a Generating Milieu of Gang Delinquency," *Journal of Social Issues*, 1958.

day, man, what do I think of the nature of the universe? I think it's pretty nice." And it's people that talk to you that have ah . . . they're really getting down into the real nitty gritty of life kind of people.

Or establishing contact with a straight person may qualify as a happening. Our part-time carpenter continued:

> I go into the doughnut shop and ah . . . go back and watch him make doughnuts and, you know, and he hands me doughnuts behind his back and stuff like that, you know. . . . I go spend, you know, half an hour a day with him probably when I was well, now the guy in the gas station at night time, you know we live late hours and it's an all night gas station.

A happening may also involve being in an extremely dangerous situation which evokes the response of courage on the part of the Colony member. Because of their dabbling in narcotics they are likely to come in contact with the police in public places. From the police point of view the public places where heads are likely to congregate are considered high delinquency areas. For the Colony member who is a head his very presence in public, dressed in a certain way, may constitute a situation of suspicion and hence require a certain amount of risk taking.

Nothing is likely to happen to you, you are not likely to experience a "happening" if you are not open to it. A 21-year-old episodically employed male, a part-time student, characterized this openness:

> If you try to offend [your host in a drug setting], try to hurry him, or disagree with him on dosage or really disagree with him very much and it isn't that blatant—"I completely disagree with you"—there is an open minded disagreement where you both leave your selves open for a change. And I really enjoy that very much because it shows that a person realizes that he might be wrong at every point and that if you bring up valid points, he'll make the change for you and expect the same of you . . . you are as open as he is, if you know what I mean. You're open to change, to new ideas that might be totally different than yours and this is on all levels.

The language heads use reveals the importance attached to the happening. When greeting another person rather than ask "what have you been doing" the query is likely to be "what's been happening to you?" or "what's been happening with your mind?" A 21-year-old unemployed male who lived in a house commune described the language:

> I always say "what's happening" because I hate to say "what have you been doing" because it's such a hell of a thing to answer, you know. If you say "what's happening?" that means they can pick anything. You know that they decide what's happening, you know and you know whatever is current kind of thing. Like "what's the scene" type thing, it just puts it down.

SOURCE OF IDENTITY

The status disclaimers indicate that identity does not come from the usual sources in American society: socioeconomic status, educational achievement, age, or race. Identity is constructed in situations where choices are made. Choices are directly related to "being." Heads speak of "having being" which points to the experience of being wherein one's choices lead to understanding of the true meaning of existence, to the truth of life. The person who has being has life and vitality. Their position is a philosophical one. The notions of self-affirmation, growth and creativity related to identity seem to be drawn from two principal sources—pragmatism, primarily William James,[3] and the radical existentialists, primarily Sartre.[4]

Our more articulate respondents recognized some historical antecedents —their debt to artists who represented an existential revolt against an inhuman and objectified world: the French impressionists; Cezanne, Van Gogh and Munch; Baudelaire and Rimbaud in poetry; Flaubert and Dostoievsky in the novel; and Ibsen and Strindberg in the theater. More directly, however, they saw themselves as the second generation of the "beats" fathered by Kerouac. They were more directly an outgrowth of writers and artists that emerged from San Francisco in 1956.

One of their heroes is Camus.[5] His emphasis on choice is what appeals to heads. Choice gives one the unlimited freedom to change, to make a person what he wants to be. Man creates what he is. Nothing is given to him to determine his creativity. The substance of his being—the "should be," the "ought to be," is not something he finds—he makes it.

This position rejects the unconscious. Man isn't a plaything of the unconscious since he creates what he is. Consequently there is a rejection of psychoanalysis, psychiatry, and conventional clinical psychology as ways of suppressing nonconformity. One can't be victimized unless he permits it. Even in situations which appear very confining there is still room for the operation of choice.

What follows for Sartre from his analysis of the human situation is revolutionary activity. For the heads it does not. Their analysis leads to a striving for compassion.

The emphasis on love and compassion seems to be a direct importation

[3] W. James, *Varieties of Religious Experience* (New York: Longmans, Green & Co., 1911).

[4] J. P. Sartre, *Being and Nothingness*, translated with an introduction by H. Barnes (New York: Philosophical Library, 1956).

[5] A. Camus, *The Myth of Sisyphus and Other Essays* (New York: Alfred A. Knopf, 1958). Also *The Rebel* (Knopf, 1959) and *Resistance, Rebellion and Death* (New York: Alfred A. Knopf, 1961).

from the mystical writings of the East, especially Zen Buddhism.[6] A 21-year-old former student, living in a small house commune, explained his attraction to Buddhism:

> Well, certainly with views toward the world I tend to put my Buddhist philosophy of love into the whole world. . . . The basic problem as I see it is the immaturity of the human race which necessitates killing and wars and which is why I think any specific action is going to be rather futile unless you change the minds of men which is why I think love is going to be the way mature mankind [will go].

VALUES

There is a great deal of emphasis placed upon choice as a precondition of morality. There is likewise an emphasis on seeing a very wide range of human behavior as the operation of choice instead of being predetermined. Heads refuse to see themselves as victims to whom things happen. For example, a young man who has flunked out of college will view the event, in retrospect, as an act that he willed. He did not flunk because he was in the grip of something larger than himself, but because the whole idea of "having to do something" is seen as deceitful, a way of reconciling something that has happened with some standard by way of excuse. An interesting example of this thinking concerns the use of opiates. Our subjects often said that addiction is a matter of choice; a person in that state of being chose it. If he had willed otherwise, he would either not have used the drug or would have stopped. They do not accept the view of the "junkie" as a victim in the sense that he is compelled to use drugs but as a person who chooses to be a victim. In commenting on heroin they express a rather casual orientation, heroin being another drug that some people can handle and others cannot.

The problem with all drugs (coffee and cigarettes included) resides, from this point of view, in the user. The discussions of such matters found in the press and other media that talk about "addiction" as a force beyond the user's control make very little sense to heads. From their point of view all such discussion is a joint effort by people who want to be seen as victims and those who want to see them that way collaborating to provide a system of excuses for bad behavior.

Choices are made in the context of a benevolent universe. Mass society may be corrupt, but the forces which regulate the universe are benign. There is the recognition that there are forces operative in the universe

[6] See D. T. Suzuki, *Studies in Zen* (London and New York: published for the Buddhist Society, 1955); *Zen and Japanese Buddhism* (Tokyo: Japan Travel Bureau, C. E. Tuttle distributors, Tokyo and Portland, Vt., 1958); and *Zen Buddhism: Selected Writings* (Garden City, N.J.: Doubleday & Company, Inc., 1956).

which are not visible. These forces, however, are not placated, as in the lower class, nor exploited in a coldly calculating way, as with the middle class, but attuned to. Heads come from backgrounds which have given them a sense of being able to control their own destiny so there is a certain confidence attendant upon their choice. The person who exercises choice in a wide variety of situations takes risks but is not likely to be destroyed by forces over which he has no control.

The choice element is much broader than middle-class decision making. Middle-class decisions are limited to "making it" in the conventional world, to mobility striving. This, from the head's point of view, is the only way in which middle-class choice is operative. Middle-class choice is linked to ambition. From the head perspective, ambitious people create coercion and misery. Middle-class choice also seems restless, anxious, and unhappy.

To the middle-class person the head seems to be one who is not decisive. This the head would deny. His choice is related to searching for true values, for exploring his own mind and others. The passivity perceived by middle-class persons involves a choice. It is a response to the coerciveness of institutions and a decision not to collaborate with them. The major choice made is to drop out of conventional society and opt for independence in personal relationships. This is not viewed as withdrawal but as the first step in exploring those facets of the world and the self ignored by mass society. Choice is necessary to create one's own self and one's scene.

Choice is also operative in the relationships between men and women. One actively searches out and becomes involved with someone else rather than passively waiting for an affair. The expectation is that the relationship will not be a long-lasting or permanent one. Relationships are initiated on the basis of mutual attraction which includes both physical and spiritual elements. When these elements disappear, then the expectation is that the relationship will be terminated. Relationships can also be ended if one or both of the parties diagnose it as unhealthy. Usually this means that it is tainted with dishonesty. There is the recognition that disruptions in a personal relationship can be utilized to bolster an inauthentic conception of love. This is viewed as a danger to be avoided. Love is not placed in the hands of fate. It is actively controlled by the lovers, not something which unwittingly happens to them. Consequently, heads are not likely to talk about "falling in love" since it refers to a romantic conception of man-woman relationships which they reject.

The romantic conception of love sees the relationship as externally controlled. Love is perceived as an object or a commodity rather than something the lovers mutually create. Love frequently appears as something to be "won" or something which is subject to theft. This is incompatible with the notion that love is jointly created by the lovers and not external to their relationship.

By rejecting romantic love the head is opting for an expansion of the relationships between men and women. He sees himself providing for different levels of involvement between two persons in addition to whatever physical and spiritual basis there is. This, from his point of view, allows for a maximization of personal freedom in a relationship and helps avoid unhealthy involvements.

The speech of heads is shot through with terms like "automated," "robots," "puppets" to signify how they think most people behave—not making choices but following the program that is set for them. A 22-year-old housewife described some people she and her husband met as an illustration:

> One night we went over to the Hotel ———— to have dinner, and it's a pine table, and everyone sits down at the table, everbody being together. There were some Air Force couple . . . but here was a younger guy that I was talking to mostly, and his wife. And they were defending the business of the war, and they were saying that you have to kill these people, so that they don't come under the horrible Communist rule, and that Communism is horrible, a terror. And they just have these crazy arguments like, you know, they have to go over there to kill them so that they won't be under Communism. It's a better dead than red kind of thing. But they're doing it for other people. And defending the war. And, I got the feeling, that because the war was there, it must be right. Because, you know the President is the President. They, you know, they seem to accept an awful lot of things. You know, they accept that you are supposed to have a house and a garden and a lawn. And, you know, lawns around here are fantastic. They are always mowed, and the dogs are all in the back yard, except for ours.

Choices are seen as private matters in the sense that one person is not justified in making choices for another. It is immoral either to try to make choices for others or ask them to make yours. The implication is that it is necessary to do something about one's life, to think for oneself no matter what the consequences. A 30-year-old graduate student in social science stated:

> I think the Beatles put it very well—"do what you want to do. Go where you're going to. Think for yourself cuz I won't be there with you."

CHOICE AS RELATED TO DRUG USE

The private character of choice is also illustrated by their views of who should use LSD. Recreational users commonly launch into a long description of the circumstances and proper psychic makeup of a person who is fit to use the drug. Heads would probably say that persons who express the desire should use it with the proviso that they have some idea of what it is all about so that they have grounds for making the choice. This is not limited to adults. It is quite within reason for six-year olds to want to use such drugs, in which case they ought to be given the chance. Their conception of the society they live in also reflects this position in that they see the citizenry as not making choices and, hence, living lives that do not give evidence of any moral position. It is necessary to make choices in order to be either good or bad.

Such choices can be interfered with in any number of ways. As mentioned before, the demands of people to be given authority is seen as a touchy point. On whatever grounds the demand is made—tradition, office or charisma—these people are very reluctant to let others make up their minds, to plot courses of action or lay down the lines of discipline. Thus, there is great disrespect for tradition as a guideline for present action whether in politics, dress, or manners. This is probably indigenous to any of the populations that have been know as bohemian. There is likewise great disrespect for authority claimed on the basis of office or similiar institutional attachment. Perhaps the most acceptable form of authority is that based on personal attributes, charisma. There are people that could be called "folk heroes" such as Ken Kesey, the Rolling Stones, and other flagrant, dissident spirits. It might be noted that none of these heroes make any demands that they be followed.

Naked force is likewise a sensitive point. Heads are close enough to police surveillance to realize that force is used to back up other demands for compliance. It is something that must be come to terms with, and how a person reacts gives some clue as to his character. The commentary made on this matter reflects the view that most people are "servile" because they easily give in to the thought of force being used against them even if they manage not to lend authority blindly to the pronouncements of others. A 28-year-old married graduate student observed:

> I think that the . . . middle class person is very servile, therefore will only do things that are normally classified as illegal only when he's told to. Like if he's in a section that has really strong anti-Negro sentiments and a Negro moves in, he knows that it's all right to burn or break bones or something like that, so he'll do it. And it's not a matter of being non-violent or good natured, I think it's just a matter of servility, and for that reason they won't try drugs either. I mean they haven't been told to, if they were told to, they would.

Beginning with the premise that people know what they ought or want to do, a term is in use that expresses disfavor toward not doing so. To "cop out" is to fail to follow one's own dictates, to do something second best because it is easier to let others dictate a course of action.

The term is applied to people who try to "pass" and still keep a foot within the legitimate order. Such people are "cop outs" in greater or lesser degree; less so if they are "out front" and do not deny their involvement and more so if they try to excuse it thereby compounding their dishonesty. Once adopting the view that the established order is morally bankrupt, it is a cop out to try to excuse one's presence in its folds. A 23-year-old laboratory technician on his way to becoming a head put it this way:

> My biggest fear, or the thing that I would mostly reproach myself for doing is what I and most people would call selling out, leading a straight life and having money and having a family, and you know, the regular thing . . . [I have] a certain amount of missionary in me, the revolutionary. Christ thing, you know, feeling that if you are not going to sell out, then you have to be poor and, you know, and can't compromise.

The cop out is putting yourself in a situation by your own choice which negates the possibility of choice at some later point. The person can then talk in terms of being victimized when some unfavorable event occurs.

SIGNIFICANCE OF THE POLICE
IN TERMS OF VALUES

The police become important because they focus and illustrate so many features contrary to the values of the heads. They demand respect on the basis of office and have the force to make it unpleasant for those who are reluctant to give it. They are taken, very literally, as the representatives of the straight world in the sense that they are behaving in their uniforms in a fashion that every other citizen would like to emulate, insisting that their demands for respect and deference be taken seriously. The police are so significant in this symbolic sense that their behavior has been turned into a term used to apply to varied circumstances. They speak of "policing" behavior and some people try to police others. Respondents also spoke of their parents as "police." Likewise it is possible to "police" oneself by denying real desires. It is all the same—people want to do things and sometimes they, or other people, stand in the way; to do that is to "police." A 21-year-old unemployed model stated a common theme:

> I think it's bad. It gives you guilt complexes and it stifles you, you know, really, and everything you want to say you know. A girl, a chick wouldn't walk out without all her makeup on, you know, or she won't go to bed with a guy she likes—so she stays a virgin until she's 35, you dig? It's a bad scene.

Much of the important activity that goes on every day for our respondents somehow involves the law and the police. They speak about various encounters with police, or how someone they know got busted, personal characteristics of particular policemen, or what the shifting administrative concerns within police departments mean for street enforcement. The discussions about particular policemen are usually intended to show that they are corrupt, ignorant, and brutal. Everyone, however, seems to have a story about police that show them to have moral character. They may be kind, interested, or genuinely convinced that the laws they are inforcing are bad laws. More rare, though not nonexistent, are stories relating to marihuana use by particular policemen.

Though conversation reveals a great deal of concern about the police there seems to be a general recognition that encounters with them need not be a degradation ceremony for heads. Since they come from middle-class backgrounds the standard operating procedures of police departments are not unknown to them. There is a certain sense in which organizational imperatives are understood—what is more difficult to understand, from their vantage point, is why someone would become a policeman in the first place. Police seem to have a vested interest in moral indignation and be concerned about it 24 hours a day. A 21-year-old part-time carpenter characterized his reaction to the police:

> If they had anything about them, they wouldn't be cops. They live their occupation. You know just because an officer is off duty, you know. ——— (a police friend) isn't a policeman then because there are more beautiful things in life. It takes a real dope to be a policeman, and it shows.

Heads are also aware that the discussions police engage them in are for the purpose of gaining information. When police are in pursuit of someone who has just committed a felony, they don't waste time conversing. Essentially they are on a fishing expedition. The nature of the game is such that you've come out ahead if you do not give information, if you confound or confuse the police or if you make it an occasion for an expression of love for them.

You have something to say about whether the encounter takes place or not. Again it is partly your choice. Heads are aware that their dress and actions make them ipso facto suspicious persons so that encounters with the police are always a possibility. Hence one must take precautions not to be placed in a situation where he can be arrested. The encounter provides an opportunity where the person can exercise ingenuity and possibly courage. Despite this, most heads would define a police encounter as an unpleasant one. Once a person is stopped and questioned he can partly determine the outcome no matter what the individual policeman may want to do. Our 21-year-old respondent further described a situation where he resisted the feeling of being victimized and instead communicated it to the policeman:

Like when we was coming here tonight two Oakland police were going by on their motorcycles and we were just coming out of a gas station. The guy just caught a quick look at us and we were both looking at him like that (a hard stare) and he just couldn't watch us because we busted him before he busted us, you know. He just went on by like he was the one who should be paranoid. . . . (Describing a situation in another city watching the "get drunk college set" on a bus bench). We never said a word to anybody, we just watched all this madness going back and forth and a man walked up to us and, you know, Palm Springs dress, you know and said "Hi Fellas. What are you doing here?" Because we both had very long hair at the time and you know looked really sort of Berkeley, if I may say that ah . . . and he was a cop and you knew it, you just knew. And so you turn around and say "we're here for the 4th of July weekend *officer*. And then he can't say anything because ah . . . his whole setup was to dig you out man and you've already established what is so—OK where do we go from here? Now what do you want? Rather than beating around the bush about it man.

Another strategy in encounters with police is to try to play some kind of joke on them. This is risky unless the police are amused by the joke also. A considerable amount of stylized kidding goes on between the police and persons he suspects may be heads. "Are you holding any today?" or "How many people have you turned on today?" Queries such as this can usually be responded to in kind. A 26-year-old male and part-time artist told of playing a little game with someone he suspected of being an undercover agent for the police.

I sold one of their agents a Lucky Strike rolled up in brown paper, 'cause he's been bugging me and my friend (about) selling weed for weeks and weeks because we were selling weed. He bugged me at a club about it in front of two girls, just came up to the table and said "I've got to have some weed, here's a dollar." So I took his dollar and I went to the bathroom and I rolled up a Lucky Strike in brown paper and gave it to him. They busted us when we came out of the club.

The "joke" wasn't as much appreciated by the police as it was by the friends of the person who played it on them. It led to his intensive questioning and a search of his apartment and car. From that point on he became in his words, a "police customer."

Relationships with the police may generate a considerable amount of paranoia about what they are up to. Our respondents described various periods in their own lives when they suspected that they were being followed and under observation by police and undercover agents. This is a serious "hang-up" and must be overcome in one way or another. Some describe moving from one apartment to another or from one police jurisdiction to another to escape paranoid feelings. A 29-year-old unemployed man described his own way of dealing with paranoia about the police:

The Berkeley police are out to get me for anything they can get me for. They all know me. You know like the very typical sort of thing that happens is, I am riding my bicycle down the street and I don't have my light with me and some cop stops me and says "Hello Mr. X —how's your book coming?" Or ah . . . let me see, "Say can't you keep your friends from carrying the hypes?" . . . I went down to the Berkeley police station to report a stolen bicycle. The desk sergeant when I mentioned this, he went back—about 30 seconds later a policeman came out and said "got your bicycle stolen again, huh?" They know all about me; they know everything that I'm doing. But that's a gas ah . . . knowing that you're being watched is a hell of a lot better than paranoia. Like so many of my friends are so fucking paranoid, and feel there's a cop car around every corner or their phone is being tapped or something like that.

There have been several reports of heads who tried to get beyond the external trappings of office to the underlying essence in relationships with police. The tale of the arrested LSD user who proceeded to kiss the arresting officer is an extreme example of trying to get beyond the uniform to relate at some fundamental human level. One 21-year-old part-time carpenter described the kind of "power" released by LSD that enables people to confront and foil the police:

There's a definite thing—when we talk, when we use the word "power" kind of thing. It's not a sort of power in the sense that it's a vicious thing or anything. It's just the people that have a realization that they have the power. Sometimes . . . there were some people riding around in SF at night. They had just taken LSD, just enjoying the city, very beautiful ride kind of thing, you know, just really enjoying the buildings and the sidewalks and the people and all and the police car came up beside them and saw that they were, you know, like loaded and just sort of crunched them over into the curb and forced them over and the five of them got out of the car and the police were behind them and for some reason they all just ran around and didn't say anything and looked at the police, just like that, you know, that sort of look, and the police got back in the car and drove away. It's 'cause they knew they couldn't overcome that presence. It would be ridiculous for them to even talk to those people. They couldn't even communicate with them. They just—the best thing for them to do was just go away and let them alone.

Almost all of our respondents had contact with the police at one time or another related to their use of drugs. Some had been arrested. Getting busted was not a desirable thing nor did the experience add luster to anyone's reputation, as it does among some lower-class delinquent groups. If a person was arrested, he had somehow collaborated in the process which led to this eventuality and his response at that point was to make sure that experience didn't violate his integrity: Our 21-year-old part-time carpenter continued:

It doesn't really bother me to spend the night in jail or to spend time in jail here or there ah . . . because there are interesting things happening in there. I'm sure I wouldn't like to do time—but I'm sure if it ended up that I had to do a year—you have to get behind it no matter what it is—if you get behind it you can enjoy it—make yourself enjoy it.

Arrests or busts often occurred in the process of buying or selling drugs, and heads were aware that information was passed to police somewhere in the distribution system that enabled them to intervene. This realization was usually treated rather lightly in conversation as "one of the breaks of the game." If you thought about it much you could get paranoid. A 28-year-old graduate student in social science described one situation which might have resulted in an arrest:

Let's see, the first I bought was, when I was staying back on X street. Oh, this is kinda funny, the first can I bought, I ordered a ten lb shipment from Los Angeles. And, the night it came in, I was waiting around anxiously, working around in the dark room and all of a sudden the door opens and there is a whole lot of light, and these guys with flashlights come into the dark room and I said "hey my prints" (photographic prints) and somebody turned on the lights and put handcuffs on me (laughter) and they looked over all the prints. . . . Somehow word had leaked out about this thing. And, the cop never got the grass, because the guys who brought it up never went back to their car [nor did they deliver it because] they realized it was a bust.

There is always the possibility that someone you know may tip off the police. The strategy of enforcement in crimes without victims which dictates the use of informers decisively affects the relationships among those who might be informed upon. It seems to affect relationships in opposing ways. First of all, by being involved in illegal activity you are likely to come into contact with many people whom you would not meet under ordinary circumstances: A 24-year-old unemployed ex-student put it this way:

There's a nice camaraderie in doing the same thing and having a common vice and . . . it's kind of doing the thing together against the law, you know. It's kind of dangerous, you know.

A 29-year-old unemployed man with a wife and child agreed:

Much of it is spreading and people are constantly, every day, you know, meeting, bumping into each other and it's sort of like you can walk down the streets now in Berkeley or you can go up to campus at 2:00 in the night you walk through the campus and there's some other guy walking down the sidewalk with a beard and you sort of look at each other—like you know, you just know (laughter). Some people you just walk up to you know, and you reach out and you touch each other.

Heads move in a broader circle of people who are related to the drug scene who may be known, known about, or not known at all. Within this wider circle of persons relationships are possible even if only the fleeting relationship of identifying, as above, a like-minded soul. The relationships are also given a peculiar intensity by virtue of their underground character. That which gives them their intensity also poses a threat in terms of getting arrested. As mentioned earlier, persons can be pressured to function as informers for the police in exchange for dropping or reducing charges against them. They are more congenial to the idea the more they have to lose. The very force that thrusts people together in exciting kinds of relationships also can disrupt close relationships by use of the informer system and the suspicion it generates. In what ways do heads cope with this threat? One way is to limit the number of persons with whom you are completely open. If your circle of friends is small and tight knit and you do not sell or buy drugs from people you do not know then the chances of being busted are quite small. In other words a certain amount of discretion in relationships with others is protective. The second method of coping with the threat of disruption is to focus on the element of *trust* in close relationships. If one thing can be said of these intimate relationships, it is that they are trusting. A 21-year-old episodically employed male, a part-time student, discussed trust:

> Many times a person in a heavy dope scene will purposely criticize you to see how you react to it. If you're one to get all mad about it, he'll know that he can't trust you because it all comes from this fear and who you can trust and to what degree. I catch myself evaluating people on how much I can trust them and this is the basis. If I got in a real bad situation, would they run on me, would they tell on me, would they tell on me or would they stand with me? Sure, all of this might be perpetuated by fear of the police . . . but it still exists.

It is no wonder that much of the important activity, for these respondents, somehow involves the law and the police. Their reaction to them is invested with a tremendous amount of significance, telescoping their conceptions of themselves and the world into the encounters with real flesh-and-blood policemen on the street.

MEANING AND DRUGS

Within this life it is a virtue to see oneself clearly, the hang-ups and all. Such perception of self goes hand in hand with the emphasis placed on choice, knowing one's desires and obligations, and on the virtue of coming to terms with reality. One is enjoined to discover the self and the world about him. A 27-year-old married woman, a research technician, talked about this discovery:

> Heads aren't hiding. That's my impression. That's how I define a person as a head. A head is a person who is going out into his world and seeking it. Not hiding from it. You can use turning on to hide, but I don't define those people as heads.

A person who has a clear vision of himself and the world in which he lives is said to "know where it's at," the spatial terminology conveying simplicity. Indeed such reality is viewed as a simple affair but one that is obscured by petty biases, excuses, and neuroses. Underneath such impediments it is felt that reality is an easy thing to grasp, and there is a premium on simple expression and not on lengthy wrangling discussion about what is basically real.

LSD is said to break down these impediments and open the person up to things that have been obscured. There is no effort to deny that LSD experiences can be very painful and, similarly, no attempt to argue that the drug should not be used for this reason. Part of reality may be very ugly; the effect of the drug might be to bring into the open parts of the person that have been carefully hidden for a long time which can be a shattering experience. Regardless, this is seen as a good thing because it is a way of confronting what is there in any event. There is no attempt to convince people that they should not use because it might be unpleasant since the unpleasantness is a sign that a beneficial process is at work. There is no virtue placed on ignorance of self even if the ignorance provides stability or happiness.

Drugs also provide a media for confronting the social world. Their use provides direct violation of laws which are felt to be violations of the user's rights. For example, drug experiences are felt to be very private, and the law is seen as a violation of privacy. The law also activates the police as the representatives of society in a way that lays bare to these users what authority and force are about. They are being ordered to comply and are effectively robbed of choice. They watch the "experts" fall in line and attempt to justify legislation that violates their felt rights.

The laws and police become symbolic actors in this dissension from the straight and narrow path, and it is doubtful if anything could bring this about more clearly than drugs because of the nature of the offense. It is clearly a crime without victims that is being enforced with considerable zeal, bringing into play spokesmen from every sector of society from the pulpit to the press to the medical profession to the academic profession. The arena is crowded with actors expressing their point of view. No other violation could so vigorously arouse so many people, letting them identify themselves by their stand on drugs.

The idea of confrontation also meshes with the mode of presentation of these users. It is a cop out to try to appear as a person who does not use drugs, to appear straight. Part of the value system demands that there be a certain openness, not to the point of arrest, but enough to signify that compliance has not been given. There is value in being "outrageous," flagrant in expressing dissension. Such behavior is a "put on" that acts as a self-fulfilling prophecy since the authorities react to noncompliance by increasing their demands and by increasing their efforts to do something about these users. For example, undercover agents are employed or minor harassment is begun. Newspaper editors call for the destruction of their hang-outs; letters to the editor demand that they all be put in the army, etc. In this way a style of use provides a revealing reaction from the society they live in, one that confirms what they felt about it all along. It provides one way of taking a close look at some of the seamier practices in society, the day-to-day operation of a police department, perhaps the inside of jails, and one gets the decided impression that civics texts are not "where it's at."

Characteristically, the reaction to the less pleasant features of society that they see is not to become politically active even in the "New Left" because it is felt to be, underneath it all, just as hostile to their style of life as the legitimate order. It is suspected that the radical, left political organizations also demand compliance or would if they ever had enough power to do so. They certainly try to exact some discipline in matters of illegality as it is, frowning on drug use among their members because it could compromise their position. Some of our respondents would demonstrate, though not go to organizational meetings. But theirs is more on the order of offending the citizenry than expecting to effect a change: they hitchhike on already unpopular causes, providing warm bodies for protests of widely varying aims. The issue of reform is not, as far as I could tell, very well detailed. Instead of programs, these people are apt to mention massive changes in character as necessary preconditions for improving the world. Often it is said that persons must learn how to love one another before anything significant can happen to improve conditions, a sentiment reflected in the popular song: *Say the word/the word is love.*

Clearly, heads react quite belligerently toward the law and its enforcers in the area of drugs but their reaction to the warrants which validate these laws is more complex. It is not simple outrage but rather puzzlement and the occasion to invoke social theory to account for them. In short, they find the reasons given for the existence of laws governing drugs like marihuana nothing less than fantastic. From their perspective none of the rhetorical terms like "dangerous" or "addictive" make sense. And it is rather hard for them to envision the kind of people for whom such terms would make sense. Consequently, reaction to the words of a public-spirited senator talking about the menace of drugs to public health or those of a chief of police or newspaper editor might be made up of a simple "Wow!" to express amazement at wordy nonsense that is the everyday occurrence when people try to make sense of the "drug problem." Unlike recreational users who try to argue with the given warrants in their own terms—e.g., is LSD dangerous or not—heads are much less willing to speak of such matters other than to speak in terms of their own experience. When we asked such questions we often received answers like, "It didn't hurt me." Likewise they are less willing to promote specific reforms like the so-called British System and more likely to say the only reform is when people stop minding other people's business.

Behind this amazement is a marked disbelief in the credibility of the warrants at face value. They do not believe the given reasons are the real reasons for suppression but look to more involved matters that include the psychic make-up of the framers and enforcers of law. The reaction to use and their particular version of use is seen as the result of their violations of convention generally, rather than for specific infractions of law. The law is seen as an instrument to suppress unconventional behavior. The mechanisms to account for this focus on the psyche of the man in the street which converts fear to hatred. As mentioned, people at large are seen as automated or extremely rigid, bound to the props which hold their lives together and give what they do meaning. Using drugs or doing other "outrageous" things is presumed to put these people "up tight," to provoke anxiety by not revering the same symbols and pointedly showing that there exist alternative ways to spend time. As a result of this, it is supposed that hatred is produced and directed at them as the most exemplary dissidents. Likewise, they feel that people who are in positions usually accorded authority are markedly upset when people refuse to accord it because this dissension attacks one of the major ways they make sense of their lives.

Those who are made "up tight" react with hatred which only coincidentally takes the form of law enforcement since that is the means of suppression most readily available. Actually what is suspected is that total suppression is actually desired which culminates in apocalyptic visions of the outcome of "outrageous" behavior. The head feels that he lives in a land filled with psychological cripples who will destroy him if given the chance because that act would defend his madness from contradiction. This feeling is sometimes expressed in sardonic inquiry as to what the Americans are up to today.

8

The Response of the
Larger Community

The Colony members who contributed to this study considered themselves to be part of a general social movement. They felt that it was
beginning to take shape, but at this point there is little indication where
it is going. It is largely unorganized—there is little official leadership
or recognized membership. Progress toward whatever goal seems to be
uneven. But of one thing they were sure: the movement, which can be
characterized as bohemian, represents an extraordinarily powerful force.

This new bohemianism evidences both continuities and discontinuities
with its historical antecedents. Persons involved in the movement see
themselves as part of a "subversive tradition" which has always existed
in America. Though they may not be writers, they perceive themselves
in a direct line from Emerson and Thoreau, D. H. Lawrence, Melville,
and Whitman. They, like previous generations of literary subversives
come from the middle class. Consequently, recent immigrants, second-
generation Americans or minority-group members are not to be found
among them in substantial numbers.

Bohemianism in America and in Europe has exhibited some similar
characteristics. Bohemians have tended to celebrate originality in art
and personal life as against the more prosaic life style of "philistines."
Authenticity is valued highly in artistic creations and in individual feelings and moods. Heroes tend to be musicians, poets, novelists, or primi-
tives who exhibit this authenticity. Conventional society is rejected
because originality and spontaneity are stifled, and voluntary poverty
is embraced as a way of maintaining one's purity. Finally, the emphasis
on mutual aid and sharing points to an attempt to develop a sense of
community which is impossible in conventional society.

The most recent descriptions of American bohemians by Lipton,[1]
Rigney, Smith,[2] and Polsky[3] delineate these concerns as they apply to
a particular group of persons living on the West Coast in the late 1950's

[1] L. Lipton, *The Holy Barbarians* (New York: Julian Messner, Inc., 1959).
[2] F. J. Rigney and D. Smith, *The Real Bohemia, A Sociological and Psychological Study of the "Beats"* (New York: Basic Books Inc., Publishers, 1961).
[3] N. Polsky, "The Village Beat Scene, 1960" in *Hustlers, Beats and Others* (Chicago: Aldine, 1967).

and in Greenwich Village in 1960. The values represented in this choice of life have shifted somewhat in this new movement. The most obvious difference between the heads described here and the earlier bohemians is in their relative numbers. The absolute increase of the number of young people who feel themselves to be part of this social movement is fairly evident and highly visible. It is difficult, however, to demonstrate that the new bohemians represent a higher proportion of college-age young people than in the late 1950's. The proportion of young persons to adults has increased since then, as has the proportion of young people going to college. If earlier estimates on drug usage are an indicator of bohemian sentiments, however, we can safely say that its relative size and influence have increased. The diffusion of this life style among young people generally is likely to increase in the near future rather than decrease.

Another obvious difference between the heads and the earlier bohemians is the more frequent use of drugs because of their accessibility. Among young people of college age there is a consensus that the effects of drugs like marihuana and LSD are pleasurable; there is also a much more discriminating attitude toward the alleged evil effects and a sense that the risks in taking them are slight and diminishing. This, combined with scientific breakthroughs in creating new drugs, has drastically affected drug availability. What was formerly a small and isolated phenomenon among some bohemian groups is now taking on mass proportions.

Concomitant with the increased availability of drugs like marihuana and LSD has been a shift in public attitudes toward them. One Colony member pinpointed the change in public attitudes toward marihuana in 1962. An article in *Playboy*[4] had the effect of legitimizing marihuana by indicating that a large number of middle-class persons were also using:

> It's become stylish. *Playboy*. More people read *Playboy* than anything else . . . they think it's maybe the Indian Bible. And *Playboy* says grass is all right. And it's one of the few, you know, like really telling effects of the fact. Artists and people have been at it for a long time, authors, etc. And they've come out and said it's all right. And, people have listened. Intelligent people have listened. Norman Mailer's *Advertisements for Myself* and he comes out and says, 'I've been killing time for a few years just getting loaded, and turning on, and I've written a lot of nice paragraphs, man . . . pretty soon I'm going to come along and write the great American novel.' It's the American dream. And now, he's burying Marvel comic books like everybody else, and digging it. People listen to cats like this because they know what they are saying. And Norman Mailer really knows where it's at. And if Norman Mailer says grass isn't, you know, it ain't bad for you, it hangs up a little bit, but it's all right. A lot of people listen to it,

⁴ D. Wakefield, M. Harrington, and A. Huxley, "The Pros and Cons, History and Future Possibilities of Vision Inducing Psychochemicals," *Playboy Magazine*, 1963, p. 10.

because Norman Mailer hasn't by-and-large done any lying to the public. If President Johnson says grass is bad for you, he's done a lot of lying to the public, and . . . you don't quite listen to this sort of thing.

It would be a mistake, however, to view the more extensive use of drugs by the new bohemians as the only characteristic which distinguishes them from the "beats." The meaning and significance they attach to drugs can only be ascertained within a broader context of shared values.

The new bohemians are much like the beats in their emphasis on originality in art and personal life. There seems to be a shift, however, in the range of heroes. No longer is the primitive the only hero. Our respondents seemed to be more critical of the idolization of the Lumpen-proletariat or the lower-class Negro or Mexican-American. The lower class is not viewed as the only true source of values. The celebration of proletarian work by the earlier beats no longer seems part of the present scene. The kinds of jobs which are preferred suggest a change in orientation. Our respondents still preferred artistic work of one kind or another, but increasing acceptance was given to low-level bureaucratic jobs. The low-level bureaucrat who manages to survive and retain his integrity was always acceptable but now he seems to have been elevated to the status of a folk hero. Another hero which has emerged is the person who manages to survive quite substantially and at the same time beat the system at its own game. Some of the rock and roll groups fall into this category. They flaunt some of society's basic values in their songs and get away with it, they make a great deal of money, and they are not physically beautiful. The fact that recognition is accorded to someone who is not poor also indicates a fundamental shift in the value attached to voluntary poverty. Poverty is not good in and of itself as it was for the beats. The notion expressed is that poor people can be pretty obnoxious too, that they have their hang-ups. Hence, a more critical and discriminating view is taken of values enshrined in lower-class culture. Poverty is good only in that it demonstrates that you can live without a lot of things—that you can be detached from them.

Philosophers, novelists, or religious persons who exemplify by their works or life the importance of the existential choice are also revered. The new bohemians seem as much aware of French existentialism as their earlier counterparts. Camus is looked upon as a kind of folk hero. His analysis of the human situation is accepted but not his prescription—engagement in terms of revolutionary activity. Rather they choose disaffiliation. The political detachment seems to be a direct importation from Zen Buddhism. The Zen influence does not come directly today any more than it did for the earlier beats.[5] What the present generation of bohemians seem to find most attractive in Zen is the idea of the holiness of

[5] Tallman, commenting on Kerouac's *Dharma Bums*, states that "it is an obvious attempt to adjust the practices, the flavor, the attitude of Zen to an American sensibility"—

the personal impulse and the dramatic role of the Zen lunatic. The lunatic is the perfect expression of the bohemian commitment to spontaneity and authenticity. He incorporates within himself a basic quest for transcendence which is suppressed in mass society. The recognition accorded to the lunatic among the new bohemians is substantially that accorded by the beats.

The mood of the present generation of bohemians, however, represents a shift from earlier patterns. Among the earlier beats, there was a profound strain of pessimism.[6] For some, the diagnosis of society as corrupt led inevitably to a sense of hopelessness. Among our respondents the strain of pessimism seemed to be completely absent. They shared the conviction of earlier beats that political activism is no solution to the corruption around them, but they were not depressed by it. The mood was one of profound optimism. They seem to be expecting a cultural revolution which will occur no matter what happens in the political arena. They feel themselves to be part of the new world which is taking shape. They feel on the verge of a major advance in the development of the human race. What makes this development of consciousness so imminent, they feel, is the discovery of hallucinogens.

The new bohemians share the diagnosis of the earlier beats as to the absolute corruption of our bureaucratic-industrial society. They favor a simpler kind of existence, and the interviews were filled with rustic allusions. Almost all of our respondents had spent some time living in seclusion—usually some kind of wilderness camping where they were required to depend completely on their own resources. The experience with LSD seemed to develop a much more pronounced attraction to nature than was evident among the beats.

The new bohemians also resemble the older generation of beats in their attempt to establish an authentic community of love characterized by mutual sharing and a set of common living arrangements. What John Clellon Holmes has said about the beats can be said just as accurately about the new bohemians:

> . . . their response is a return to an older, more personal, but no less rigorous code of ethics, which includes the inviolability of comradeship, the respect for confidences and an almost mystical regard for courage—all of which are the ethics of the tribe, rather than the community, the code of a small compact group living in an indifferent or hostile environment which it seeks not to conquer or change, but only to elude.[7]

in T. Parkinson, ed., *A Casebook on the Beats* (New York: Thomas Y. Crowell Company, 1961), p. 226.

[6] See J. Kerouac, "The Origins of the Beat Generation" in *A Casebook on the Beats*, p. 73.

[7] S. Krim, ed., *The Beats: A Gold Medal Anthology* (Greenwich, Connecticut: Fawcett Publications, 1960), p. 22.

Finally, the manner in which the beliefs associated with bohemianism are communicated is distinctively different among the new bohemians and the earlier beats. Values are still communicated in painting, poems, or novels which have for the most part a limited circulation. Much of it is underground. But a new vehicle for the dissemination of beliefs has appeared: rock and roll music. The lyrics enshrine the values associated with this new phenomenon.

Finally, within this evolving social movement there is pronounced emphasis on mutual aid. This flows from the fact that identity is not developed in terms of the possessions a person owns. Property, food, and drugs are shared. In this, of course, they are like their earlier counterparts living by the rule of the smaller group which is faced with the problem of survival in a hostile world. The response is to establish a community of love and try to extend beauty into an ugly world. This can be done by telling people how beautiful they are or can be and by telling them that they are basically good. This usually entails passing out leaflets, buttons, or food as many of these small communes do. The mutual aid anticipates a new social order where honesty, authenticity, and self-realization are presumably possible.

WHAT DOES THIS PHENOMENON REPRESENT?

The rapidity with which this movement is spreading, if we accept increasing drug usage as one index of it, is due to the widespread dissemination of its beliefs among receptive individuals.

Certain conditions must be present for a social movement of this sort to develop. Among the most important of these conditions is the unavailability of means to express protest or grievances among a population suffering from some kind of strain.[8] Alternative means for reconstituting the social structure are perceived as unavailable. The age group which constitutes the recruits for this movement, those between approximately 18 and 25, despite their largely middle-class status, rank low in wealth, power, prestige or access to the means of communication. Their experience, consequently, is one of deprivation—not deprivation in any material sense, but a deprivation of participation. The disaffection springs from a sense of powerlessness in the face of inflexible political structures. This is the condition which generates the sense of disillusionment discussed earlier. Smelser has observed the relative deprivation which precedes movements of this sort:

[8] See N. J. Smelser, *Theory of Collective Behavior* (New York: The Free Press, 1963), Chap. 3.

Such deprivations are relative to expectations. By an absolute measure, groups which are drawn into value-oriented movements may be improving . . . improvement on absolute ground [may] involve deprivation on relative grounds; for the same group, with their new gains in one sphere (e.g., economic, cultural) is often held back in another (e.g., political).[9]

Internal migration and a shift in the composition of the population generally produce a strain which precedes the generation of any value-oriented beliefs. The concentration of population in large cities after World War II [10] combined with the increased birth rate set the stage for the new bohemian movement. The increase in the birth rate altered the proportion of youth to adults significantly.[11] The mixing of unlike populations in larger cities further contributed to social strain. As Gillin points out, one fundamental factor in the rise of religious movements is "The heterogeneity of the population of any social group . . . or its social unlikeness which results from the imperfect assimilation of population elements suddenly brought together . . ." [12] A third element contributing to the strain is the dramatic change in work practices, mainly those changes associated with automation, which have been made obsolescent old skills and increased the importance of re-education in a person's work life. This has had the effect of lengthening the time span between basic schooling and desired employment among a group of people always noted for their questioning attitudes and profoundly moral stance on social issues.

The direction this movement will take depends on the response of the larger community through its agencies of social control. If consistent and firm repression is the reaction, then it is likely to be driven further underground and possibly eliminated. This may happen because of a general American reaction to the use of certain kinds of drugs by the new bohemians. The use of marihuana, the hallucinogens, and the amphetamines is popularly considered to be in opposition to fundamental American values of self-restraint and earned pleasure. It may be helpful to characterize the specific view of drugs in America today preliminary to any discussion of the future possibilities of this bohemian movement.

[9] *Ibid.*, p. 340.

[10] Hauser points out that about 122 million people lived in urban places in 1960—some 68 per cent of the total population as contrasted with 56 per cent in 1950. The major shift took place during the war years and is expected to continue. See P. Hauser, *Population Perspectives* (New Brunswick, N.J.: Rutgers University Press, 1960), p. 97.

[11] "The decade of the fifties was in a unique way the decade of the elementary school child. The number of youngsters 5–14 years of age increased by 49 per cent during the fifties, as contrasted with a gain of less than 9 per cent during the forties. The sixties will be the decade of the older teenagers and young adults. During the sixties youngsters 5–14, as a result of the leveling off of the postwar birth rate, will grow in number by only 18 per cent, whereas persons 15–19 years of age will gain by about 44 per cent. During the fifties teenagers 15–19 increased by only 26 per cent." *Ibid.*, p. 41.

[12] J. L. Gillin, "A Contribution to the Sociology of Sects," *American Journal of Sociology*, XVI (1910–11), pp. 240–41.

PUBLIC VIEWS ON DRUGS

The American response to heroin is central to any discussion of marihuana or LSD-type drugs. It is important to examine the reaction to these
two substances in the light of American experience with heroin.[13]

In the United States, the response to and the general strategy in dealing
with drug use has been the enactment of legislation to eliminate the drug
habit. Various control mechanisms and prohibitory regulations have been
erected so that individuals can function in the society without resort to
drugs. In this respect, of course, the response is very similar to earlier
prohibition on the use of alcohol.

The first federal laws regulating the sale and use of narcotics were passed
in 1914. The Harrison Act was the beginning in a series of legislative en-
actments relating to drug use. In part, such legislation was intended to
carry out treaty obligations, but its main purpose was to aid states with
problems beyond their own control.[14] Federal enforcement of narcotics
laws has been based upon that act, and several others: The Narcotic Drug
Import and Export Act (1914 and 1922), the Narcotic Information Act
(1930), The Uniform Narcotic Drug Act (1932 and 1956), the Marihuana Tax Act (1937), the Opium Poppy Control Act of 1942, the
Narcotic Control Act of 1956, and the Narcotics Manufacturing Act of
1960. Federal enforcement of another set of regulations, "the dangerous
drug laws," has been based on the Federal Food, Drug, and Cosmetic Act
of 1906 as amended in 1962 and 1965.[15]

[13] We exclude the consideration of barbiturates, alcohol and amphetamines from this
discussion because the use of them is so insignificant in the Colony. Barbiturates are
defined as dangerous drugs though alcohol, by popular consensus, seems to escape this
definition. In this connection the report of the Ad Hoc Panel on Drug Abuse is interesting: "Alcohol qualifies on all counts with the World Health Organization definition of addiction. It is the outstanding addictive drug in the United States and is
available without control because of public demand . . . The magnitude of alcoholism, involving as it does the partial or complete incapacitation of an estimated five
million Americans (a number far exceeding all other types of drugs combined) demands
attention." Ad Hoc Panel on Drug Abuse, *Proceedings, White House Conference on
Narcotic and Drug Abuse*, (Washington, D.C., 1962), p. 276.

For a comprehensive summary of barbiturate use, see J. Fort, "The Problem of Barbiturates in the USA," *Bulletin of Narcotics*, XVI, No. 1 (1964), 17–35.

For a summary of amphetamine use, see J. Sadusk, "Size and Extent of the Problem,"
Symposium: Non-narcotic Addiction, *Journal of the American Medical Association*,
CXCVI (May, 1966), 707–9.

[14] See Rufus King, "The Narcotics Bureau and the Harrison Act: Jailing the Healers
and the Sick," *Yale Law Journal*, LXII, No. 5 (1953), pp. 736–49, and W. B. Eldridge,
*Narcotics and the Law: A Critique of the American Experiment in Narcotic Drug
Control* (New York: American Bar Foundation, 1962).

[15] The Harrison Act established the pattern for dealing with the regulation of mor-
phine-like substances (morphine is the active principle of opium and heroin is a simple
derivative of morphine), cocaine-like substances (derived from cocoa leaves) and those
that are cannabis-like (marihuana). Legislation dealing with these kinds of drugs are

The three major pieces of legislation are the Harrison Act, the Marihuana Tax Act, and the Drug Abuse Control Act. They cover five substances: opiates, marihuana, hallucinogens, amphetamines, and barbiturates. The acts were passed at different times and involve different units of the federal government in enforcement: the Federal Bureau of Narcotics for the Harrison Act and the Marihuana Tax Act and the Food and Drug Administration for the Drug Abuse Control Act. The acts are separated by fifty years of experience in attempting to control drug trafficking. The emphasis in the later legislation is on the manufacturing and distribution of drugs rather than possession, and the user himself is depicted as a "victim." [16] This reflects the origin of the bill in a congressional committee on juvenile delinquency, and the public health justifications supplied by the Public Health Service, the FDA, and the medical profession. Proponents of the amendments to the Food, Drug, and Cosmetic Act saw this as an opportunity to initiate a fresh approach to the national drug problem. It was a major attempt to re-define the problem in medical terms—the individual user was not the target of attack and generally the penalties were less severe than those invoked in narcotics legislation. On the face of it, the approaches to narcotics and dangerous drugs seem quite divergent. The two acts, though separated in time, however, do show some continuity. The same congressional committees took testimony at the same time on narcotics and dangerous drugs. Their questioning of witnesses and response to testimony reveals their conviction that they were dealing with one fundamental problem. Since the passage of the Drug Abuse Control amendments, pressure has increased to make individual possession of dangerous drugs a crime. California and New York have since passed laws making possession a misdemeanor. The implementation of the Drug Abuse Control amendments also indicates that the high hopes of some of its proponents are not to be realized. The pattern of enforcement represented by the Federal Bureau of Narcotics seems to have been taken as a model by the newly constituted Bureau of Drug Abuse Control. The early arrests made by the new agency reveal a concern with the distribution level rather than with manufacturing.

Research on drugs developed in terms of the questions asked by legislative bodies—who uses certain kinds of drugs, what effect does it have on

part of the Internal Revenue Code and the enforcement machinery is located in the Treasury Department. The attempt to regulate manufacturing, production, and sale of these drugs was based on a tax warrant different from the public health warrant used in the later "dangerous drug" legislation. This involves the imposition of a heavy transfer tax for the purpose of regulation. The imposition of a heavy transfer tax has been held to be a legitimate exercise of the taxing power despite its collateral regularity purpose and effect. See *U.S. vs. Sanchez* (340 U.S. 42).

[16] The remarks of the President on signing the bill included this statement: "We know all too well that racketeers in the field are making easy victims of many of our finest young people." U.S. Department of Health, Education and Welfare, Food and Drug Administration, *Fact Sheet, Drug Abuse Control Amendments of 1965* (Washington, D.C.: Government Printing Office, 1965), p. 1.

them, in what way is it connected with other kinds of crime, what causes addiction and how can it be cured? This has given an eminently practical cast to the investigations conducted. It has also resulted in a body of literature on drug use which is not distinguished by its high quality. A summary of what has been accomplished reveals few high points.

If we analyzed the content of the research done over the past fifty years, and the assumptions which underlie it, we would note several things: the archetype of the drug user is the heroin addict, and the schemes developed to explain his dependence, and to deal with it, have, by and large, simply been transferred into the investigation of other kinds of drug use. Investigators have tended to explain both youthful use—the concern of the recent legislation—and adult use—the subject of the earlier legislation—in the same general terms, even though the pattern and purpose of use seem to be different.[17]

There is little in the literature about younger users which accounts for behavior in terms of the social systems of young people. Such an exploration presumably should include distinctive rationales for use and the vocabulary of motives of young drug users.[18] The question can be raised whether the imagery which shaped the view of the older narcotics user is adequate to describe the youthful user, much less the user of other than narcotic drugs. The fact that investigators tend to regard all drug users as a single type and all drug scenes as part of a single piece would be of no consequence if it did not affect social policy. Views of the problem have necessarily led to certain conclusions and the researchers have wittingly or not been caught up in a *disposition* game. Plans of action for dealing with the user emerging from these investigations have been proposed to legislative or control bodies.

The literature on drug use can be summarized in terms of the dispositions favored, either implicitly or explicitly, by the investigators. At least two major vantage points can be distinguished in terms of how the problem is formulated and what should be done about it:

The *official morality model* exemplified by Harry Anslinger, formerly of the Federal Bureau of Narcotics, and law enforcement officials.[19] The overall aim is to increase penalties for sale and use. The individual user is viewed as a criminal who should be incarcerated.

The *medical view* is exemplified by Lawrence Kolb.[20] The aim here

[17] Brief recognition of this fact is given by the New York Academy of Medicine, *Conferences on Drug Addiction among Adolescents* (New York: The Blakiston Company, 1953), p. 5.
[18] Zimmering et al. note the importance of distinctive adolescent motivation in youthful drug use. See Paul Zimmering, James Toolan, Renate Safrin, and Bernard S Wortis, "Drug Addiction in Relation to Problems of Adolescence," *American Journal of Psychiatry*, CIX, No. 4 (October, 1952), 272.
[19] H. J. Anslinger and W. Oursler, *The Murderers: The Story of the Narcotics Gangs* (New York: Farrar, Straus & Giroux, Inc., 1961).
[20] Lawrence Kolb, *Drug Addiction: A Medical Problem* (Springfield, Ill.: Charles C Thomas, Publisher, 1962).

is hospitalization of the user. He is viewed as a patient rather than a criminal. Civil commitment is posed as an alternative to prison.

THE OFFICIAL MORALITY MODEL

The community stereotypes about the drug user which have evolved within the last fifty years represent a fusion of several strands within the American experience. It is not our purpose to explore this development, but rather to trace its implications for the community's response to this problem. However, an excellent analysis of the formation of the "drug fiend" stereotype is given by Lindesmith and is an important background to this discussion.[21]

The principal proponent of the official morality view has been Harry J. Anslinger, the former Commissioner of the Federal Bureau of Narcotics, and currently the U.S. representative to the UN Commission on Drugs, who has written at length from the enforcement perspective.

Marihuana and the Opiates

Reports published by the Federal Bureau of Narcotics describe marihuana's effects as very strong, frequently accompanied by nausea in the early stages, often leading to violence, wild hallucinations and exotic emotional outbursts. The user is subjected to a loss of moral control, resulting in a loss of will power so that any suggestion is likely to be followed; vast distortions in time and space are created, and the user often blanks out—either on the scene or retrospectively so that whatever unusual behavior occurs is forgotten the following day.[22] At first it was not argued that marihuana led to heroin use,[23] but rather that marihuana in and of itself was a menace to the user and to society. The description of marihuana encompassed the following assumptions: Acts of violence, including rape, murder, and kidnapping are often committed by persons using or addicted to marihuana.[24] Both men and women are sexually stimulated

[21] A. Lindesmith, " 'Dope Fiend' Mythology," *Journal of Criminal Law, Criminology and Police Science*, XXXI (1940), 199–208.

[22] The reports of the Federal Bureau of Narcotics relied on the work of Bouquet, a Tunisian active in marihuana research for over three decades, and Munch, an American pharmacologist who was a leading consultant for the Bureau in the 1930's. See J. Bouquet, "Marihuana Intoxication," *Journal of the American Medical Association*, CXXIV (April 1, 1944), 1010–11; and James C. Munch, "Marihuana and Crime," *UN Bulletin on Narcotics*, XVIII, No. 2 (1966).

[23] FBN Commissioner Anslinger testified in Congressional hearings in 1937 that the marihuana- and opiate-using populations were distinct: "The drug is not used by those people who have been using heroin . . . [but] by a much younger group of people. . . . I think it is an entirely different class. The marihuana addict does not go in that direction." This view was later modified: ". . . the danger of progression to the use of and addiction to the opiates always lurks in the background for the user of marihuana." H. Anslinger and W. F. Tompkins, *The Traffic in Narcotics* (New York: Funk & Wagnalls, 1953), p. 20.

[24] As late as 1961 Anslinger wrote: "Those who are accustomed to habitual use of the

and become promiscuous and/or inclined to commit sex crimes when under the influence of marihuana.[25] Marihuana can cause insanity and organic brain damage if used in heavy amounts. It generates an overall moral deterioration.[26] The drug brings in its wake numerous negative physical effects such as insomnia, nausea, reddened eyes, throat and lung problems.[27]

Individuals, especially teen-agers, are introduced to drug use through the active proselytizing of "dope peddlers" who may or may not be addicted themselves. They are generous in giving away free drugs in order to expand their market.[28] The pattern is to start with marihuana and gradually encourage the use of heavier drugs. Those individuals who experiment with marihuana will eventually turn to heroin, not only because of peddler encouragement but because they desire a "bigger jolt." This, combined with its other perceived effects, makes it especially dangerous.[29]

An important part of the official version of the marihuana user and what should be done with him involves the notion that he and the opiate user are linked. The marihuana user has the same characteristics as the opiate user though he tends to be somewhat younger. Essentially marihuana use is viewed as the early stage of the addiction process which culminates with heroin use. This can be partly explained in terms of the official enforcement apparatus. Because of their primary concern with the opiates,

---

drug (marihuana) are said eventually to develop a delirious rage after its administration during which they are, temporarily, at least, irresponsible and prone to commit violent crimes." (*Ibid.*, pp. 38–39.)

M. L. Harney, a former assistant of Anslinger, repeats the same observation on the relation of marihuana to violent crime. See M. L. Harney and J. C. Cross, *The Narcotic Officer's Handbook* (Springfield, Ill.: Charles C Thomas, Publisher, 1961), pp. 104–5.

[25] *Ibid.*, p. 106. New York City's Narcotics Commissioner, a practicing psychiatrist, wrote in 1921 that marihuana leads to rape by arousing animal passions and lessening inhibitions. He stated that "Hash Eesh is the greatest aphrodisiac known to man." (S. Carleton, "From Hash Eesh to Opium," *Scientific American*, 1921.)

[26] See Anslinger and Tompkins, *op. cit.*, pp. 20 ff.

[27] Munch, *op. cit.*

[28] See Chapter 2 for a discussion of the official version of drug trafficking.

[29] Graduation from marihuana to heroin is a persistent theme on the literature representing the viewpoint of official morality. See, for example, John B. Williams, ed., *Narcotics* (Dubuque, Iowa: William C. Brown Co., 1963). A reprint of the Merck Report on Drug Addiction by Harris Isbell, M.D., states: "Abuse of one drug predisposes to abuse of another drug. Individuals who smoke marihuana are likely to 'graduate' to heroin or morphine." (p. 4)

See also W. Trembly, "The Typical Addict" in *ibid.*, p. 33. The Bureau of Narcotic Enforcement, Department of Justice of the State of California, makes the same point in its publication: *The Narcotic Problem: A Brief Study*, 1962.

The motivation to experiment with drugs in the first instance and progress to heavier usage is "defiance." Drugs appeal only to those individuals who are defiant of authority and use drugs as an outlet for this feeling. See T. Brown, *The Enigma of Drug Addiction* (Springfield, Ill.: Charles C Thomas, Publisher, 1961), p. 36.

federal enforcement officials tended to see marihuana users when they were on heroin cases and considered the two to be part of the same pattern. The law itself, by treating marihuana and opiate use in similar terms, forged links between the two which otherwise did not and would not exist.

Several additional elements are added in the official morality discussion of opiate use. Heroin is considered a more dangerous substance than marihuana in terms of its effects on the human body. The confirmed addict can be expected to have problems with the functioning of his stomach and intestines, his skin coloring and sex organ. Some of the descriptions indicate that the addict's life span is shortened.[30]

De Ropp suggests that society finds the use of drugs as a shortcut to happiness or tranquility to be essentially immoral to those who feel that these ends should be achieved only after years of arduous self-discipline.[31] Addiction is felt to be antithetical to such values as self-restraint, independence, sobriety, earned pleasure and leisure, and sexual propriety. Heroin use violates these traditionally esteemed American values. Some of the qualities or characteristics cited for the identification of addicts are polar opposites of desirable behavior and values. One of the manifestations of addiction is "increased dependence upon others and a marked aversion to work. . . . Drug addiction itself directly causes a cancerous invasion of the moral structures . . . with an absence of ethics, scruples, and even the minimum demand of human decency.[32]

That addicts and addiction are seen as inherently evil can be noted in the terminology used to describe them. Addiction is a "hideous, unnecessary social evil founded on crime and aimed at the destruction of masses of individuals." [33] Addicts themselves are viewed as predatory and parasitic individuals who contaminate all they come into contact with. The addict's general moral degradation even extends to the way he walks.[34]

Addicts are seen as criminals not only by virtue of their illegal possession and use of drugs but because they are driven to criminal acts in order to support their habits. The criminal character of the addict is not a result of

[30] Some police training materials are particularly lurid in their description of the physical ravages of heroin: e.g. from a police journal entitled "The Scourge of Narcotics" in Richard Kuh, "Dealing with Narcotic Addiction," *The New York Law Journal*, June 8, 1961: "Veins collapse and livid purplish scars remain. Boils and abscesses plague the skin; gnawing pain racks the body. Nerves snap; vicious twitching develops." (p. 4)

[31] R. S. De Ropp, *Drugs and the Mind* (New York: Grove Press, 1957), pp. 3–4.

[32] R. G. E. Richard, M.D., in Harney and Cross, *op. cit.*, p. 87.

[33] *Ibid.*, p. 115.

[34] J. Skolnick, *Justice Without Trial* (New York: John Wiley & Sons, Inc., 1966) quotes a police training manual which states that addicts can be identified by their "furtive movements" and a kind of shuffling walk (p. 120). Addicts are also characterized as "unnatural." They will go to great lengths to connive or steal sufficient money to pay for the drugs necessary for their euphoric effects. They prefer to be "high." See Brown, *op. cit.*, p. 55.

his addiction but precedes it.[35] Hence it can be expected that addiction finds its recruits among criminal elements.[36]

The picture of drug trafficking is an important element in the official moralist's view of opiate use. The traffic is controlled by organized entrepreneurs who profit from the dependency of their victims. Anslinger suggests that there is an international conspiracy of evil which in well-organized fashion imports drugs into the United States. Red China is cited as the main villain.[37] The penetration of the American market is for the purpose of imposing a subtle and diabolical form of conquest and enslavement.

Official Morality and LSD-Type Drugs

The concern over LSD-type drugs has been so recent that little has been written yet from a law enforcement perspective. That which has is unpublished and consists of reports prepared for legislative bodies or training materials developed for local departments. The information is drawn from case summaries of police departments and represents their experience in enforcing the laws.

Possession of LSD-type drugs was not illegal until recently, and the law enforcement experience with it reflects this fact. Most of the cases supplied by Peter Pitchess, Sheriff of the Los Angeles County Sheriff's Department, to the Assembly Criminal Procedure of the California legislature in 1966 involved other drugs. The LSD was usually uncovered in connection with a narcotics investigation. The implication is that there is a definite link between LSD and narcotics, much as there is between marihuana and heavier narcotics. The description of the LSD users is also very much like the older description of marihuana users. Pitchess classifies LSD users into four major groups:

1. People who are primarily and preferentially narcotic addicts, but who will use the hallucinogenic drugs occasionally for "kicks" or "curiosity." These persons usually take the hallucinogenic drug after a "fix" of their own addictive drug. At the present time, this group is in a decided minority.

2. The "professional potheads" who have had extensive experience with various drugs—carefully avoiding the highly addictive opiates . . .

3. A small number of people use hallucinogens repeatedly over a sustained period of time to the exclusion of all other drugs. These people do not take drugs in a group setting, but tend to take the drugs while alone in order to attain some personal "soul searching" goal, increased

[35] Harney and Cross, *op. cit.*, p. 86. See also Bureau of Narcotic Enforcement, California, State Department of Justice, *op. cit.*, p. 15.

[36] Peter E. Terranova (testimony), U.S. Congress, Senate Committee on the Judiciary, Subcommittee to Investigate Juvenile Delinquency, *Juvenile Delinquency: Treatment and Rehabilitation of Juvenile Addicts* (Washington, D.C.: Government Printing Office, 1957), p. 79.

[37] Anslinger and Tompkins, *op. cit.*, p. 69.

sensitivity to nature, "closeness to God," and other esoteric experiences.

4. Probably the largest single group of persons using LSD would include the so-called intellectual, pseudo-intellectual, artistic and literary persons and the beatnik varieties, on and off the college campuses . . .[38]

John Storer, Chief of the California Bureau of Narcotics, testifying before the same committee as Sheriff Pitchess, indicated that the use of heroin is dropping off and that LSD is being substituted for it. His point is that the social composition of users has changed somewhat but use itself is still related to slum conditions.

> . . . at one time we felt that it was a product of the slum area and it certainly does proliferate there, but it would appear more and more that we have the people who are pseudo-intellects or looking for thrills or looking for things that drugs can bring them, more than the drug just starting in deprived areas because of the dissatisfaction with life as they find it and they seek the drug to escape an intolerable social condition.[39]

The picture that emerges is that LSD is a drug used by narcotic addicts and that we can expect it to become one of the drugs of choice in the future by the same hard-drug-using population. The one complicating feature of this portrait is the fact that LSD use is overwhelmingly a middle-class phenomenon at the present time. Law enforcement recognition of this fact comes in terms of descriptions of "so-called intellectuals," "pseudo-intellectuals," and "beatniks" who use. The other group of middle-class users recognized by the law enforcement portrait are "thrill seeking juveniles" who may end up eventually as addicts. The use of LSD by juveniles and the implications this may have for the larger community seem to be the main concern of law enforcement representatives, and their arguments and testimony usually emphasize this point.

In summary, there is an attempt to link LSD with the older kind of narcotics both in the social composition of users and the social significance of use. Sheriff Pitchess states:

> While the discovery of LSD may rank with ether or penicillin in medical history, LSD may in the meantime prove to be as dangerous as heroin which once was hailed as the drug to cure morphine addiction.[40]

The solution to the problem posed by LSD is to increase the penalties associated with possession or sale. This will have a double effect: many otherwise curious people will be discouraged from experimenting with it

[38] Los Angeles County Sheriff's Department, Peter J. Pitchess, Sheriff, *LSD*, Los Angeles, 1966, pp. 7–8.

[39] John Storer, California Bureau of Narcotics (testimony), Assembly Committee on Criminal Procedure, California Legislature, Los Angeles, 1966.

[40] Pitchess, *op. cit.*, p. 11.

and the police will be given the resources to deal with the LSD distribution network.

The Impact of the Official Morality View

A strategy for dealing with drug use flows from this description of the user. The strategy for eliminating drug use is to increase the severities of the penalties. Severe penalties discourage new recruits, and their effect can be noted almost immediately.[41] The proper approach is through legal controls of the drug traffic aided by legislative and penal sanctions. Since addicts are criminals prior to their addiction and continue to commit crimes to support their habits, the problem should be handled mainly at the police level. The literature representing the viewpoint of official morality is replete with pleas for greater police discretion—including the use of wire tap, and relaxation of search and seizure restrictions in investigating and apprehending drug law violators.

Spokesmen for official morality are quite aware of and responsive to the possible political implications of research into drug use. A good part of their own literature, in fact, is polemical,[42] warning, as Harney and Cross do, against the situation where the "busy professional leaves too much of the program to some starry-eyed employee who needs most of all a few years of real indoctrination as to what this business is all about." [43]

The view of official morality has been incorporated into much of the legal code surrounding use and sales of drugs. Its assumptions underlie much of the present legislation. The Daniel-Boggs Act of 1951 and the Narcotic Control Act of 1956 both make convictions easier to obtain and stiffen the penalties. A system of graduated sentences, including 40-year maximums, has been substituted for the previous 10-year maximum.[44] Maximums of 40 years and life are found in many state laws, and in some states there are provisions for the death penalty on conviction of sale of narcotics to a minor.[45]

The emphasis of official morality has been primarily functional or

[41] Wm. F. Tompkins, "History of Legal Patterns in the United States," *Narcotic Drug Addiction Problems: Proceedings of the Symposium on the History of Narcotic Drug Addiction Problems*, Robert Livingstone, ed., National Institute of Mental Health, Bethesda, Maryland, March 27–28, 1958, p. 55.

[42] Lindesmith refers to exchanges between himself and then Commissioner Anslinger of the Federal Bureau of Narcotics including copies of departmental memos which identify Lindesmith as a "so-called Professor of Sociology." A. R. Lindesmith, The Addict and the Law (Bloomington: Indiana University Press, 1965). Anslinger was quite vitriolic when discussing those professionals who were urging more liberal consideration of the problem. In his book *The Murderers* he states: "Much of the campaign for relaxing narcotic controls and setting up clinics emanates, in fact, from organized syndicate sources. Reefers and propaganda too, go hand in hand." Anslinger and Oursler, *op. cit.*, p. 294.

[43] Harney and Cross, *op. cit.*, pp. 32–33.

[44] Lindesmith, *op. cit.*, pp. 25–28.

[45] Eldridge, *op. cit.*, p. 65.

expedient: How can the user or trafficker in illicit drugs be identified, apprehended, and punished? And the form of punishment most preferred is that which permanently removes this socially evil one from the community. Spokesmen for official morality do not like the term "clinic," nor do they believe that any version of the British system has any applicability to this country. Indeed, if clinics were set up, it is felt that this would raise a "grave moral issue"—that is, whether or not the governmental sanction of a narcotic clinic would provide drug addiction with a source of official respectability, and whether it is morally desirable to maintain individuals in a perpetual state of disease.[46]

Although the official morality view has not contributed much to the rigorous investigation of drug use, it has contributed the only tentative statistics on the extent of drug addiction. Official statistics are kept by the Federal Bureau of Narcotics, U.S. Customs, and parallel state and city organizations. However, a number of factors make these official statistics difficult to interpret.

Because of the severity of the law, many judges resist applying it. Selected statistics on marihuana are illustrative. In California in 1964, 64 per cent of those persons under 20 who were arrested for possessing marihuana were released, acquitted, or dismissed—as were 54 per cent of those over age 21.[47] Hence, only a very small percentage of those arrested are in fact convicted. A second complicating factor is the police use of possession statutes to go for bigger arrests. Eldridge claims "the real value to law enforcement officials is that such [addiction] statutes provide an effective bargaining point in the search for further information. Addicts turn informer much more readily with the threat of imprisonment facing them." [48]

Statistics would be difficult enough to interpret if the only major obstacles were the court's reluctance to prosecute many offenders and the enforcement agency's desire to free marihuana users as bait for bigger game. But, in addition, available data rarely differentiate between small and large users or small and large pushers, and seldom yield evidence of social class. In short, official statistics on drugs suffer from the same limitations as other official statistics and are further complicated by the fact that information is more meagre and mainly concentrated in the agencies also charged with the enforcement of the laws.

Summary

The views of the spokesmen for official morality stem largely from the narrow range of experience that law enforcement agencies have had

[46] See "Treatment and Rehabilitation of Narcotic Addicts" in Williams, *op. cit.*, p. 115.

[47] Bureau of Criminal Statistics, State Department of Justice, *Drug Arrests and Dispositions in California, 1965*, Sacramento, California, 1965.

[48] Eldridge, *op. cit.*, p. 62.

with drug users rather than from any systematic research. The experience is narrow in the sense that it is limited to the kinds of contacts law enforcement personnel are likely to have with violaters of drug laws, usually during or just after an arrest.

Whatever validity this view may have had in describing other drug scenes we can be sure of one thing: it is completely inadequate to describe the kind of usage prevalent in the Colony and other communities like it. These middle-class users of marihuana are not violent, do not graduate from milder drugs to heroin, and are not inducted through the active proselytizing of dope peddlers.

A brief examination of the official morality view of the LSD user and the amphetamine user suggests that the older stereotype of the heroin addict is shaping its perception of this new phenomenon and consequently of what the community should do about it. The likelihood that the official view will be shifted to take into account new groups of users is slight. A more realistic picture of this emergent youth phenomenon would require a different picture of the relations between pushers and users, which would essentially repudiate the older version and call into doubt the credibility of agencies like the FBN. A more realistic picture of contemporary college-age usage would also require that the enforcement apparatus at the federal level be joined so that information gathering and analysis could be coordinated.

THE MEDICAL VIEW

There has been a shift in the last fifteen years or so in some circles regarding narcotics and illegal drugs in general. The warrant has shifted from one emphasizing the criminal nature of drug use to the "new Humanism" which speaks of disease, illness, contagion, and the like. It is a shift from a legal to a medical warrant.

Doctors and psychiatrists now call for the transfer of social control to the medical profession.[49] There has been growing support for this approach as opposed to the official morality view. The widespread acceptance of the medical-motivational approach parallels the growth of the mental health movement in the United States. A massive attempt was made during World War II to screen recruits on their psychological ability to perform in the armed services. This created an enormous demand for trained psychological and psychiatric personnel. In 1946 the National Mental Health Act was passed, establishing the National Institute of Mental Health within the United States Public Health Service. This act provided a substantial measure of federal support for research on the diagnosis, etiology, and treatment of mental illness. One index of the

---

[49] See the Joint Report of the American Medical Association and the American Bar Association, *Drug Addiction: Crime or Disease?* (Bloomington: Indiana University Press, 1961).

growing acceptance of the mental health movement is the increase in membership of mental health professions. Prior to World War II, there were some 4,000 members of the American Psychiatric Association. In 1960, there were approximately 10,000 members. There has been an equivalent increase in other professions related to mental health: social workers, psychologists, psychiatric nurses, and occupational therapists.[50]

Fifty years after the first regulatory law, the awakening interest of the medical profession in medical solutions comes at a time when the trend in legislation is to define a broader range of behavior in relation to drugs as criminal.[51] The chorus of criticism against labeling the addict or user as criminal began to develop in both the medical and legal professions only after World War II. However, their joint report, *Drug Addiction: Crime or Disease?*, seems to have had little effect on current drug narcotic legislation. Both the Daniel-Boggs Act of 1951 and the Narcotic Control Act of 1956 make convictions easier to obtain and increase criminal sanctions.

One of the main recommendations included in an appendix of the joint report of the AMA and the ABA was for a wider use of a civil commitment approach in dealing with addiction. Civil commitment is the process by which a person could admit addiction and volunteer for treatment without criminal prosecution, or an addicted person could be committed to a state hospital when he was determined to have lost the power of self-control. The overwhelming proportion of candidates for this alternative to prison, however, have been persons arrested on a criminal charge, who also manifest addiction. It is also possible to use the leverage of a criminal charge to keep the addict in custody before commitment. Essentially, the person is given the choice of one kind of confinement or another.

In fact, civil commitment, as it is practiced, does not involve medical control or a real medical program, although as Lindesmith points out, it does use some of the vocabulary of the healing professions. It is an

[50] J. A. Clausen, "Sociology of Mental Health," in H. E. Freeman, S. Levin, and L. G. Reeder, eds., *Handbook of Medical Sociology* (Englewood Cliffs, N.J.: Prentice-Hall, Inc., 1963).

[51] The provisions of the Harrison Act did not apply to the dispensation of narcotic drugs to a patient by a physician "in the course of his professional practice only." Enforcement officials concerned over physician distribution of narcotics presented a succession of cases to the Supreme Court for interpretation. Dispensing large amounts of narcotics to addicts without attempting to withdraw them was termed "improper professional practice." (*Webb v. United States*, 249 U.S. 96, 1919; *Jin Fuey Moy v. United States*, 249 U.S. 96, 1920; *United States v. Behrman*, 258 U.S. 280, 1921). This had the effect of discouraging medical intervention in the narcotics problem.

Clinics were set up in a number of cities to provide relief for addicts who could no longer obtain drugs from physicians. The experiment lasted four years, from 1919 to 1923. The AMA passed resolutions in 1920 and 1921 condemning ambulatory treatment. The second of these resolutions requested the federal government to close all narcotic clinics and the Treasury Department complied. See C. F. Terry and M. Pellens, *The Opium Problem* (New York: The Bureau of Social Hygiene Incorporated, 1928), Chap. 12.

approach which has been advocated by the FBN, and its current popularity is probably largely due to the fact that "it seems to offer advantages to both the police and the medical philosophy of addiction. To the former it offers the continuation of the old practices of locking up addicts and of dodging the constitutional guarantees of the Bill of Rights which are built into the procedures of the criminal law. To the liberals and the medically-oriented, it offers a gesture toward a new and more humanitarian approach and a new vocabulary for old practices." [52]

The vocabulary has also been enlarged by the expansion of the medical model to include an interest in the personality of the drug user. The warrant for community action is a public health one: drug use is a contagious disease and, therefore, the carriers must be quarantined or isolated from the general population.[53]

Marihuana and Opiate Use

Marihuana is a non-addictive drug which comes from the plant *Cannabis sativa*. Research on marihuana—on its psychological and cognitive effects and on its use—is negligible, and the sparsity of intellectual or scientific research can be attributed to the particular history of marihuana in American society. Use and sale of marihuana has been a felony in this country for thirty years; scientific study of the effects of the drug by objective investigation has been greatly discouraged by the drug's illegality. Most of the writing which has been done has been a justification for the drug's illegal status—that is, it has tried to show that marihuana is harmful to the individual and dangerous to society. Medical doctors and psychiatrists have lent support to the view that the drug induces aggressive and anti-social behavior. For example, Gaskill wrote in the *American Journal of Psychiatry* in 1945 that marihuana, occasionally used, is not harmful, and produces euphoria; however, he went on to warn that the habitual user of marihuana exhibits "major personality defects" and marihuana use may be the determining factor in turning a poorly integrated social conscience to a social behavior.[54] Bouquet, a doctor writing in the official organ of the AMA, states that if marihuana is taken in large doses, there is a danger of chronic intoxication, and that many serious accidents occur under the influence of the drug.[55] The Council on Mental Health of the American Medical Association takes the position that repeated marihuana usage is indicative of underlying personality problems.[56]

[52] Lindesmith, *op. cit.*, p. 90.

[53] G. Rosen, "The Evolution of Social Medicine," in Freeman, Levin, and Reeder, *op. cit.*, pp. 17–61.

[54] S. Gaskill, "Marihuana an Intoxicant," *American Journal of Psychiatry*, CII (1945), 202–4.

[55] Bouquet, *op. cit.*

[56] See Council on Mental Health and Committee on Alcoholism and Drug Dependence, "Dependence on Cannabis (Marihuana)," *Journal of the American Medical Association*, CCI, No. 6 (August 7, 1967). "Persons who use marihuana continually

Psychiatric reports on marihuana usage have been based almost exclusively on very unusual samples. Psychiatrists usually report on persons they have seen because of gross psychiatric problems, or persons who have committed themselves for analysis and treatment, or prisoners. Several articles on the personality of the marihuana user appeared late in World War II and shortly thereafter. This was the period of greatest interest in marihuana users to judge by the number and size of the articles. They dealt with the experience of base psychiatrists with dissatisfied recruits. The reports reveal the psychiatrists' acceptance of many of the prevailing myths about marihuana users.[57]

The investigations into opiate use also rely on unusual samples. The subjects are usually in confinement of some kind, and the relationship to the researcher is usually not a voluntary one.

The picture that has been developed is essentially a model of the heroin addict. There are a number of assumptions which this view makes about the user:

1. The user or addict has an inadequate or psychopathic personality. He has a low frustration tolerance and needs continued reassurance in any threatening situation. He seeks to avoid the stress of a taxing environment and to escape to a fantasy world by means of use.[58]

---

and as the symptomatic expression of a psychological conflict, a means of gaining social acceptance, or a way of escaping painful experiences of anxiety or depression may be said to be psychologically dependent on the substance. . . . The major focus of effective treatment cannot be on the repeated drug abuse alone, because psychological dependence is almost universally symptomatic of serious underlying personality problems, severe neurotic conflicts, or psychotic reactions."

The Council recommends civil commitment of the habitual marihuana user: "During the initial phase, ambulatory treatment of the person with psychological dependence . . . is generally not satisfactory because of the tendency to relapse. At least brief hospitalization is usually recommended to separate the patient from his supply, establish relations, and initiate treatment. Complete cessation of the use of the drug is necessary, and circumstances may require the family or others to seek legal means by which the patient can be brought to treatment in those states where this is possible."

[57] Users told incredible tales of what they did under the influence of marihuana and claimed overwhelming craving for it. Tales of tea-pads and tea-parties where users would dance naked before strangers, engage in public sexual intercourse often with the same sex, engage in unusual sex play occasionally with animals, and so on were cited as evidence of the weird madness which marihuana induces. Statements by other users that marihuana was fairly harmless, enjoyable, not earth-shaking and "you oughta try some doc" were taken as evidence of stupidity and belligerence. If the psychiatrists didn't understand the users very well the opposite doesn't seem to be true. Each article—each base psychiatrist—strongly recommended psychiatric discharges for marihuana users. See S. Charen and L. Perelman, "Personality Studies of Marihuana Addicts," *American Journal of Psychiatry*, CII (1946), 674–82; and E. Marcovitz and H. J. Myers, "The Marihuana Addicts in the Army," *War Medicine*, VI (1945, 382–97).

[58] Herbert Wieder, "Recognition and Classification of Addiction in Young People," *Conferences on Drug Addiction Among Adolescents*, New York Academy of Medicine (New York: The Blakiston Co., 1953), p. 12; D. W. Maurer and V. H. Vogel, *Nar-*

2. The user is childishly hedonistic and unable to postpone immediate gratification in favor of a long-term goal.[59]
3. The addict fails to visualize adult roles in society and is unable to fulfill normal heterosexual roles.[60]
4. Use is a symptom of an underlying character disorder; the personality insufficiency persists after use has been terminated. There is always the strong possibility of relapse.
5. Treatment strategies should be designed to reinforce the weak individual. This should involve a structured environment so that temptations are reduced and immediate help is available. The first step must be the withdrawal from physical dependence. This can be most effectively carried on in an institution like a hospital where access to drugs is completely controlled. After withdrawal occurs, there should be a long period in a drug-free environment. Patients should not be allowed to leave the hospital prematurely. However, if kept in an institution too long, the addict may become dependent upon an institutional routine. The overall goal of treatment is summarized by the Ad Hoc Panel on Drug Use in 1962 ". . . in the US the prevailing philosophy is based on the premise that it is better to terminate the drug habit and create conditions wherein the former addict can function in society without resorting to drugs . . . We believe that in the US, the treatment and rehabilitation program for addiction should be based on such a philosophy, rather than on the perpetuation of the dependence through sustained and supervised administration of the drugs." [61]
6. If the addict is to live in the community, some external control must be substituted for the inner control which is lacking. The Nalline Clinic is recommended as a very effective program It combines medical and law enforcement authority in a way designed to keep the user abstinent.[62]

---

cotics and Narcotic Addiction (Springfield, Ill.: Charles C Thomas, Publisher, 1962), pp. 162–63; E. Rosenfeld, "Teenage Addiction," in W. C. Bier, ed., Problems in Addiction: Alcohol and Drug Addiction (New York: Fordham University Press, 1962), p. 173; and Zimmering et al., op cit., p 275

[59] H. Isabell, "Causes of Addiction," in What to Know About Drug Addiction, Public Health Service Publication, No. 94, 1951

[60] U S. Department of H-alth, Education and Welfare, Public Health Service, Rehabilitation in Drug Addiction, Mental Health Monograph 3 (May. 1963), pp. 12–13. Zimmering and his colleagues also make the same point See Zimmering et al., op. cit., p. 275. See also New York City Youth Board, Report of the Three Day Conference on Narcotic Addiction and the Teenager, In-Service Training Department, New York, October, 1959, p. 9.

[61] Ad Hoc Panel on Drug Abuse, Proceedings, White House Conference on Narcotics and Drug Abuse, Washington, D.C., 1962, p. 44. This is substantially the position taken by the AMA. See American Medical Association's Council on Mental Health and National Academy of Sciences—National Research Council's Committee on Drug Addiction and Narcotics: "Narcotics and Medical Practice the Use of Narcotic Drugs in Medical Practice and the Medical Management of Narcotic Addicts," Journal of the American Medical Association, CLXXXV (September 21, 1963), 976–82.

[62] See J. T. Carey and A. Platt, "The Nalline Clinic: Game or Chemical Superego?"

The Medical View and LSD-Type Drugs

The important element in the medical-motivational outlook on LSD-type drugs, as with other drugs, is the personality of the user. Is he stable or unstable? Most attention is given to the unstable personality and the damaging effects these drugs may have on him. They may also decisively effect the stable person.

> There is no doubt that even apparently well-adjusted persons can be thrown into acute psychosis requiring days or weeks of hospitalization. This is true even in the hands of an experienced physician who carefully selects his patients. In uncontrolled circumstances, the incidence of acute psychosis is increased; in addition, there are dangers of prolonged reactions. [Thus, some persons who have hallucinogenic experiences with LSD will undergo the same, often terrifying experiences weeks or even months later in times of stress, without any further ingestion of the drug.] Persons with personality instabilities such as neuroses or borderline psychosis often deteriorate markedly under its influence and may develop acute psychoses which may require prolonged hospitalization.[63]

A critical problem is how a stable person is distinguished from an unstable one. Louria suggests that the differentiation can only be made after careful evaluation by a physician. He even goes so far as to state:

> Those who are tempted to take LSD in uncontrolled, illicit situations are likely, whether they know it or not, to have considerable personality instability. For such people, the drug may be definitely harmful and may result in prolonged hospitalization.[64]

Issues in Criminology, II, No. 2 (Fall, 1966). The ironic part of this development is that clinics are again reinstituted but with a completely different purpose in mind. Medical aims disappear in the service of a surveillance strategy.

Since users are perceived to be "impulse ridden" and lacking in controls some management and guidance to help them change is necessary. Brill notes that the experience of several rehabilitation programs suggest the use of authority or some kind of "authoritative structuring" in dealing with addiction-prone persons. (See L. Brill et al., "Rehabilitation in Drug Addiction: A Report on a Five Year Community Experiment of the New York Demonstration Center," Mental Health Monograph No. 3, Public Health Service Publication No. 1013). Pescor studied what he characterized as "voluntary" and "involuntary" patients at Lexington and found the voluntary patients less likely to abstain after treatment than the involuntary ones. He concludes that the optimum conditions for a patient to remain abstinent were for him to be hospitalized as a probationary prisoner and discharged on parole. (See M. J. Pescor, "A Statistical Analysis of the Clinical Records of Hospitalized Drug Addicts," Public Health Report, Supplement 143, Washington, D.C., 1943.)

One can take issue with Pescor's definition of voluntary and involuntary. All of his subjects seemed to be involuntary. A more reasonable comparison would be with the most favorable group at Lexington matched with a group of private patients who seek assistance without any pressure from the law.

[63] D. Louria, *Nightmare Drugs* (New York: Pocket Books, 1966), p. 49.

[64] *Ibid.*, p. 49.

There is usually a recognition that the drug may be potentially useful to those patients who are highly resistant to the more conventional forms of psychotherapy. However, none of these claims have been subjected to investigation free from bias and distortion. Cole and Katz[65] are especially critical of investigators who have taken LSD or substances similar to it and suggest in inquiries explicitly or implicitly that they can be beneficial to others. Louria summarizes emphatically this view: "Indeed, at present, it can be stated categorically that there is no specific medical situation in which the administration of LSD has been clearly demonstrated to be useful." [66] Since LSD-type drugs might have beneficial effects, further exploration is usually encouraged in a variety of settings and with different classes of people. However, one crucial ingredient of the setting is that a doctor or a psychiatrist be present. Any research on human subjects conducted under nonmedical auspices is vigorously discouraged.

Exponents of this particular view draw their knowledge from two principal sources: the experiments conducted on the effects of LSD-type drugs, and reports of hospital personnel on LSD admissions. The latter source is more decisive and seems to account for the increasingly urgent tone in the medical literature.[67] The increase in admissions for LSD-induced psychosis is sufficiently alarming to call for more effective controls on the drug by local medical societies. The careful investigation of LSD impact on psychological states reported by Cohen and Ditman supported this view.[68] Their sample was drawn from admissions to a Los Angeles hospital during 1962–63. They noted that LSD may produce a psychotic break by releasing overwhelming conflictual material which cannot be handled by the patient's defenses. The hallucination of ego dissolution seems to make rigid or over-conscientious people depressed. More important, the drug seems to release "pre-existing psychopathic or asocial trends

[65] J. Cole and M. Katz, "The Psychotomimetic Drugs: An Overview," *Journal of the American Medical Association*, CLXXXVII, No. 10 (March 7, 1964), 758–61. There they state: "There has also been concern over the possibility that investigators who have embarked on serious scientific work in this area may have been subject to the deleterious and seductive effects of these agents." (p. 761)

R. Grinker makes the same point more strongly in "Boot Legged Ecstasy," *Journal of the American Medical Association*, CLXXXVII, No. 10 (March 7, 1964), 768, where he calls into question the conclusions of those who have experimented with LSD: their conclusions are "biased by their own ecstasy."

[66] Louria, *op. cit.*, p. 45.

[67] For an example of this "emergency ward" perspective, see J. T. Ungerleider, D. Fisher, and M. Fuller, "The Dangers of LSD," *Journal of the American Medical Association*, CLXXXXVII (August, 1966), 109–12. In a later article they comment: "Delusions (under LSD) are not infrequent. We treated, in crisis intervention, a young man who became convinced, a few hours after ingesting LSD for the first time, that he had to offer a human sacrifice, that is, kill someone, or die himself. He was prevented from throwing his girl friend off the roof of a Hollywood hotel." J. T. Ungerleider and D. Fisher, "The Problems of LSD and Emotional Disorder," *California Medicine*, CVI, No. 1 (January, 1967), 50.

[68] S. Cohen and K. Ditman, "Prolonged Adverse Reaction to Lysergic Acid Diethylamide," *Archives of General Psychiatry*, VIII (1963), 475–80.

and an abandonment of social responsibilities." They conclude that patients who have difficulty with LSD are "emotionally labile, often hysterical or paranoid personalities." Many may already be in treatment. They are hypersuggestible according to Cohen and Ditman:

> Although a number of patients recognized that the LSD had caused their psychotic or neurotic break, nevertheless they believed that the treatment had been extraordinary and often sought additional drug exposures. Such faith reflects the unusual nature of the experience and the personality of the patients concerned.[69]

Finally, they request that the drug be administered only in controlled settings with responsible investigators, presumably medical, present. More significantly, they link LSD with other kinds of drugs:

> It appears that antisocial groups have embraced LSD and mescaline in addition to marihuana, the amphetamines, the barbiturates, and the narcotics. . . . Easy access to the drug will result in its accidental or deliberate administration to people without their knowledge, and this can be a devastating event. We can only repeat that carefully screened, maximally supervised patients given the drug by responsible, experienced investigators will avoid many difficulties in the post drug period.[70]

Impact of the Medical View of Addiction

The medical approach under its psychological label has focused attention on the personality of those who use but has not successfully depicted the addiction-prone personality. Any attempt to do this must take into account that persons who become addicted undergo the same processing by the legal apparatus that makes them appear alike. The post-addiction similarities are then assumed to have been in existence prior to addiction. As Lindesmith observes:

> The manner in which addicts are characterized is strongly influenced by the nature of the observer's relationship with them. Because American addicts are generally observed in captivity, characterization of them tends to reflect the authoritarian nature of the relationship. When addicts are seen in other situations—as for example, in private medical practice, at large on the streets, or in the clinics that operated in this country from 1919 to 1923—the characterizations are typically different. Most observers who saw the addicts who came to the New York clinic, for example, were impressed by the variety of types rather than by the similarities.[71]

[69] *Ibid.*, p. 479.

[70] Cohen and Ditman, *op. cit.*, p. 480. The American Medical Association links LSD with both marihuana and heroin. See Council on Mental Health and Committee on Alcoholism and Drug Dependence, "Dependence on LSD and Other Hallucinogenic Drugs," *Journal of the American Medical Association*, CII, No. 1 (October 2, 1967), 142.

[71] A. R. Lindesmith, "Basic Problems in the Social Psychology of Addiction and a

Goffman originally described the distinctive characteristics of the medical view in his observations on mental hospitals.[72] The model is now extended to include drug users as well as the mentally ill. The patient is seen as a kind of object that bears the problem within himself, and he can be "tinkered with"—made well. The major treatment strategy implied or advocated in the medical-motivational model is some kind of hospitalization or outpatient therapy. The problem is that those who are defined as sick will not voluntarily seek assistance. Civil commitment has been proposed as a forceful intervention in the life of the addiction-prone person. No effective way has yet been worked out to encourage addicts who are not facing criminal prosecution to commit themselves for treatment.

A minority position within the medical-motivational approach rejects any use of authority in treating users although there is no disagreement on the personality characteristics of the addict. This is the view of a sub-committee of the New York Academy of Medicine and Dr. Marie Nyswander.[73] An experiment in the use of maintenance therapy is now being conducted in New York City by the Rockefeller Institute. Several maintenance units have been established in municipal hospitals under the control of the New York City Inter-Departmental Health Council. Applicants are voluntarily hospitalized after an initial screening by physicians and psychiatrists for a period of six weeks. They are given methadone after their discharge. The user still remains dependent on drugs but it is no longer heroin. The figures suggest a rehabilitation rate much higher than in any other treatment program.[74] The program is controversial and has generated much hostility in law enforcement circles. The majority medical viewpoint, however, was summarized by Ausubel in 1960 where ambulatory treatment was characterized as "both impractical and dangerous." [75]

Summary

A brief review of the medical-motivational approach to the understanding of drug use reveals little of relevance to any systematic knowledge of the meaning and purpose of use by differentiated groups within the community. The focus on addiction-prone personalities has done nothing

---

Theory," in J. F. Mulcahy, ed., *The Chatham Conference: Perspectives on Narcotic Addiction*, September 9–11, 1963, Chatham, Mass., p. 15.

[72] E. Goffman, *Asylum* (Garden City, N.Y.: Anchor Books, Doubleday & Co., Inc., 1961), pp. 321 ff.

[73] M. Nyswander, *The Drug Addict as Patient* (New York: Grune & Stratton, Inc., 1956), Chap. 10. The New York Society's report of 1955 is reprinted in full and commented on favorably by the author.

[74] P. Dole and M. Nyswander, "A Medical Treatment for Diacetylmorphine (Heroin) Addiction," *Journal of the American Medical Association*, CXCIII, No. 8 (August, 23, 1965), 80–84.

[75] D. Ausubel, in Williams, *op. cit.*, p. 125.

more than suggest an extension of a traditional classification of mental disorders to those who use drugs. The research conducted has not yielded new insights or basic knowledge of the causes of drug use. Rather, the focus on unstable personality as a critical factor in use has suggested a whole range of treatment strategies devised originally for those persons defined as mentally ill.

Some observers, while critical of the medical perspective on drug use, have concluded that in our society a major advance has been made if a person is classified as a patient rather than a criminal. Hence, drug use should be mainly viewed as a medical problem. The more ominous features of medical intervention in the lives of those who do not view themselves as sick has not been seriously discussed to date.

The as yet unrealized contribution of the medical approach may come from an unexpected source—that small group interested in demonstrating the effectiveness of maintenance therapy. They share their more traditional colleagues' views of the characteristics of the addiction-prone personality, yet it does not automatically lead, for them, to some kind of authoritarian treatment. Their attention to the conditions under which a person may voluntarily respond to some kind of treatment may, in the last analysis, provide a rationale for changing public policy. Despite the harsh criticisms leveled against maintenance therapy by proponents of the present policy, the real test will be the proportion of those treated who can be defined as rehabilitated. In a field where success has been so meagre any small gains will have broad ramifications among legislators and opinion leaders.

We can only speculate on why the medical approach has become more popular in dealing with drug use. It may be due to the increased awareness that the older legal warrant was incoherent and mistaken. It is difficult to argue today that addicts are out to corrupt the young, and the notion that crime and addiction are inextricably linked has been seriously questioned.

There is some question whether the change from a simple legal warrant to a medical one is going to alter the fate of users. The change seems to be nothing more than a change in vocabulary. In short, the medical-motivational view of addiction is a revised version of the official morality approach. Despite its sophisticated terminology, it turns out in practice to be less responsible than the earlier view in terms of the constraints of law.

The emergence of a medical warrant is of considerable significance since it seems to be a new rationale for organizing social action in the most diverse behavioral aspects of our society. Except for the work of E. Becker, Szaz, and Goffman[76] on the mental health movement, few have explored it as a potentially powerful new warrant for social action.

[76] E. Becker, *Revolution in Psychiatry: The New Understanding of Man* (New York: The Free Press, 1964); T. Szaz, "The Myth of Mental Illness," *American Psychologist*, XV, No. 113 (1960); and Goffman, *op. cit.*

The Sociological Perspective

There are a small group of researchers who have advocated no explicit disposition of the drug problem. They do not easily fit into the two dominant views; on the contrary, they may be strong critics of these approaches. Some of them are physiologists, pharmacologists, and psychologists interested in drug effects. Others have been sociologists interested in providing a picture of the conditions and circumstances within which drug use takes on meaning. If a vantage point can be inferred about the character of the problem it is that the user emerges out of a particular set of social relationships. Hence deviance is located within social processes and social structures not within the individual. To the extent that there is a policy implication it suggests a reorganization of social structures. The impact of this view has been slight. Its main appeal has been to university researchers and a handful of sociologists in public agencies. Representatives of this view, with the outstanding exception of Alfred R. Lindesmith, have shown a reluctance to being drawn into the conflict surrounding drug use in America. This has meant that the official morality view and the medical-motivational perspective have not been seriously challenged as a basis for social policy.

The concern at the official level continues to be on individual users and sellers and the problems related to their adjustment to conventional non-drug-using norms. It is the emphasis on the role policy and its enforcement play in the creation of the "drug problem," however, which suggests new lines of action the community can take. This entails the description of how laws and official policies are enacted in the first instance, and the relationship of drug use to social characteristics and the development of deviant career patterns.

The emergence of this new public view of drug use would require a more careful look at the impact of the present legislation preparatory to changing it. Second, it would involve a reorganization of the machinery which has been created to enforce the drug laws. There is some question whether the official agencies charged with enforcement have the experience, inclination, information, and sophistication to change their view of the problem even if they wanted to. Finally, an acceptance of the sociological perspective would require a shift in official attitudes toward the problem. Any shift would lend some validity to the criticism voiced against the social order by users themselves and against the present enforcement policy by reformers.

WHAT NEXT?

The direction this movement takes depends on the response of the larger community through its agencies of social control. If consistent and firm repression is the reaction, then the movement will probably be driven further underground and possibly eliminated. This does not seem a likely outcome at this point for several reasons. First, the resources it would take to repress the movement are more than the community is prepared to expend—in short, public opinion is not favorable to it even though many official moralists may be. Moreover, firm repression does not seem likely because many decision makers are too ambivalent about the movement. Though they share many of the myths about drugs, their effects, and the kind of people who are drawn to them, the movement seems to be composed of their children or friends of their children.

Another possible outcome, at least theoretically, is that the sources of strain which generated the movement in the first instance will be eliminated. This is not likely to happen even if we wished it because our knowledge is inadequate to the task of reorganizing the social structure in such a way as to eliminate the sources of strain. If we were able to do it, the movement would probably disappear because the new world envisioned by young people in the movement would be here.

If agencies of social control respond with a certain amount of flexibility, then we can expect another kind of evolution. When channels are opened for peaceful agitation for change and a patient and thorough hearing is given to grievances, then the larger community's response is essentially an accommodative one. This would require some initiative on the part of agencies of social control: legislators, university and college administrators, and the police, which has not yet been forthcoming.

Whatever the outcome of this movement, it seems to bespeak a vague dissatisfaction in all of us about the quality of our lives. Hence we may heed seriously the call to slow down, to live our life instead of enduring it, to open our eyes and really see what is happening around us and in us, to respond to beauty, and finally to humanize the large-scale structures that now victimize us.

Appendix

A METHODOLOGICAL NOTE

The study of college-age drug use was funded as a part of a larger project on drug use among different age groups in the Bay Area. The research was sponsored by the President's Committee on Juvenile Delinquency and the principal investigator was Herbert Blumer. Our initial plan was to collect information on the perspectives of local drug users.

I selected four graduate students at the initial stages of the project who seemed to be knowledgeable about the local drug scene. We devised an interview guide as a starting point for a series of interviews. This proved inappropriate to capture the experience we knew was available from our first respondents. We shifted our ground after the first five interviews and asked interviewees to give us a chronological account of their life leading up to their drug experience. We decided to deal with as many people as we could interview and get them to describe intensively certain episodes in their life: their experience just prior to turning to drugs and the various stages of their involvement in the drug scene. We opted for a shorter life history with a wider range of persons as against fewer lengthier life records. In this we followed Kluckhohn's advice:

> The lifelong retrospective biography is an imperfect alternative to the contemporaneous, on-going life history, controlled by current observations and the current testimony of others.[1]

We asked questions as the chronology progressed, but tried to allow the respondent the structuring of his story as he chose rather than as a schedule would dictate. As the interviewee progressed, we attempted to make sure that he covered at least the items in the schedule which were pertinent to his biography. Sometimes the respondent provided answers to these questions without being asked. Sometimes the questions followed

[1] L. Gottschalk, C. Kluckhohn, and R. Angell, *The Use of Personal Documents in History, Anthropology and Sociology* (New York: Social Science Research Council), 1945, Chap. 5.

directly the respondent's train of thought and provided continuity to the interview. Sometimes they had to be asked out of context and directly.

The life history included the usual information on age, race, sex, background, occupation, and residence. The age when marihuana and other drugs were first used and the circumstances surrounding it followed. This included the number of people present and the respondent's relationship to the initiators. The progression from first use to more systematic use was then explored and the role which defining agencies may have played in the process. This led very naturally into a discussion of the relationship to the "straight world" and the general problems experienced by the respondent in information control. Relationships to one's circle of friends was probed and relationship to a larger bohemian world. Questions were posed on the respondent's round of life. A description of "trips" experienced by the respondent was an inevitable part of each interview without any urging by interviewers. This seemed to lead naturally into a discussion of the extent of use at the present time. The final area explored was the respondent's self-conception.

The information on round of life turned out to be somewhat meager in the abbreviated life histories, so we asked ten of our respondents to keep a log of their experiences for one week, indicating what time they got up, ate, worked, went to classes—if they did so—visited with friends and finally went to bed. On the basis of this information we developed a picture of the rhythm of life, daily and on weekends, of recreational users and heads.

The question inevitably arises of the extent to which our respondents represent the population of drug users in and around the Colony. Sampling problems are obvious. There is no sampling frame to begin with, so there is no way of comparing the adequacy of alternate samples. The investigator must use the services of those persons whom he knows to be members of the population studies or enlist the support of people who can recommend him to such persons. As he talks to his subjects, they gradually develop a degree of trust in him and his work and become more and more willing to cooperate and to encourage others they know to cooperate. The study radiated out from the selected points of contact which we were able to utilize within the deviant subculture. The news leaked out and people began to come to us to find out what we were doing. In the local drug world, news of this sort seems to spread very rapidly. In obtaining interviews we tried to correct for some of the limitations in the selection of our population. This meant trying to get as much diversity as possible. This diversity exists within the limits of participation in the system of related drug-using scenes. Care was taken to represent occasional and neophyte users as well as confirmed heads. Special concern was given to obtaining interviews from users who hold divergent points of view, so as to give as broad a scope to the study as possible.

Qualitative interviews and life histories are an essential ingredient in any naturalistic approach but require a context within which they can be interpreted. Hence we tried as far as possible to become part of the world we were studying. This involved hanging out on the Avenue, developing a number of acquaintanceships and being present in a number of social situations in which drugs were used or sold. We all kept field notes on our experiences and used them initially to make some judgments on the credibility of some of our informants. Our field notes also enabled us to distinguish between the volunteered statements versus the directed ones that emerged from the interviews.[2] In the early stages of our research we had a series of meetings to discuss how we were viewed by those with whom we were associating. We concluded that several of us were viewed very much as participants in the drug scene, i.e., were identified as heads; the rest were identified as sympathetic straight people—at worst those who would like to experiment with drugs but had not the courage to try. In our assembling of data we followed Becker's suggested procedure: we organized our field notes and interviews around a series of areas that became the topical headings for the eventual manuscript. This enabled us to describe the perspective of the recreational user, the head, and the user-dealer. The frequency of the perspective was roughly calculated and, to the extent possible, its range in the various observational situations.

At Professor Herbert Blumer's suggestion, a final check on validity was attempted. We selected ten recreational users and ten heads who had been interviewed and in our judgment were very articulate observers of the scene in which they found themselves. We asked them to meet with us in a series of group interviews where we discussed what we concluded was the perspective of each of these groups. Our description of the Colony scene was corrected and extended as a result. This enabled us to separate individual perspectives from those more collective in character and to use in a more discriminating fashion our life history data. Our presentation of material to them generated with both groups a discussion of the alternatives available to persons within their scene and the acceptable variations within them. The group setting enabled us to raise points about which we were unclear and get the reaction of our informants on the authenticity of our description. It unintentionally added to our data because it constituted a group interview. All of our attempts were to address the problem of the credibility of subjective reports.

SECOND STAGE

Our interviews with recreational users and heads revealed that a number of them had pushed drugs at one time or another but seemed to be uninformed about the distribution system that supplied the Colony. We ex-

[2] See H. Becker, "Problems of Inference and Proof in Participant Observation," *American Sociological Review*, XXIII (1958), 652–60.

plored the possibility of building up a description of street-dealing as a preliminary to looking at middle- and top-level dealing. We selected material from our interviews that related to the distribution system and constructed a hypothetical model of it. This was presented in a group setting at several different points in time to twenty former agents of the Federal Bureau of Narcotics who are now working for the FDA as agents of their newly constituted Bureau of Drug Abuse Control. They were undergoing a training program on the Berkeley campus at the time and were receptive to being queried. As a result of our discussions with them we concluded that the agents have a much more accurate picture of the traffic at all levels than do virtually any other groups, including most professionals. Agents do their work at the most elementary level, and their job requires them to understand the "roles of the others" well enough to play them without being discovered.

These interviews clarified the producer and three-step distribution system for marihuana, LSD, and the amphetamines described earlier. In many ways our method was much the same as that of the drug agents—establish trust, get close to the action, but be aware of it from the position of both insider and outsider, don't disturb the actual behavior, and expand contacts upward and outward.

There were differences, of course. Unlike agents, we did have some public identities locally and we did present our credentials openly. Our personal histories could be checked on. Twenty of our interviews contained information on street-level pushing. Our first task was to expand this information and broaden our experience at the lower levels. In some cases this meant re-interviewing respondents to get more detail on drug trafficking.

Our sample of user-dealers, if it can be called that, is difficult to describe because most of the contacts were not on a formal interviewing basis. Such procedures often destroyed the very things we were after. We personally and formally spoke to five persons who periodically dealt in amounts of over $500 at a time (i.e., top-level dealers), and have had "informal" second party interviews with two others dealing at this scale. Our field notes also included approximately twenty secondhand stories of persons dealing at this level drawn from seven persons—four street pushers and three middle-level dealers. We also interviewed five middle-level dealers—i.e., big dealers. At lower levels of trafficking, the picture is one of near chaos with pushers entering and leaving the market rapidly, some moving up, some getting arrested, most moving out or operating so part-time that they do not see themselves as pushers except for a short while. Our field notes included some 100 stories about low-level dealers drawn from all parts of the system. Our formal interviews of street-level dealers included twenty gathered in the first stage and seven interviewed formally in the second stage. In short, our description of trafficking—the material included in Chapters 2, 4, and 5—was based on thirty-seven formal interviews with dealers, two group interviews with twenty drug agents, and extensive observations over a six-month period.

Is this enough of a sample? We cannot be sure. It is certainly biased, as must be every sample of illegal traffic. We may have missed fringes and subgroups. Given the illegality and assuming a very widespread market, one cannot see it all. But our conviction was that we must start somewhere, and if our description did not prove to be reasonable, comprehensive and insightful enough, then someone would be sure to report where we erred.

It would have been ideal to use group interviews with our dealers to check on the authenticity of our account as we did with recreational users and heads, but unfortunately this was not possible. The trust we developed did not extend to the point where seriously incriminating data on how one makes one's living illegally would be discussed in a group setting. The problem of access is a major one in studying deviance, but so also is the amount and character of information which is disclosed once the access problem has been solved. This is a critical area in the study of illegal occupations and careers. The researcher is compelled to use some of the methods of drug agents and journalists (though he does not share their aims) to gather the information required. Because the data are difficult to come by, however, does not mean that the field should be left to the agents and journalists. What makes a sociological account different from a journalistic account, let us say, is the number of informants, the attempt to deal with the sampling problem, the attempt to check on the validity of informants, and the investigator's theoretical orientation.

The attempt to check on the validity of the account provided by dealers was mainly done by the use of "unobtrusive measures." For all the criticisms of official descriptions, certain official information is very worthwhile. Official arrest and seizure statistics are probably the best drug statistics there are. Seizures are reported in amounts and tend to be quite accurate. The amount and number of people arrested gives some picture of the volume of traffic. In addition to official statistics there are numerous statements, scattered here and there, which suggest how the traffic operates, and how agents relate to it. For example, in the FBN's annual report on "Traffic in Opium and Other Dangerous Drugs" there are usually one or two paragraph descriptions of ten or twenty of the largest seizures of the year. Occasionally they report the prices asked and paid, the problem and "cost" of dealing at various levels, and sketchy "social backgrounds" of the captured dealers. Similar information may appear in articles by a narcotic agent, or former agent, or in comments that agents and informers make to the press following a sensational arrest.

THE SEQUENTIAL MODEL AS A FRAMEWORK

There are some problems in using a sequential model to account for drug involvement. The reality as perceived by those who are users can be somewhat distorted by employing a developmental perspective. The first question is whether or not drug use can be viewed in terms of a career approach at all? To say that it can requires some information on the complete cycle of use. The sequence described in this book brings us from the initial stage of induction up to dealing. Since the phenomena being described are such a recent development, there were few who had been involved in the drug scene for more than a few years, and the person over thirty was hardly to be found. We asked our participants to introduce us to older users who were "in the same scene." None were over thirty. We asked them to describe "older heads." The persons they described usually emerged out of a bohemian setting in the 1930's or out of the late 1950's. One thing came through all the comments about older drug users. They were a different group of people. They were not intimately linked with the scene our participants found themselves in. And Colony members did not see them as role models. In short, they did not see themselves in the same situation a few years hence. The scene they were making, the selves they were constructing, they perceived as new and emergent. There were no older models to follow.

Another question related to the congruence between the investigator's and the respondent's views on the significance of using drugs. In fact, the role drugs play in the lives of people who use might be such that it is inaccurate to speak of a career of use. For that reason we asked our respondents to describe the particular life style of persons they knew. From that we moved to a discussion of what the meanings of use were. There seemed to be two major meanings of drugs held by participants. One was characteristic of the occasional user, and the other of the hard-core user. These meanings were intimately connected with values about life, the self, experience and so on, which bear no necessary relationship to drugs. These values have been described in Chapters 6 and 7.

The career perspective in our study of college-age drug use applies most accurately to those whose lives are literally organized around drugs—those individuals who make their living from drugs, that is, the dealers. It seemed less appropriate to talk about the recreational user's career of use, since the role drugs played in his life was not as significant.

The description of the process is a tentative one. We would want to know much more about the dilemmas experienced and resolved by older persons in this scene before we could speak confidently about the development of commitment. A crucial dilemma, of course, is how one manages to survive economically.

In summary, the sequential model, if used as a set of sensitizing concepts, can be very helpful in describing the cycle of use, and the life style and values associated with it. Caution must be taken at the early stages of the inquiry, however, to insure that there is some congruence between the observer's view of phenomena under study and the actor's.

Index

A

"Acapulco Gold" (marihuana), 33
Acid dealers (*see* LSD, dealers in)
Advertisements for Myself (Mailer), 173
Alpert-Leary experiments, 38
American Bar Association, 189
American Journal of Psychiatry, 190
American Medical Association, 141, 189, 190
Amphetamine crystals, 40
Amphetamines, 42, 43, 146, 179
Angell, R., 200*n*.
Anslinger, Harry V., 30*n*., 31, 161, 180, 184
Ausubel, D., 196*n*.
"Avenue, the" (Berkeley), 12, 13

B

Barbiturates, 179
Baudelaire, Charles Pierre, 158
"Beats," 11, 158, 174
Becker, E., 197
Becker, H. S., 4*n*., 55*n*., 57, 63*n*., 202*n*.
Belladonna, 149
Bill of Rights, 190
Blum, Richard, 40
Blumer, H., 7*n*., 200, 201
Bohemian subculture, 8, 27, 172–77
"Bono" ring, 115*n*., 116
Bouquet, Dr., 190
British System, 5, 171, 187
Brown, Thorvald, 96, 97*n*., 182*n*.
Bureau of Drug Abuse Control, 203

C

California Bureau of Narcotics, 185
Camus, Albert, 158, 174
Carey, J. T., 43*n*., 192*n*.
Carleton, S., 182*n*.
"Cat, the," 2
Cézanne, Paul, 158
Charen, S., 191*n*.
Chemists:
    as LSD manufacturers, 113
China, Communist, as source of drugs, 184
Clausen, J. A., 189*n*.
Cloward, R., 3
Cocaine, 149
Cohen, Sidney, 1*n*., 194, 195
Cole, J., 194
"Copping out," 162
Cross, J. C., 182*n*., 183*n*., 184*n*., 186

D

Dangerous Drug Act of England (1920), 5
Daniel-Boggs Act (1951), 186, 189
"Dealer bag," 98
DeRopp, R. S., 183
Deviant behavior:
    autobiographical approach to, 1
    labeling approach to, 3–5
    psychoanalytic approach to, 1, 6
    situational approach to, 6
    social structural approach to, 2–3, 6
    theories of, 1–7
Ditman, K., 194, 195
Dostoievsky, Feodor, 158

206